THE PHELAN FEUD

THE PHELAN FEUD

The Bitter Struggle for Control of a Great Canadian Food Empire

STEPHEN KIMBER

Library and Archives Canada Cataloguing in Publication data available upon request.

978-1-998841-08-0 (hardcover)

Printed in Canada

Publisher: Sarah Scott
Book producer: Tracy Bordian/At Large Editorial Services
Cover design: Paul Hodgson
Interior design and layout: Ruth Dwight
Copy editing: Eleanor Gasparik
Proofreading: Dawn Loewen
Indexing: Rhiannon Thomas

For more information, visit **www.barlowbooks.com**

Barlow Book Publishing Inc.
96 Elm Avenue, Toronto, ON
M4W 1P2 Canada

Contents

Prologue
"A Fair Will"

In the American business tradition, taking a woman into the company was on a par with taking a woman to sea: bad luck at worst and a lot of trouble at best. A daughter was considered successful and useful if she married well. A wife was expected to be an extension of her husband's property. In fact, the idea of the woman as weak and incompetent persisted well into the twentieth century. Now, social and economic circumstances have jolted many women out of these limited roles and put them in charge of their lives.

—*Family Business, Risky Business*, David Bork, 1986

Paul James Phelan called this morning's meeting to order and directed his secretary, Dorothy Pyfrom, to take minutes.[1]

The meeting's focus was supposed to be the future of the Phelan family—currently ranked 17th on a *Financial Post* listing of Canada's wealthiest families—but not all family members were present.

It was also, indirectly though not coincidentally, a meeting about the future of Cara Holdings Ltd.—witness the minute-taking and the presence of two lawyers and a family business consultant—but it did not take place, as you might expect, at the company's headquarters at 230 Bloor Street West in Toronto.

Instead, it unfolded in the elegant living room of the Phelan family home at 8 Old Forest Hill Road in one of the city's most affluent neighbourhoods, just a ten-minute drive but a world away from the bustle of downtown. The home—a 1920s-style English manor on a professionally landscaped, irregularly shaped, "more or less" 160-foot-by-360-foot lot—featured a circular drive, a four-car garage, an in-ground pool, and a tennis court. The two-storey, 7,000-square-foot stone-walled house boasted five bedrooms, four bathrooms, three fireplaces, an elevator, maid's quarters, and a separate apartment for other live-in help. The finished basement offered its own large, party-sized recreation area, exercise room, and a small 12-foot-by-6-foot lap pool.

It was May 12, 1988, a pleasant late-spring morning. The sunlight played through the large living room windows, reflecting off the pink damask wall covering and casting a warming glow on the faces of the meeting's participants. They had arranged themselves casually on various pieces of furniture around the room: an antique Victorian sofa, a scattering of French occasional chairs, two modern off-white couches facing each other in front of the fireplace, a few mismatched straight-backed chairs here and there. Coffee, tea, and sweets were available on a side table.

The family members present on this day included Paul James—PJ as he was better known—the seventy-year-old Phelan patriarch and chair of Cara Operations Ltd., the source of the Phelan fortune, and his wife, Helen, sixty-nine, who was in her own right a scion of Toronto's famous and famously successful Gardiner clan.

Their eldest daughter, Gail Regan, forty-four, president of Cara Holdings and chair of the executive committee of Cara Operations, was present too, along with her husband, Tim, and their three oldest children: Sean, twenty-four, Tim, twenty-two, and Ellen, who would soon turn eighteen.

The non-family members included Larry Hynes, Cara's legal adviser who was also PJ's long-time confidant and a fellow life member of Toronto's Royal Canadian Yacht Club. According to Gail, Hynes had been practising law with "a modest law firm" in the 1950s when her father orchestrated a deal for him to join Fraser & Beatty, a white-shoe Bay Street firm that could trace its beginnings to 1839. Fraser & Beatty, Gail says, was a more "suitable" firm for a lawyer representing Cara's corporate interests, and Hynes became that lawyer.

Gail didn't fully trust Hynes who was, after all, her father's lawyer and friend, so she'd asked Glen Macarthur, another Toronto corporate lawyer, to represent her interests during this meeting.

David Bork, a US-based family business consultant who'd been working with the family on its complicated succession issues for close to a decade—without much succession success—attended as well. Today's minutes would pointedly, if not completely accurately, refer to him simply as "Mrs. Regan's consultant."

Notably absent—though not far from anyone's thoughts—were Gail's siblings: Sharon, forty-one; Paul David, thirty-seven; and Rosemary, thirty-one, the baby of the family.

They each had their reasons for not being present today.

Rose, her husband, Michael Robbins, and their two daughters, Raewyn and infant Michaela, had relocated the year before to New Zealand where Michael had taken a job developing the tourism division of a large engineering and planning firm in Auckland.

Sharon and her eighteen-year-old daughter, Holly, were at Sharon's horse ranch in California where Sharon continued to struggle with ongoing mental health and addiction issues, demons that had deep roots in the Phelan family.

Paul David—who was called PD to distinguish him from his father—lived in a house near his parents at 63 Old Forest Hill. Although he'd been invited to participate in this meeting, he had chosen not to. As his mother noted for the record, Paul David "is totally agreeable to some form of family agreement," but Helen herself had "gently suggested that perhaps her only son should not attend as she felt he might be hurt by the demands of his sisters."

In the months leading up to today's meeting, PD's sisters, despite their own differences in age, ambition, and temperament, had forged an unlikely sisterhood, a bulwark against what they saw as the unfair and unrealistic succession plans concocted by their father and mother, and the unseemly and seemingly unwarranted ambitions of their brother.

This latest round in what had become a never-ending struggle for the future of the family had begun six months earlier, around Christmas in 1987, when PJ informed Gail he'd drawn up a new will.

"You're not going to like it," he'd joked offhandedly.

She didn't.

At issue? The ultimate fate of PJ's 1,000 voting preference (more commonly referred to as preferred) shares in Cara Holdings Ltd., the Phelan family's private holding company, which in turn controlled publicly traded Cara Operations, one of the country's largest and most successful restaurant and food services businesses.[2]

The number "1,000" near the beginning of that last sentence is significant. So too is the reference to "voting." Unlike most preference stock, PJ's lawyers had structured the Holdings company's governance structure so that these preference shares carried real voting power.

That mattered because there were also 943—also voting—common shares of Holdings, all owned by family members. PJ held 143 of them. The remaining 800 were registered to 373027 Ontario Ltd. PJ had set up that numbered company more than two decades earlier to serve as the home for four equal trusts, one for each of his children. As a result, each now-adult child owned 200 shares of the family holding company.

But, of course, when all was added and subtracted, PJ's wishes—and his 1,000 preference shares—inevitably trumped any combination of his children's votes, even if they all voted as one.

That, everyone had agreed, was as it should be. After all, PJ had personally created the wealth they now collectively enjoyed. He should continue to have ultimate decision-making power until he retired, was no longer mentally competent, or died.

Let's set aside for the moment the first two possibilities.

In his previous will, signed in 1977, PJ had instructed his trustees "to hold my voting preference shares in the capital of Cara Holdings Ltd. ... until the death of the survivor of my wife and my children ... On the death of the survivor of my wife and my children, any shares of Cara Holdings Ltd. shall be transferred to my issue then living in equal shares."

The instructions to his trustees were clear and unambiguous. Most likely, those 1,000 shares in Holdings would end up in the hands of his grandchildren after PJ, Helen, and their four children were long gone from the scene.

PJ's proposed new will changed all that. We'll come back to the new will.

If the name "Cara" rang even the faintest public memory bell, it would probably have been because of the company's long-standing but mostly out-of-the-spotlight role as the food caterer of choice for more than sixty airlines, including Air Canada. Cara's flight kitchens cooked up 60 per cent of all inflight meals served in Canada's skies. And the company controlled the concessions at most Canadian airports too. But even that significant chunk-of-change business accounted for only one-third of Cara's annual revenues. The rest came from ubiquitous but seemingly unrelated brand name fast-food chains like Swiss Chalet, Harvey's, and Steak n' Burger. The collective net result was that Cara Operations had become Canada's third-largest restaurant company after McDonald's and Tim Hortons, boasting more than $600 million in annual sales.

No wonder Barry Gruman, a retail industry analyst at First Marathon Securities Ltd., would tell the *Financial Post* a few weeks after today's meeting that Cara was "an excellent company" and its stock "very definitely a buy."[3]

No wonder too that PJ Phelan's children were concerned about what changes to their father's will might portend for the future of the family enterprise as well as their own families' futures.

"For the guidance of my children," PJ had written in that previous 1977 will, "I wish to record that in all the years of our family association, including the administration of my grandfather's estate and my father's estate, I have noted most remarkable harmony and unfailing mutual good humour and understanding. I recommend to my children that they should always work together with warmth and understanding so that any tendency to pull apart will be submerged—in unity is strength!"

PJ's optimistic call for co-operation and collaboration—if indeed it had ever been genuine—had long since lost its resonance, most recently because of one specific provision in PJ's new will.

Instead of holding on to the preference shares through PJ's generation and that of his children and then dividing them equally among his children's children, the new will established a powerful new proxy committee with the power to vote all 1,000 shares. The three-member committee—which was to be made up of PJ's son Paul David, PJ's confidant Hynes, and Cara Operations' CEO Bernie Syron—would ultimately control key decision-making at Holdings and, through that, Cara Operations.

That idea made no one in the family happy.

In February, in fact, PD himself had written a letter to Hynes, who'd drafted the new will. "It appears the proxy committee will effectively control Cara, and two of three proxy members are to be non-family," he wrote. "It seems to me then that it could be quite possible—and then perhaps probable—that the control of Cara will not rest with the family. Could you please explain this to me at your earliest convenience?"

Gail was also concerned that the majority of members of the proxy committee would come from outside the family. "There is an enormous difference between voting shares and owning shares that someone else votes," she noted. What if an investment decision by this new proxy committee "divert[ed] Cara Holdings funds from the children's trusts, thereby drying up family money?"

Larry Hynes was quick to try to reassure her. The family trusts, he explained during the meeting, had been established at a time when the value of Cara's stock was "zero ... Today," he reported happily, "Cara Operations is worth $520 million." Hynes, the lawyer, informed Gail, an MBA, that "an excellent dividend program" could be worked out for all the children.

But the current value of the trusts' shares wasn't at the heart of Gail's concerns. Neither was she fretting about the dividends themselves because, at the time, "Cara Holdings did not pay dividends."

She was worried that Paul David would be the sole family member on this all-powerful new committee. Gail harboured increasing doubts about her brother's ability to lead the company and to protect the interests of herself, her sisters, and their families.

Gail was concerned about their father too. Over the course of three decades after the Second World War, PJ had successfully and radically transformed the Canada Railway News Company, the staid Phelan family business he'd inherited, into a dynamic, ever-expanding enterprise. He'd consolidated ownership by buying out fellow family members, changed the company's name to Cara Operations Ltd., and then successfully taken it public in 1968. In the late 1970s, he'd orchestrated the acquisition of Foodcorp Limited, operators of Swiss Chalet and Harvey's, catapulting Cara into the top tier of restaurant companies in Canada. "That was dad's brilliant move," Gail says today.

By then, however, he'd begun to step away from his central role as Cara's day-to-day boss, hiring professional management to run the company instead. Bernie Syron, Cara's most recent CEO, had become Cara's public face. "People began to think of it as Bernie's company," Gail remembers. "It wasn't Dad's baby anymore." PJ lost interest, attending board meetings and carrying out other official duties, "but he didn't really work. He read sailing magazines."

A lifelong sailor and former commodore of the Royal Canadian Yacht Club, PJ had begun to see his real legacy as the architect of what he hoped would be a Canadian victory at the prestigious America's Cup sailing challenge. In the lead-up to last year's America's Cup series, he'd helped organize and fund a $14-million merger between two rival Canadian sailing consortiums. (The fact that he'd sold shares of Cara to help underwrite the deal had caused consternation within the family, but that is another story—and another part of this story.)

To make matters worse, Gail recognized that her father's increasingly prodigious drinking had begun to play havoc with his health—and his ability to focus on the needs of the business.

She also wondered—not for the first time—about her father's mysterious, perhaps even Machiavellian, plans for her. In the mid-1970s, he had convinced her to abandon an academic career "I was enjoying," postpone work on her PhD, and enrol in a master's in business administration, juggling that demanding program with the requirements of mothering three small children. After she graduated from the University of Toronto in 1978, she'd joined the board of the operating company, but it was never quite clear what her father expected of her, or where she might eventually fit in the Cara pecking order.

She was convinced her father still wanted Paul David—the eldest son, if not the eldest child—to succeed him. "I was permitted into the business because Paul didn't seem interested," she explains. "I was the backup to Paul; I would do." She had been okay with that. Until recently.

For his part, Paul David, who was still grieving the death of his five-year-old daughter, Paula, from leukemia three years earlier, had become increasingly erratic. He drank more heavily than was usual even for him and was consuming more, and more dangerous, drugs. On the one hand, he showed little interest in the day-to-day business of Cara. On the other, he regarded Gail as a rival for pre-eminence as the head of the next generation of both the family and its business, so he did his best to undermine her at every turn.

Could Paul David really be trusted with the keys to the family's valuable business?

Gail wasn't the only one who was concerned. Her cousin on her mother's side, Michael Gardiner, a lawyer and investor himself, had heard about PJ's plans to change his will and warned Gail she "needed to object." In part, his lawyerly concern was that Bernie Syron, the company CEO, should not sit on the proxy committee. "The purpose of a committee like this," he pointed out, "is to control the CEO." But, more importantly, he knew PD too well; they had had more than one difference of opinion.

"Michael did not respect my brother," Gail says today.

"I don't think your brother should be on the committee," she remembers Gardiner telling her.

During the winter leading up to today's meeting, Gail had reached out to her sister Rose in New Zealand to inform her about the proposed change to their father's will. "I have a vision of me standing by the phone in New Zealand," Rose says today, "listening while Gail tells me, 'We're out of the will. We've been disinherited.'"

That wasn't technically true, of course. Their father had established trusts for each of his children back in the 1960s, and they, and their children, would continue to benefit from their shares in the holding company. But the larger and more problematic question, which Rose quickly grasped, was who would then control the holding company? What would that mean for the company's future success and, in the end, for the family's future?

Rose also harboured doubts about her brother—for some of the same reasons as Gail, but others of her own—so she agreed to support Gail's efforts to convince their father not to change the will.

Initially, Gail wasn't sure whether she should contact Sharon. Her other sister had more pressing personal issues to deal with. Instead, she reached out to Steven Stutz, a friend of Sharon who'd been acting as her adviser.

"Does Sharon really care what happens?" Gail asked Stutz. "Because what I think will happen is that Dad and Paul David want to take control of Cara, and Paul David will head it all. Is Sharon willing to stay with them? Because Rose finds that impossible. And I will be squeezed out, so I will need to go do something else..."

"Oh no," Stutz responded quickly. "Sharon is frightened of your father, and she doesn't trust either of them. She will want to be with you and Rose."

That helped explain why, in the lead-up to today's meeting, Gail had sent a series of letters to her father on behalf of herself and her sisters. One was headed: "LETTER TO PJP FROM HIS THREE DAUGHTERS."[4] Collectively, they amounted to a *cri de coeur*.

"If you are determined that Cara Holdings should remain a vehicle for the whole family," Gail explained, "we would like to share [our ideas] with you. It is through the addressing of these issues that Cara Holdings can be preserved for all of us equally."

In addition to her concerns about the change to the will itself, which "none of us can tolerate," Gail laid out a table-setting of significant familial issues she said the family needed, finally, to face head-on if they were to move forward together with any hope of that "warmth and understanding" her father had described.

Although at pains to praise her father's past leadership successes—"As the founder of Cara in this generation, you have had to make extraordinary leaps of faith in other people and have needed depths of trust from your loved ones"—Gail made it plain that "good faith cannot be taken for granted" among her own generation. "Thus, the relationship we have developed with you over a generation cannot be instantly duplicated with PD."

Without being specific, the letter made clear that what Gail decorously described as Paul David's "acting-out behaviour" had violated the trust of his sisters and could no longer be tolerated. "We are perfectionist and unforgiving women who do not trust others easily. We are a combination of wild horses and mules, so that leading us is a tougher job than most people would willingly engage in."

If they were to succeed as a family—and as a family business—family members would need to become open about their feelings for, and about, one another, the letter added. "We are a family who, in the interests of graciousness and harmony, hides true feelings. The suppression of spontaneous perceptions and emotions, the constant biting the tongue, rolling with the punches, pulling the guts together inexorably stress the spirit ... We will have to learn to create a free environment of shared feelings—good feelings and bad, bitter, resentful ones."

"Finally"—well, not quite—Gail wrote that "the atmosphere of constant rivalry would have to be forsaken ... Positive appreciation of various ideas and interests would have to replace the continuous struggle for dominance that goes on ... I know this struggle is enlivening to you," she confided to her father, "and that it will be difficult to change. It will be especially difficult for PD to entertain a different relationship to his sisters than you have had to Mom." But that would have to happen.

Gail's actual, final "finally" concerned the oversized elephant still sucking all the oxygen out of any room in which family members gathered.

Succession.

After years of business counselling, books, family conclaves, even a sojourn at a Betty Ford addiction treatment centre, PJ was still not prepared to appoint a strong board, formally designate a successor, provide leadership training for that successor, and, perhaps most important, create "a retirement timetable" for himself.

That, Gail explained, was why his daughters had reluctantly decided to abandon the idea of trying to fix what ailed the family from within and request a "butterfly" instead. A butterfly—also known as a corporate divorce—is a financial term of art that's used to describe a tax-free method of carving up the assets of a corporation after a business or relationship breakdown. Without getting into the weeds of it all, the important point was that the sisters could walk away with their assets and start over on their own.

This could be achieved, Gail suggested—more hopefully than realistically—"without upsetting our underlying patterns of relating to one another and the inner self of each person in the family. It will free up time and energy for the family to enjoy one another. Plans for maintaining Cara Holdings in its present form without addressing the real issues," she added pointedly, "are unlikely to be productive."

That was why the sisters wanted out, *unless*—again, hope sprang eternal—their father was prepared to agree to modify his will and create a workable succession plan, not to forget addressing those other "real issues" confronting them all.

Was PJ prepared to change his will, change his behaviour toward his family, and finally address all the many elephants in this room? That was the question that hung over 8 Old Forest Hill Road on that morning in 1988.

Unhappy Families

"All happy families are alike; each unhappy family is unhappy in its own way."

—**LEO TOLSTOY,** ***ANNA KARENINA***

"Shirtsleeves to shirtsleeves in three generations."

—**ATTRIBUTED TO INDUSTRIALIST ANDREW CARNEGIE**

On page 8 of *Cara: 100 Years,* the celebratory book marking the 100th anniversary of Cara Operations, *né* Canada Railway News Company, there's a full-page, sort-of family tree/chart staring out at the reader. It's entitled "Phelan Family Members Involved with the Canadian Railway News Company and Cara Operations."

It begins with the original paterfamilias, Thomas Phelan, whose oldest son, Thomas Patrick, TP—PJ's grandfather—founded the Canada Railway News Company in 1883 when he was thirty-two years old. It was very much a family affair. TP's three younger brothers—Frederick, Eugene, and Charles—as well as his cousins and nephews all found their places in a family enterprise clearly driven and dominated by TP.

When TP died in 1932 at eighty-one, he was succeeded, briefly, by his brother-in-law J. D. Warde and then, in 1938, by his eldest surviving son, Harry Warde—HW—Phelan, who was already fifty-six when he took the helm. Seven years later, in 1945, Harry died of a heart attack on the golf course, and his cousin Eugene assumed the corporate caretaker reins for the next sixteen years until illness forced him to step aside in 1961.

That's when Paul James Phelan, then forty-four, finally entered the historical family organization chart as president of the Canada Railway News Company. On the face of it, his was an unlikely ascension. He was the eighth of HW and Estelle (Donegan) Phelan's ten children and the youngest of their surviving sons. But he was also, and ultimately more importantly, a dynamic go-getter. He consolidated the scattered stock of the stolid, privately owned and operated family transportation services company, remade the company in his own image and ambition, renamed it Cara Operations Ltd., and then, finally, took it public in 1968, creating what became a publicly traded, but still family-controlled, fast-food juggernaut.

This is where that family tree gets interesting. The third-generation line in this Cara/Phelan family tree simply shows "Paul James Phelan, 1917–" and then nothing beside or below. There aren't any names of his third-generation siblings, or—more significantly—anyone at all from the fourth generation, even though two of his own children, Paul David and Gail, were by then working for Holdings, the family company that controlled Cara Operations, and their sister Rose had been the primary researcher for the 100th anniversary book.

Intentional or not, the omissions made a symbolic point. First, Paul James Phelan wanted to be seen as—and was—the first among no equals in his generation of Phelans. He, and he alone, had made Cara the contemporary success it had become during its third generation. Second, the absence of the fourth generation suggested that PJ could never envision a family company beyond one led by him. But that was not quite true.

In theory, PJ saw Cara as an exemplary family enterprise, one that had stood the hundred-year test of time and would be around *and* family controlled for at least another hundred years. PJ was proud of all that he had accomplished, and he wanted his children, and their children, and their children after that not only to enjoy the fruits of his creation but also to respect and revere the family-business tradition that had created their wealth. At the same time, though, he refused—or was unable—to seed the ground for a smooth transition to the next generation. Now, at sixty-six, he was running out of physical and psychic runway to alter his solo course of a lifetime even if he'd wanted to.

PJ had often suggested that he hoped his only son, Paul David, would someday, some way, succeed him. But he either didn't have faith in PD's commitment or talent to take on the top job, or—more likely—still couldn't imagine anyone but himself in charge.

So, although he brought PD into the business, he never offered him a clear path to the top. At the same time, he encouraged Paul's oldest sister, Gail, to return to school and get her MBA. Then, he welcomed her into the company as well, creating an obvious rival to PD, but he didn't give Gail a role designed to lead anywhere either.

In the process, he set brother against sister to no obvious good end and unintentionally—or not—lit the match that threatened to consume his cherished family business.

None of that would have surprised Leon Danco, at the time the foremost authority on family-owned business in the United States. "Too many family-owned businesses," he said, "seem to suffer from 'corpor-euthanasia,'" which he described as "the owner's act of willfully killing off the business he started by failing to provide in his lifetime a viable organization with clear continuity. This disaster occurs because the owner of the business cannot face the fact that at some point, he will become incapacitated or die. And because he has not taken time to prepare a successor, he takes the business right into the grave with him."[5]

That sounded very much—too much—like the story Paul James Phelan was busy writing. Had he inadvertently salted the ground that would lead to the end of his cherished Phelan family business?

~

Family businesses, we are told often enough, are the "backbone" of the Canadian economy, with families owning or controlling 80 per cent of all businesses in the country. But then there is always this asterisk: barely 30 per cent of family businesses survive through the second generation, and only 10 per cent make it beyond the third.

Like many asterisks, this one comes with its own asterisks. For starters, as Lloyd Steier, who directed the Centre for Entrepreneurship and Family Enterprise at the University of Alberta School of Business, put it: three generations "represents an admirable longevity—50-plus years—in the life of almost any business."[6]

That said, there has always been an expectation that family businesses *should* survive and thrive forever. When they fail, as almost all ultimately do,[7] that failure seems somehow more personal and painful.

Canada's corporate landscape is littered with the leavings of major, well-known family businesses. You will know many of their names.

Think of the T. Eaton Company Limited, which, like Cara, was also founded by an Irish immigrant, this one in 1869, fourteen years before the Canada Railway News Company got its initial charter. Over the course of its first three generations and one hundred years, Eaton's claimed to be "the largest retail organization in the British empire" with landmark retail stores from coast to coast, sales catalogues that occupied an iconic space on the Canadian cultural library shelf, and even its name at the head of the largest Santa Claus parade in North America. But then in 1999, one hundred and thirty years after it began, Eaton's was ignominiously shunted into bankruptcy and out of what had become its corporate misery, a victim of many failings, including a fourth generation that had tried to be "too involved" in its day-to-day operations.[8]

Family business is fraught. Even when a family business survives, family harmony often does not. In 1994, for example, the board of family-owned global food giant McCain Foods, during a struggle over succession, pushed one of its two founding brothers out of his job as co-chief executive. Lawsuits followed.

A decade later, Eric Molson, the long-time chair of Montreal's legendary Molson-family brewing business, squeezed his cousin, Ian Molson, off the board in a battle ostensibly over how much Ian, who was considered Eric's logical successor, should be paid as deputy chair but, more significantly and truthfully, over which of them should chart the future of the then-218-year-old company.

More recently, there were the Stronachs. In 2019, Frank, the eighty-six-year-old founder of Magna, the multi-billion-dollar auto parts empire, sued his own daughter, Belinda, fifty-three, a former federal member of parliament, for more than $500 million, claiming she had defrauded him to wrest control of the family fortune. Belinda countersued her father. And then her brother and niece sued her too. "Their dysfunctional machinations have been laid bare in a web of litigation so complex it could keep them bound up in court for years to come," Leah McLaren wrote in *Toronto Life*, adding pointedly that, "unlike most wars, theirs isn't just about power or money. It's also about love."[9] A year later, they settled out of court, but the result split the family fortune between Frank and his wife on one side and their daughter, Belinda, on the other.

And even more recently, there was the Rogers family.[10] Edward Rogers, chair of the board of Rogers Communications Inc.—and not coincidentally, the son of Ted Rogers, the late founder and prime architect of one of Canada's largest telecom and media empires—wasn't happy with his CEO, Joe Natale. In 2021, Rogers secretly manoeuvred to replace him with the company's chief financial officer, Tony Staffieri, and get rid of most of Natale's senior managers in the bargain.

Edward's planned C-suite coup was set to unfold at a critical juncture in the history of the sixty-year-old family-controlled telecommunications company. Rogers was in the middle of finalizing a deal to acquire rival Calgary-based Shaw Communications Inc. for $26 billion, including debt.

But Edward's scheme suddenly and spectacularly came a cropper, thanks to what some would later call the "world's worst butt dial." Natale accidentally overheard Staffieri and another company insider discussing how Staffieri would lead the company "once Mr. Natale was out of the way."

Natale immediately notified one of Rogers's independent directors, who raised the alarm. During an emergency weekend board meeting, the majority of board members backed Natale against Rogers, their chair and supposed leader. What made that unexpected outcome even more stunning was the reality that Edward's own mother, Loretta, Ted's eighty-two-year-old widow, and Edward's sisters, Martha Rogers and Melinda Rogers-Hixon, the deputy chair of the board, voted against Edward.

Even the board's rebuke of its own chair didn't end a family—and family-business—saga that the *Washington Post* would later compare to "a Shakespearean drama full of twists and betrayals, a clan-vs-clan tangle worthy of CBS soap, *The Young and the Restless*, and infighting and intrigue akin to the HBO series, *Succession*." Edward's sister Martha would liken it to another HBO series, "the bloody fantasy epic, *Game of Thrones*, with its tyrant kings, wedding massacres and fire-breathing dragons."[11] On October 21, 2021, the Rogers board twisted the knife, voting to replace Edward as chair of Rogers Communications.

Within hours, Edward—who remained the chair of the Rogers Control Trust, a family trust that, like Cara Holdings, effectively controlled the voting shares of the operating company—responded with a news release of his own. It announced his intention to replace Rogers's independent directors, including the director who'd replaced him as chair, with directors of his own choosing. He expected that his new board would then reinstate him as chair of the operating company.

But then, in yet another head-twisting spin of the chair's chair, the original board, including Edward's mother and sisters, ruled Edward's new board invalid, so the reappointment of Edward as chair was too.

What? Who was really in charge here? This was no trifling matter, given the reality that, as Andrew Willis noted in the *Globe and Mail*, "Rogers is on the cusp of an extraordinary achievement." If its plan to take over Shaw was approved by regulators, "the once-in-a-generation transaction will make Rogers the national platform that Ted Rogers always dreamed it would be."

Unsurprisingly, all sides lawyered up, submitting hundreds of pages of inevitably conflicting briefs to the Supreme Court in British Columbia where Rogers was officially incorporated. On November 5, Justice Shelley Fitzpatrick ruled that Edward Rogers did indeed have the right to replace the directors and was therefore once again the chair of Rogers Communications. Two days later, the now former Rogers board, including Edward's mother and sisters, capitulated in a one-sentence statement, announcing that it "will not seek an appeal of last week's British Columbia Supreme Court ruling."

The war for control of the company was over. Edward had won. The women—his mother and sisters—had lost.

In one sense, that is where this book begins.

Rosemary Phelan watched the Rogers family tragedy unfold with sadness for the Rogers women, but also with a deep personal sense of déjà vu few others could understand. She had been there, done all that and more, survived more than twenty long years of frustration, family estrangement, anger, tears, and heartbreak. The ultimate outcome of her family dysfunction had been different, but the pain and frustrations were familiar. What had been gained and what had been lost, and at what cost?

Friends had told her often enough she had a story to tell, one that was worth the telling, that was important to share. She didn't disagree, but she wasn't sure she was ready to revisit those too-many painful chapters. Eventually, she talked it over with her surviving sister, Gail, and they agreed to co-operate in the telling of their family's story.

The two women not only sat for hours of interviews but also shared boxes of documents—official corporate minutes, unofficial family correspondence, lawyers' letters, consultants' reports. They pointed me in the direction of various company insiders, family members, and associates who could flesh out the narrative and help make sense of a sometimes senselessly Byzantine, often ineffably sad human tale of family turmoil.

While Tolstoy may have been right about unhappy families, there is still some sense to be made—and lessons to be learned—from their unhappiness.

No "Meek Little Newsboy"

There is much we do not know about James and Mary, the original Canada-bound Irish Phelans, the ones whose children's children would come together on a bright, sunny August day in Montreal in 1883 to create the company that became the cornerstone for one of Canada's most successful family business empires.[12]

That said, there are things we do know, and others we can assume.

Start with the name Phelan. It's the anglicized form of *Ó Fialáin*, meaning "generous," "modest," "honourable." It's a "bardic" name, so its descendants can trace their own beginnings back to a thirteenth-century Irish bard whose family members were "often employed by the lords of the isles as poets, lawyers and physicians." But we can reasonably assume there wasn't much of that lords-of-the-manor connection connecting James Phelan to his roots by the time he arrived on the scene five centuries later.

James Phelan and his wife, born Mary Tobin, hailed from Waterford, an historic port city in the southeast of Ireland. Since early in the eighteenth century, fishing vessels from Bristol, England, had made Waterford their final European port of call on their journeys across the North Atlantic to the rich fishing grounds off Newfoundland. In Waterford, the captains would take on provisions as well as hire men from among the city's desperate but dependable Irish labourers, those who were willing to perform fishing's most brutish scut work—handlining from small open boats in the frigid, storm-tossed North Atlantic; salting and drying the catch on a rocky, unwelcoming coast; filling the holds for the return journey east.

Over time, some of those Waterford labourers brought their families and settled permanently in Newfoundland, an island the Irish called *Talamh an Éisc*, or "land of fish." The settlers' tales about Newfoundland's abundance of fish—they probably did not share stories of the grinding poverty in which they still lived, even in their newfound land—eventually made it back to Ireland and no doubt sparked the hopes and dreams of many among the hopeless dreamers they'd left behind.

In the early 1800s, as Ireland's population grew and its economy shrunk, many, including many in Waterford, determined to try on new futures for themselves and their families in Newfoundland, or in one of Britain's other North American colonies, or even in the new and fledgling United States of America. Those territories were in the process of expanding ever westward, offering what must have seemed like limitless opportunities for the ambitious.

James Phelan was one of those. In the mid-1820s, he left Ireland and found work in Lewiston, New York. Created in the aftermath of the War of 1812, Lewiston—the first European settlement in western New York—sprawled along the Niagara River beside the US–Upper Canada border just north of Niagara Falls.

Soon after James had established himself in Lewiston, he sent word for Mary and their two small children, Thomas and Mary, to join him. Unfortunately, before the family could reunite, James was killed in a railway accident in Lewiston. Then James's wife, Mary, fell ill with cholera during the voyage from Ireland to North America and died at sea. By the time their ship docked in Montreal in 1826, seven-year-old Thomas and his five-year-old sister, Mary, were orphans.

There are differing versions of what happened next. According to one story, Thomas was hired on as a cabin boy on a ship bound for Niagara where he was able to join some of his father's relatives. In another account, the two children spent their first winter in Quebec in an Ursuline convent, after which they were dispatched westward with cardboard name tags hanging around their necks so their relatives would know who they were.

Regardless, we do know young Thomas did make his way from Montreal, first to Chippawa on the Canadian side and then across the river to Lewiston, New York, where he eventually found work as an apprentice to a local tailor. Later, he would acquire his own haberdashery on the town's Main Street, a business that conveniently came with its own orchard as well as the coal concession that fuelled the steamers ferrying tourists down the river to experience the natural wonders of Niagara Falls. It was convenient because, in just a few years, those add-ons would come in handy for Thomas's own children as well as those of his sister, allowing them to plant the seeds that would eventually grow into Cara Operations.

Meanwhile, Thomas's younger sister, Mary, had been farmed out to work for a local landowner. In exchange for her domestic duties, her employer generously agreed to foot the bill for her education at the local school in Stamford, a Loyalist township across the river from Lewiston. That turned out to be doubly fortuitous; not only did Mary get an education but, in 1839, she also married her Scottish-born teacher, Alexander Chisholm. They would have eight children, nicely balanced between four boys and four girls.

Six years after the Chisholm nuptials, brother Thomas married Jane Dillon—"the daughter of a captain of the King's Hussars and, by all accounts, a beauty"—in a ceremony at Niagara-on-the-Lake. They would have ten children, also a matched set of five sons and five daughters.

Perhaps because the Chisholms tracked a few years older than their Phelan cousins, Mary's two oldest sons, Colin, who was not yet twenty, and Hugh, barely a teenager, became the pioneering family entrepreneurs. In the late 1850s, they sensed an opportunity to wrest some spare change from the tourists on the steamers that passed through Lewiston on their way to Niagara Falls. The boys harvested baskets of fruit from their uncle Thomas's orchard and carted their bounty down to his coal dock. Hiring a "band of Niagara street urchins" to do the actual selling, they peddled apples and other fresh produce, along with copies of the latest newspapers and magazines, to the hungry, bored, captive passengers waiting while coal was loaded on the vessels.

Once they realized the tourist steamboat season was, at best, only five months long, the Chisholm brothers broadened their sales horizons to include the Grand Trunk Railway. Its original rail line between Toronto and Montreal had already pushed past those boundaries west as far as Sarnia, Ontario, and southeast to Portland, Maine, adding connections to other rail lines running across the northern United States.

Hugh convinced a conductor at the Grand Trunk station in Lewiston to let his young sellers board and hawk their wares—by then including newspapers, stationery, games, greeting cards, postcards, sheet music, hardcover books, even sporting goods—to passengers on the trains heading off to Buffalo. As the company's history would note, "grim persistence and a powerful set of lungs" paid off on the trains.

After the Chisholms added the train to Hamilton to their sales routes, they realized they would need more hands to handle this new business. Enter their young cousin Thomas Patrick, probably not yet in his teens. The oldest of Thomas Phelan's children—who would become known as TP, the first in the long line of initialled Phelans—was designated to oversee the Buffalo run.

Later, when they added the concession on the Hamilton-to-Chicago route as well, TP assumed responsibility for that while his younger Phelan brother Frederick joined the family enterprise, taking over TP's Hamilton duties.

By 1866, Colin had moved to Toronto, the centre of the action for both trains and ships. There, he operated not only a newsstand in the old Union Station, then an unprepossessing wooden structure at the foot of York Street, but also news outlets at other Grand Trunk Railway locations in Montreal and Portland, Maine.

TP was just twenty when he joined the Chisholms in Toronto in 1871. "Haphazardly educated in Lewiston's schools," as *Cara: 100 Years*, the official history of the family business, notes delicately, Thomas Patrick would eventually become the most successful of the lot. But in his formative years, he was best known as an outgoing, adventurous, swashbuckling, push-the-boundaries young man. "I wasn't a meek little newsboy," he would boast later. "I was a big rough kid who could do things." He could.

During the summer when he was fifteen, for example, he swam "naked as a jaybird" across the Niagara River against the current from Lewiston, New York, to Queenston Heights on the Canadian side, and then back again. Later, he would join a travelling circus where he assisted the acrobats with their performances. He learned the art of boxing—a lifelong passion—up close and personal, studying with Harry Gilmour, a Canadian lightweight champion who ran his own boxing school.

The year he arrived in Toronto, TP earned local fame for rescuing a small child who'd fallen into Toronto Harbour at a spot where raw sewage was piped directly into Lake Ontario. "Undeterred by floating refuse and lethal fumes," TP leaped into the murky water and "hauled the hapless tot to safety." Years later, the by-then brawny youth showed up at the offices of the fledgling Canada Railway News Company and demanded TP give him a job. He did.

TP was equally adventurous—if not initially successful—when it came to business. In 1873, he bought 1,600 barrels of apples from a Grimsby, Ontario, farmer and shipped them to England where he hoped to turn a profit. Instead, the sailing ship took so long to cross the Atlantic, "the apples were in very bad condition when they were unloaded in the old country." TP barely managed to off-load them for enough to cover his costs to ship them there. "It was speculation," he acknowledged later, "and it didn't work."

Much else that TP tried, however, worked very well. For example, at one point, he made a deal with John Ross Robertson, founder of the *Toronto Evening Telegram*, buying up twenty-five thousand copies of a pamphlet the paper had produced containing the full texts of serialized stories from the newspaper. TP paid five cents per copy and then sold each for a quarter, turning a tidy profit for himself.

Although he was still officially the junior partner in the business, *Cara: 100 Years* notes that "a picture of the young entrepreneur begins to emerge: an excellent salesman, tramping the streets, buttonholing, cajoling and exercising his considerable charm, settling matters with rival suppliers 'over a bottle of Old Cliquot at the Queens Hotel...' [and] formulating a vision that went beyond that of his employers." Thanks largely to the efforts of TP, "the firm held news and advertising privileges with just about everything that moved on land and sea" in the recently confederated Canada.

By 1879, when the Chisholms decided they needed a loftier corporate name and established the Dominion News Company, they wisely made TP both the manager and a co-partner. Three years later, TP's younger brother Frederick joined the firm as another co-partner.

On August 3, 1883, Hugh and Colin Chisholm and Thomas Patrick and Frederick Phelan—along with a lawyer and four other Montreal men "in the publishing and bookselling business"—gathered at 496 St. James Street to ratify the charter of a new business, which was to be known as the Canada Railway News Company. It was to be "a body corporate and politic" whose expansive boilerplate objective was to pursue "any purpose or object," except building and running railways, operating banks, issuing paper money, or selling insurance. But in the real world, its overriding ambition was to continue and expand the work the family had been pursuing now for close to thirty years, winning "all rights and powers to sell books, newspapers, periodicals, publications and so forth upon the different lines of railways throughout the Dominion of Canada."

The capital stock of CRNCo. was arbitrarily established at $50,000, made up of 2,000 shares, each valued at $25. (Eighty years later, TP's grandson Patrick James [PJ] Phelan—the third and most entrepreneurial Phelan to run the family company—would take on the daunting, all-the-king's-men task of gathering the by-then scattered shares of CRNCo. and reassembling them into the Humpty Dumpty of the publicly traded juggernaut that became Cara.)

During CRNCo.'s first shareholders' meeting in 1883, Colin was elected chairman of the new venture and the Chisholms acquired 1,040 shares to the 960 the Phelan brothers held. But there was little doubt about which branch of the family was in the ascendancy.

"Basically," as the author of *Cara: 100 Years* later sifted the corporate tea leaves, "Colin had correctly identified TP as the company's most valuable asset, with Frederick on his heels." But, as later Phelan generations would come to understand, "elder statesmen have cause to fear young Turks." That may explain why the Chisholms retained effective control. "Every contingency had been provided for in an atmosphere of grudging admiration mingled with mistrust."

By the time of the company's annual shareholders' meeting two years later, however, the records indicate the Phelans had assumed majority control of the company's shares. Neither Chisholm brother even showed up for the proceedings. A year after that, TP officially became identified in company documents as CRNCo.'s president.

By 1890, the Phelan brothers—primarily Thomas Patrick—controlled the Canada Railway News Company.[13] Because the new company had done very well for all concerned, "the directors reviewed a gilt-edged balance sheet, congratulated themselves 'for having at last brought the company's affairs to such a state,' and recommended 'a dividend of 50 percent be paid to the stockholders from the last six years' business.'"

With the business at hand in hand, *Cara: 100 Years* notes, "TP, seizing the moment, went off to found the Queen City Stables."

Demonstrating he could be as successful in pleasure as in business, TP bought his first horse for his new stables—a mount named Hercules that was "highly charged with what they called the blood of the killers"—for $1,000 cash, then bet $1,000 on his new horse in its first race. Hercules came through at three to one, meaning TP "strolled away with both purse and horse for no outlay at all." In fact, he was $1,000 to the good as a result.

Later, TP would become famous across North America for his passion for horses and horse racing, especially steeplechase racing, a sport that had originated in Ireland in the eighteenth century. TP, who took up the sport at thirty-six, would eventually be credited with "having won more steeple chases than any one man in North America," often riding his own mounts.[14]

Even at the track, he seemed somehow both larger than life and always on the edge of the rules that governed others. At one point, for example, he planned to ride a mount called Driftwood in the Hunters' Handicap event at Toronto's Woodbine Racetrack, only to discover that an official had started the race without Driftwood or his rider.

Enraged, TP fired off a letter to the city's newspapers, demanding the chance to prove his horse would have won the race if he'd been allowed to participate. Race officials countered that, despite "repeated warnings," TP had chosen "to stand in the centre of an admiring throng" rather than line up for the race, forcing the official to start without him. Other sportsmen, however, did take up TP's challenge, organizing a competition pitting Driftwood against another horse named Silver King. "Driftwood won by a neck despite a subsequent claim of foul." TP, it was alleged, had "whacked Silver King over the head with his whip while approaching the final hurdle." The judges disallowed the claim; Driftwood and TP remained victorious.

Perhaps distracted by such pleasures, TP had been blindsided in 1894 when "a person rejoicing in the name of Azro Buck Chaffee, the publisher of something called the *International Guide*, crept up and low-balled a deal with the Grand Trunk, making off with the lion's share of CRNCo.'s business."

TP, as both president and managing director of the Canada Railway News Company, was "directly responsible for the botch" and just as directly responsible for cleverly countering it.

First, he handed Chaffee $5,000 in cash, then bought $7,500 worth of stock in Chaffee's International Publishing Company, and finally hired Chaffee himself at a salary of $1,200 a year, plus expenses. Under the terms of the deal, Chaffee would spend some part of his time working in CRNCo.'s advertising department while continuing to publish his *International Guide* on the side.

In return, TP promised that CRNCo. would not only "fulfill all Chaffee's commitments to the Grand Trunk" but also promote Chaffee's *International Guide* to the exclusion of all others, a clause that *Cara: 100 Years* notes, without comment, "seems to have been honoured largely in the breach."

Thanks in part to the Chaffee scare, TP refocused his attention on "the nuts and bolts of business." He would willingly suffer occasional small financial losses to block anyone who might aspire to become the next Chaffee.

He struck a deal, for example, to provide newsboy services aboard the irrelevant-in-the-bigger-picture Temiscouata Railway's once-a-day, 131-kilometre run between Riviere du Loup, Quebec, and Edmundston, New Brunswick. "There is no future in the railway," TP would acknowledge, but "we will stop the other fellow"—who was never identified—"from going into business in this place and establishing a supply depot."

More importantly, TP began pushing the boundaries of what had been CRNCo.'s news-and-sundries-only business model. In 1895, he bought a two-storey frame building beside the Gravenhurst, Ontario, rail station

170 kilometres north of Toronto for $2,100. The purchase price included "kitchen, woodshed and all other buildings ... stocks and fixtures ... [and] two cows and one sow." CRNCo. then spent $2,700 more to transform the facility at the southern tip of the popular Lake Muskoka tourist district into one of the Canada Railway News Company's first restaurant operations.

As a result, the company began advertising itself on its letterhead not only as "publishers, booksellers and general news agents" but also as "caterers and lessees of refreshment rooms."

The following year, as passenger rail traffic experienced a boom in Canada, the company built "a posh restaurant on two levels" at Toronto's new Union Station, now the "hub of Canadian transportation." Fixtures included "stained glass windows, a 31-foot oak counter, a 27-foot bar with brass rails, marble facings and copper taps."

Thomas Patrick Phelan had a vision: he wanted to create a truly national company but one that reflected the regional reality of the new country. So, he divided the business into geographic divisions run by trusted family members who were given autonomy over their areas.

Before the century turned, the company had applied for supplementary letters patent, officially allowing it to "carry on the business of catering and keeping restaurants and hotels."

The Canada Railway News Company was ready to welcome the twentieth century.

In the early years of the new century, TP began "spending capital with unholy glee." He bought and built a string of hotels and resorts, starting with the Queen's Hotel in Palmerston, Ontario, "a singularly un-opulent structure on leased railway land, for which he paid the sum of $12,000."

Four years later, in 1908, he opened the next-step-up Wawa Hotel on Lake of Bays near Huntsville, Ontario. It was billed as "low-budget accommodation for the cost-conscious holidayer." In 1914, TP opened Minaki Lodge, a stunning—and stunningly expensive—full-featured resort north of Kenora in Ontario's lake district. It boasted scenic shorelines, boreal forest, and colourful sunsets, attracting well-heeled guests, many of them in search of the region's abundant trophy fish. The cost to construct the 250-room resort: $229,000, nearly twenty times as much as he'd spent on the Queen's Hotel a decade earlier.

TP's many travels in Northern Ontario produced more than just new hotels and resorts for CRNCo. In 1913, as the *Toronto Telegram* breathlessly informed its readers, TP returned home with the "richest hunting tale that has come out of the woods this year." It starred none other than "TP Phelan, the well-known president of the Canadian Railway News Company, and a big black bear of maternal instincts."

TP, it seemed, had gone on a deer hunting expedition with friends in a forest about 30 kilometres west of Timmins, Ontario. While TP and the other hunters hid themselves, a member of their party assembled the hounds and used them to—everyone hoped—drive the deer through the forest toward the waiting hunters. It didn't work. "The afternoon had worn on and no fleet-footed prey had appeared in the neighbourhood of Mr. Phelan, whose patience was beginning to ooze."

That was when he heard a yelp from nearby and noticed three tiny black bear cubs wandering on their own. "He realized that there would likely be a mother not far off and secreted himself in a clump of heavy underbrush to await her coming." But when she hadn't come back after half an hour and his own search of the nearby woods failed to find any trace of the animal, "he could not resist the temptation to adopt one of these little balls of fur and started back to the camp with it under his arm."

Suddenly, he heard something behind him. It was a very angry mother bear. TP dropped the cub, grabbed his rifle, and fired a shot at the mother bear, hitting her "somewhere," as he would explain. He fired again, but "the second shell failed," so he did the smart thing: dropped the rifle and ran for his life. He managed to scramble up a tree and onto the precarious safety of a tree branch. But the mother bear, hot on his trail, camped out under the branch and showed no signs of leaving. "For four hours, the bear remained in his company."

Finally, the other hunters found their missing companion and felled the menacing mother bear. Incredibly, TP and the other hunters then collected the three baby cubs "and took them back to the camp." The story didn't make clear whether TP brought the orphan cubs back with him to Toronto, but his son, Harry, who told the story to the newspaper reporter, said he was "confident that his father will at least bring enough of the old one down to mount it."

By then, Thomas Patrick was not only one of the country's most prominent businessmen—worthy of such fawning press coverage—but also a well-established family man. On February 2, 1880, when he was twenty-nine, he'd married Mary Kate Warde, twenty-four, the daughter of a retired army officer.

Nine months later, their first son, Frederick James Phelan, was born. Harry Warde—the father of Paul James, PJ—followed less than two years later. Then came a daughter, Irene, in 1885, and finally a third son, Arthur Thomas, a decade after that.

By the early 1900s, the family was living in a mansion at 149 South Drive in Rosedale, befitting a man of TP's wealth and power. *Cara: 100 Years* reports that even into his sixties, TP, still the showman, could be found turning cartwheels on his Rosedale lawn to the delight of his seventeen grandchildren and three great-grandchildren.

It sometimes seemed he would live forever.

But death inevitably caught up even with the larger-than-life Thomas Patrick Phelan. He died on August 9, 1932, in Toronto's St. Michael's Hospital after a brief two-week illness. He was eighty years old.

"What can be said about this extraordinary man?" asked the author of *Cara: 100 Years* a half-century after his death. "He left behind him a firm built up from scratch to span the nation, earning the universal respect of his employees and business associates ... He was the sort of man you wish you'd known—a visionary, a shoestring entrepreneur, a devout Catholic and almost total abstainer, a man of public and private honour, and a sly old fox."

While some of that is no doubt 100th anniversary celebratory hyperbole, it's still worth parsing.

TP Phelan, after all, did rise from the most "humble beginnings ... to head one of the largest railway news distributing agencies in the world" during a career that not only spanned two centuries and sixty-five years but also laid the foundations for a family business empire that would survive him and several more generations of Phelans.

How did he do it?

Some of it, of course, was good timing. The Phelans and Chisholms got into the passenger transport servicing sector before most of their potential competitors even understood there was such a sector. TP then rode the wave of an expanding country that wanted—and needed—everything he had to offer. And he had plenty to offer, from the latest newspapers and chewing gum to full-course meals and every class of accommodation from coast to coast.

He and his company survived war, the stock market crash, the beginnings of the Great Depression, the emergence of the automobile, and dozens of other potential business destroyers. In the process he created a national network of branches—newsstands, lunch counters, dining rooms, even hotels—in and around railway stations in every province that included, as his obituary put it, "the chain of restaurants which the company owns from coast to coast in Canada, a chain of more than 1,000 branches."

"Look at those branches," Harry Warde Phelan, TP's son and eventual successor, told his own son, PJ, years later, "everyone bringing in a little money here and there. And if one loses, you do your best to minimize the loss, but then the profits are picked up in Toronto to Montreal or Winnipeg or Vancouver. What a fascinating business! And the most marvellous thing is that it runs itself."

That wasn't true, of course. TP was able to not only create but also maintain a virtual monopoly with his business model primarily because he delivered well and consistently—for his customers, for his employees, and for himself.

He didn't do that all by himself. Sometime after the Chisholms took their leave, James D. Warde, TP's brother-in-law, joined the company. Warde was the opposite of the voluble, flamboyant TP. He was, as one company official remembered, "a very proper man. Dapper too, and pompous. He and TP sometimes didn't get along."

But that was more than okay, because Warde's passion for detail provided the ideal counterbalance to his brother-in-law's passion for the ever-larger vision.

TP could be unpredictable but often in ways that endeared him to both customers and employees. There was the time during the early days of the Depression, for instance, when someone complained to him that George Bond, the manager of his restaurant at Union Station, had been giving away food.

TP confronted the manager. "They tell me you're giving food away," he said.

"Yes, Guv'nor, I did," Bond replied. No one called him "Mr. Phelan." He was always "Boss" or "Guv'nor." "I gave six loaves of bread and some meat and fruit to a mother and four children," Bond explained. "They were in the baggage car heading for Winnipeg with nothing to eat." He paused. "Now, if you want me to pay for that, I'll pay for it."

TP brushed aside the offer. "If you hadn't given it to them," he said breezily, "I'd have fired you."

TP, in truth, treated his employees well, offering low-rent accommodation and subsidized meals on the trains. They rewarded him with loyalty. "Whole families would work together," reports *Cara: 100 Years*, "the wife seeing to the kitchen, the father busying himself with the newsstand, and the kids boarding a passing train, papers in hand, little knowing that they followed in the footsteps of the company's founders."

TP could also be generous—or not—in his everyday life, depending on his mood. One of his CRNCo. board members recalled that TP would often have to run a "virtual gauntlet" of beggars during his daily ten-minute walk from his Union Station office to the National Club on Bay Street, the downtown gentlemen's business and social club where he often lunched. He would usually arm himself with a pocketful of bills to hand out to the needy, the man explained. But on other occasions—"when philanthropy failed"—he would instruct the company official "to bring a stepladder round to a certain window so that TP could clamber down, unseen, making his escape from indigent cronies who were trying to put the bite on him."

Thomas Patrick Phelan was, in short—like many in the Phelan clan before and after—a walking contradiction. He revelled in it.

By the time TP died in the summer of 1932, the Canada Railway News Company was experiencing the same fiscal contractions that had been forced on the entire country by the Great Depression. CRNCo. closures had begun the year before in the Northern Ontario bush country but then spread to company outposts in the West and the Maritimes.

With TP's death, the mantle of leadership passed briefly to brother-in-law James D. Warde, a man lacking the founder's vision and daring. One of the new president's first pronouncements was "an all-points memo, announcing that 'a general cut in wages be made in our several branches according to the best judgement [*sic*] of each region.'" For the next two years, as revenues plummeted and closures and contractions continued, the company's board declared no dividend at all.

Then J. D. Warde himself fell seriously ill and had to be replaced.

By the usual determinants, TP's eldest son, Frederick James Phelan, would have been his logical heir and successor, but he had died of typhoid in 1911 when he was only thirty years old. That left Harry Warde Phelan, TP's second son, who, according to *Cara: 100 Years*, "reluctantly assumed the presidency."

Reluctantly? HW was already well into his fifties when he was tapped to run the company. He was, in the dismissive words of his own son, Paul James, "a rich man's son." And he'd married a rich man's daughter.

In 1905, Harry Warde had connected Toronto's Irish Catholic establishment with its Los Angeles counterpart by marrying Mary Estelle Donegan, the only daughter of Daniel Donegan, "one of the leading contractors of Los Angeles and prominent in all civic affairs," a man who had laid out most of the streets of Pasadena, California, and, in 1893, had even patented a "crematory" in Los Angeles. Estelle grew up on South Bunker Hill in Los Angeles in a twenty-room mansion known locally as The Castle.

According to a society report of their wedding, the bride was "led to the altar preceded by choir boys in blood red velvet with soft ermine waving sweetly as they walked, and by dainty bridesmaids with pretty picture hats and arms filled with blooming roses."

Although HW had served a stint as the company vice-president, he seemed more comfortable running the Queen City Stables established by his father, or presiding at Toronto's Lakeview Golf Club, of which he had become the "proprietor" in 1911.

Luckily, Harry Warde Phelan arrived in the president's office at a propitious moment. The Depression had begun to recede, war was looming, air travel was in its infancy. Some of the old optimism crept back. A new rail station opened in London, Ontario, with a ceremony conducted by the lord mayor of London, England.

More significantly, for the company and the country, Canada's first airport restaurant, the Tea Wing, opened in the new Dorval airport in Montreal in the fall of 1941. Within five years, the airport would be playing host to a quarter of a million passengers a year; within the decade that number would nudge one million—most of them needing food and refreshment.

Under normal circumstances, given that airports were under the control of the federal Department of Transport, there should have been an open bidding process in which various companies could compete for lucrative contracts to supply exclusive services like restaurants and newsstands at Canadian airports.

But these were not normal times. Dorval began operations in the early days of the Second World War when the Department of Transport was too busy training pilots to ship overseas to worry about a "frankly experimental facility at a time when nobody knew what to do with airline patrons ... No other firms were asked to bid on airport development since no others were in fact equipped to do the job."

CRNCo. already knew how to do what needed to be done. They had, of course, serviced railway passengers for decades and passenger ships before that. And they had already begun providing cafeteria services and hotel accommodation for the Royal Air Force's Ferry Command, a secretive operation based at Dorval. Its goal in the days before the United States entered the war was to speed urgently needed aircraft from their manufacturers in Canada and the United States to the front lines of the war in Europe.

No wonder Ottawa turned to the Canada Railway News Company to get the necessary meals moving quickly. In 1941, the company, which had already been putting together box lunches at its Bonaventure Station restaurant and trucking them to the airport, opened Canada's first flight kitchen in a house next to the Ferry Command complex. It was, suggests *Cara: 100 Years*, "a wing-and-a-prayer culinary shot in the dark"—but it worked.

CRNCo., as it so often had, quickly applied what it had learned at Dorval to Toronto's Malton Airport northwest of the city. It prepared meals in its Sunnyside rail station, then carted them to an old farmhouse that had seen previous service as Malton's first terminal building. Its first floor was quickly converted to a primitive flight kitchen. CRNCo. employees bunked upstairs. When they were needed, they "rushed downstairs and buttered sandwiches at all hours of the day and night." CRNCo.'s first in-the-airport public space was a ten-seat coffee house, also known as the Tea Wing, that opened in Toronto a few months after Dorval.

Despite what was happening all around them, "the elderly men" who controlled CRNCo. still "viewed air travel with skepticism." They looked instead at the company's existing "branches" and noted with satisfaction that most were still profitable. The few that had racked up losses reported losing no more than $700 over a full year. Those losses, as HW Phelan had suggested, could easily be managed, thanks to profits from other, larger branches.

No one paid much attention to the underlying problems—an aging workforce, systems under strain, and the seemingly inevitable collapse of an outdated railway system being overtaken by improved highways, more and better private automobiles, and, yes, the coming dramatic expansion of air travel.

According to *Cara: 100 Years*, however, the company's interest in the possibilities of air travel wasn't "spurred by the lure of instant riches, but by a pardonable desire to get in while things were still being handed to them on a silver platter."

In 1944, the company's directors agreed to form Aero Caterers Limited (Aero), with the majority of shares held by CRNCo. Most of the rest were held by Phelans, which may explain why TP's nephew Charles C. Phelan, who was already running CRNCo.'s western division from Winnipeg, which also happened to be where Trans-Canada Air Lines (TCA) was headquartered, was elected its president.

The following year, on September 23, 1945, Harry Warde Phelan, who was just sixty-three, died "after suffering a seizure while golfing at the Lakeview

Golf Club in Toronto." He was succeeded by his cousin Eugene Dillon Phelan, who also happened to be Charles C.'s brother.

The two brothers could trace their corporate lineage back through their father, Charles A. Phelan, TP's brother, who had served as a vice-president of the Canada Railway News Company. They now might have been expected to be the leaders who would guide the company into its post-war future.

They weren't. Instead, it would be Harry Warde Phelan's eighth child and fourth son, Paul James Phelan, who would return from wartime service to wake the sleeping corporate giant. He would become, in every way, the true successor to swashbuckling founder Thomas Patrick Phelan and the man who would lead the company to its greatest successes.

Waking the Sleeping Giant

The wedding was low key, unremarked upon in the society pages of the Toronto newspapers of the day. In part, of course, that was because the marriage of Paul James Phelan, twenty-five, and Helen Doris Gardiner, twenty-four, took place in the relative privacy of the rectory of Holy Rosary Church on St. Clair Avenue West in Toronto. It was Friday, October 2, 1942, which not coincidentally happened to be in the middle of the darkest, deepest depths of the Second World War.

Paul James—PJ—had wrangled a brief leave from his posting as Royal Canadian Air Force (RCAF) squadron leader in remote Newfoundland to come home for the ceremony. He wore his blue dress uniform. Helen was dressed in a simple blue suit. The bride would remember that the Roman Catholic church, which had been modelled after a fifteenth-century Gothic church in Huntingdonshire, England, was "lovely," but that the rectory, where they exchanged their vows, seemed tired, its floor covered with a "cheap looking" linoleum.

Their courtship had hardly been the stuff of high romance either. They'd met by accident early in the war. PJ, who was training for wartime service at the RCAF's Camp Borden base 100 kilometres north of Toronto, had decided to take advantage of its location not far from Ontario's ski slopes and spent one off-duty day skiing. Helen happened to be skiing that day too. She would recall later how impressed she'd been to think a young officer with so little time off would spend those hours in such healthy activity. She learned later it was the only leave day PJ would ever spend skiing.

No matter. They fell in love. For much of the nearly two years that followed, their blossoming relationship was necessarily conducted from a long distance. Still, that had obviously been enough for Helen to say yes to the handsome, adventurous PJ and no to another suitor, a young man named Harold Kirby whom her parents might have considered a more suitable match. (He was later killed in the war.)

But there was more to the understatedness of their wedding day than just the fact it was wartime.

It is fair to say Percy and Gertrude Gardiner did not look with favour on their only daughter's choice of husband. Percy finally decided to attend the wedding only reluctantly and at the last moment.

He had his reasons. For starters, he believed Helen was marrying beneath the social station to which he had long aspired and now achieved.

There was no question Helen herself was "a catch." She was a beauty who'd once dreamed of becoming a movie star. She had even auditioned in a Hollywood screen test. But she was also academically bright and unusually ambitious. She became one of the few women of her generation to attend university. As an undergraduate at University College, a division of the University of Toronto, she had combined her by now extracurricular passion for acting—she starred for three years running in the UC Follies with future Canadian comedy icons Johnny Wayne and Frank Shuster—with outstanding scholastic achievement. She earned her honours degree in psychology in 1940, then won a scholarship to do post-graduate work in the United States. "But my father wouldn't let me accept it," Helen complained many years later. "My mother wasn't well; the war was on. But my brother would have been able to go. My father never thought of my life. He thought of the family."[15]

By the 1940s, the Gardiner family—Percy, Gertrude, son George, and daughter Helen—were members in excellent standing of Toronto's Irish Protestant aristocracy. Percy Ryerson Gardiner was a partner in Gardiner, Wardrop & Company, a successful stockbrokerage he had founded in 1926. The following year, he and his wife had acquired 57 acres in Emery Village near the Humber River in the western suburbs of Toronto. There, they built Rivermede, a lavish "cottage" specifically designed for hosting charitable fundraising events and entertaining Toronto's business, cultural, social, and sporting elite. Rivermede, which included tennis courts and a $75,000 swimming pool, was where Canada's Olympic swim team—of which the Gardiners' only son, George, was a member—trained for the 1936 Berlin games.

Percy and an entrepreneurial stockbroker colleague, Ronald Graham, also branched into various money-making ventures, purchasing a controlling interest in the Toronto Dairy Company, which they later sold for a million-dollar profit, and buying Atlantic Sugar Refineries, "which earned them an average of a million dollars a year during the Depression."[16]

During the 1930s, they'd also acquired the Toronto, Hamilton, Ottawa, and London, Ontario, outlets of an American-based restaurant chain known as Bowles Lunch. Named after its shoemaker-founder, Henry Leland Bowles—who had grown tired of "disappointing" meals on his travels around the United States and opened his own first restaurant in Springfield, Massachusetts, in 1897—Bowles's unique men-only establishments became popular gathering spots wherever they were located.

There were no locks on the doors, so the restaurants remained open twenty-four hours a day. "Women were not barred," the *Ottawa Citizen* would insist years later. "It was just not a place women wished to go. The atmosphere was masculine, loud, and often bawdy." The menu was whimsical: a dish of baked beans was billed as "Musical Fruit"; prunes were "A Dish of CPR Strawberries"; and two poached eggs on toast were advertised as "Adam and Eve on a Raft." Distinguished by "an interior that consisted almost entirely of white porcelain"—one wag referred to it as "Early Men's Bathroom"—a patron ate at a small table that ingeniously doubled as the arm of their chair.

What Bowles restaurants boasted in abundance, however, was atmosphere, the sense of being an in-the-know insider. Partly because of their downtown locations, often near city halls, Bowles's regular lunchtime patrons included businessmen, journalists, and politicians. That made Bowles an excellent investment for an upwardly mobile businessman seeking acknowledgement of his own place within that circle.[17]

By the beginning of the Second World War, Percy had become well respected in Toronto, not only as an entrepreneur but also as a philanthropist and supporter of worthy civic causes. In 1937, for example, he was one of a small group of investors who bought the city's Maple Leafs baseball club just to prevent the International League team from being acquired by US interests and moved to Albany.

Despite his outward trappings of old wealth and noblesse oblige largesse, however, Percy Gardiner himself was hardly a gentleman to the manor born. One of seven children of Percival and Mary Gardiner, he was born in 1896 in Mount Forest, a small town 150 kilometres northwest of Toronto. Orphaned at thirteen, he made his way to Toronto three years later with just $20 in his pocket. After landing work in the purchasing department of a brass company, he taught himself enough about the intricacies of the metal business to open his own company while still in his twenties. He became a self-made millionaire.

What happened after that would become a public history that gauzed over Percy's down-at-the-heels personal beginnings.

Set side by side, there wasn't all that much to distinguish the Gardiners from the Phelans as family-business families. By some measures, in fact, the Phelans would have been considered the more established of the two. Paul James could already trace his own family's business beginnings back through two increasingly successful generations. The Canada Railway News Company operated coast to coast; owned hotels, restaurants, and newsstands; and employed thousands. PJ, the son of its late president, was already poised to climb the executive ladder, maybe even become president himself when the war was finally over.

So why, then, did Percy Gardiner consider PJ Phelan such an unworthy suitor for his daughter?

"Because he was Catholic," PJ's daughter Gail explains with a laugh. Ironically, she adds, Percy's own wife, Gertrude, had also been born Roman Catholic, "but she gave it up to marry Percy." That skeleton having been long since neatly tucked—and forgotten—in the back of the Gardiner family closet, PJ's Catholicism must have served as an unwelcome reminder of a past Percy himself would just as soon forget.

Compounding PJ's original sin of Catholicism—in the eyes of the Gardiners at least—was the reality that the Phelans were, well ... "from the other side of the tracks." The Phelan clan were, in Rose's telling, "far more good-looking, glamorous, and flashy" than the dour Gardiners. They also enjoyed, adds Gail, "much more partying." As businessmen, the Gardiners were "very disciplined and very astute. Dad was more seat of the pants, but Dad was very talented too, and he had a vision for business."

All that helped stoke natural lifelong rivalries—not only between PJ and Percy, his new father-in-law, but also between PJ and his wife, Helen. After Percy died of a heart attack at the age of sixty-nine in 1965, Helen would become not only a benefactor of her father's estate but also, ultimately, a corporate director in her own right.

The inter-family rivalry also extended to include PJ and George, Percy's son. George was the same age as PJ and would—like PJ—become a "very successful, brilliant entrepreneur." George would launch two stockbroking firms, including Canada's first discount brokerage; serve as president of the Toronto Stock Exchange; and found both Gardiner Oil and Gas Ltd. and Scott's Hospitality Inc., the Kentucky Fried Chicken business that would ultimately become a fast-food rival to PJ's Cara Operations.

To complicate that rivalry, Helen herself served on the board of Scott's Hospitality, which was one-quarter owned by Percy's grandchildren, including PJ's own four children. It was, well, complicated.

In business, PJ could always more than hold his own. But that never seemed to be enough for his in-laws.

After Percy died, Helen once asked her brother, in hopefulness, "Wouldn't Dad be proud of how well PJ has done?"

George didn't miss a beat. "He would have been surprised," he retorted.

Despite Percy's personal and religious misgivings about his soon-to-be son-in-law, the truth is that he also quietly employed his considerable influence within Canada's political-military establishment—even before the wedding—to keep PJ as far from the worst of the deadly air war in Europe as possible. Perhaps his concern had less to do with PJ's safety and more with his daughter's happiness. No matter. The concern was well grounded. By 1945, more than 17,000 Canadian airmen would die in action. According to the Bomber Command Museum of Canada, "of every 100 airmen who joined Bomber Command [in the Second World War], 45 were killed, six were seriously wounded, eight became prisoners of war, and only 41 escaped unscathed."

As one of Canada's famous dollar-a-year men—a select group of businessmen who had been seconded to Ottawa to help with the war effort while their companies paid their salaries and Ottawa covered their expenses—Percy knew exactly who to call and what to say. The sell probably wasn't all that difficult. PJ's two younger brothers, Jerome and Donnie, who'd also joined the air force, had been killed already. No single family deserved to lose so many of its sons. And no daughter of Percy Gardiner should end up a war widow.

So PJ, a squadron leader, had been dispatched to a massive, jerry-built military station in the tiny, isolated town of Botwood on Newfoundland's rugged northern coast. There, he and members of his squadron occupied their days and nights on anti-submarine patrol in the skies above the frigid eastern North Atlantic. While not as dangerous as making bombing runs over enemy cities, their role was at least as vital to the war effort. Flying amphibious Canso aircraft—"flying boats" specially designed to cover long distances and land anywhere, including the ocean—PJ and his crew of ten scanned the sea for signs of German U-boats, provided early warning of danger ahead to convoys carrying vital supplies across the ocean to Europe, occasionally engaged the enemy, and scrambled as needed to provide search and rescue assistance when ships were sunk, as they often were. Between March and September 1942, German submarines sank Allied merchant ships at the rate of one hundred per month, killing thousands of sailors and sending tons of precious cargo to the sea bottom.

Many of those attacks happened in an area of the mid-Atlantic known as the "Black Pit," a swath of the ocean beyond the range of Allied aircraft stationed on the eastern edges of North America or on the west coast of Europe. Finally, in late 1943, thanks to a deal between Great Britain and ostensibly neutral Portugal, the Allies were able to use a landing strip on Terceira, one of nine small volcanic islands off Portugal known as the Azores. From there, they would be able to patrol that otherwise inaccessible expanse of the mid-Atlantic.

Sometime after that agreement, PJ and his crew were instructed to relocate there. But when their aircraft was more than halfway on its 2,500-kilometre journey across the Atlantic to its destination, the crew received an emergency radio message from Newfoundland, instructing them to turn around and immediately return to their home base. The Azores were being battered by a hurricane and they wouldn't be able to land. Too late, PJ radioed back. They were already more than halfway to the Azores; they didn't have enough fuel to return to Newfoundland. You must return, came the order. So, PJ and his crew stripped the plane of its seats, guns, anything they could toss into the sea. And then they turned, nose back in the direction from which they'd come, climbed as high as they could, shut off the engine, drifted slowly downward, restarted the engine at the last moment, climbed again, repeating the manoeuvre over and over as they edged closer and closer to their destination.

They made it, "but there wasn't a drop of fuel left when they finally landed back in Newfoundland," his daughter Gail says today. She never heard that story from her father, who rarely spoke of the details of his wartime experiences. She heard it from one of his fellow fliers nearly sixty years later as part of a tribute at her father's funeral.

After their wedding, PJ and Helen didn't have the time or opportunity to enjoy a real honeymoon. Instead, PJ hurried back to his base in Newfoundland. Helen joined him soon after. By then, PJ and four fellow officers had built a single cabin for themselves and their wives near Botwood. Though the cabin had privacy partitions and a shared stove for heat, conditions would have been "primitive," certainly a far cry from the tennis courts and pool at Rivermede where Helen had spent her formative summers. Gail remembers her parents telling her about the night Helen found herself being frightened in the outhouse by a wild horse. Perhaps it's no wonder Helen returned to Toronto in the summer of 1944 to give birth to Gail.

By the time she and the baby reunited with PJ, he'd been transferred to the RCAF's Shearwater base in somewhat more urban Dartmouth, Nova Scotia. On the way to the new posting in October 1944, PJ and Helen enjoyed a brief belated honeymoon/vacation at the elegant Algonquin Resort in St. Andrews by-the-Sea, which was much closer to the life Helen had lived before the war. "I went with them," says Gail, "but I don't remember." She would have been barely three months old at the time.

The rest of the war passed relatively uneventfully, at least in PJ's and Helen's later telling. The most interesting moment happened in early May 1945 in Halifax when several thousand servicemen, merchant seamen, and civilians celebrated victory in Europe with a two-day riot—payback, in part, for the shabby way servicemen believed the city had treated them during six long years of war. PJ didn't take part, but as squadron leader, he had to bail out some of his exuberant airmen who'd been caught "urinating in public because they had too much beer."

In November 1945, PJ was finally discharged from the RCAF. He, Helen, and the baby headed back to Toronto. Paul James Phelan was twenty-eight, and he was eager not only to take his place in the Phelan family business but also to make it his own.

Paul Phelan was frustrated. Yet another beside-the-point meeting of the board of the Canada Railway News Company. This one was about coffins, of all things. At least on this day the old-men directors—and they were, in Paul's view, *old*—had fretted about something that mattered to them, if not to CRNCo.'s shareholders, employees, or customers.

"In an excess of thrift," as the author of *Cara: 100 Years* described it, "the senior partners had bought shares in a funeral home and occupied their morning in hot debate on the merits of wholesale coffins, literally measuring one another for the great beyond with rulers borrowed from an astonished secretary. Then, the powers of Canadian Railway News adjourned for lunch, problems unresolved, directions undetermined."

PJ feared there was a different coffin the directors would soon be measuring: the company's own. In fact, Paul Warde, JD's son and PJ's cousin, who handled the Canada Railway News Company's insurance dealings, warned

PJ not to join the company. The railway passenger trade, he confided, was "a dying business."

The stark reality, rarely spoken of around the boardroom table, was that one man, the federal minister of transport, could, with a flourish of his pen, wipe out the majority of the company's business, which at that point consisted largely of contracts with the federally owned railway and the federally owned airline.

Canada's railways, of course, were in a steep decline that was getting steeper by the day. No wonder Canadian National, which previously had signed five-year contracts with CRNCo. without bothering to ask many questions, was now demanding a full-scale mid-term renegotiation of the latest deal because, well, business was bad and getting worse.

It was 1954, and PJ Phelan—back from the war and now both a CRNCo. shareholder and director—began preparing himself, heedless of the warnings and portents, for a lifetime in the family business.

He had signed up for a restaurant management course at Ryerson Institute of Technology, "which was more than any of the company's managers had bothered to do. Nobody," he would recall later, "knew anything about fine-tuning the back of the house."

He had also been "saddened and enraged" to discover that CRNCo. was no longer doing railway servicing business in its—and his—home city of Toronto. "He declared that unless the company could maintain a presence in Union Station, it had become 'effete' and was engaging in a betrayal of its roots." Two years later, thanks largely to his efforts, the company took over the station's elegant Oak Room restaurant, plus its lunch counter and luncheonette. But even that didn't—couldn't—halt the rail industry's decline.

CRNCo.'s issue with Trans-Canada Air Lines was the reverse. Airplane traffic was growing at the rate of 20 to 30 per cent a year and CRNCo., through its Aero subsidiary, struggled to keep up. In 1947, 180,000 passengers at Malton Airport "funneled through a totally inadequate wooden building" that was "bursting at the seams." Within the decade, the number of passengers passing through would nudge one million.

When he returned from wartime service, PJ had set out to "revolutionize" Malton's ten-seat coffee shop. That project took an incredible—and exhausting—fifteen years to bring to fruition. In 1946, the board assigned him to look for a suitable property near its old farmhouse to "plug the gap until permanent quarters became available. His interim solution was a pair of wartime dormitories, and for the next few years Aero played tag between these and other temporary structures." In 1949, he presented plans for a fifty-eight-seat restaurant coupled with a new flight kitchen, but it would take another dozen years for the $100,000 restaurant-kitchen upgrade to become reality. In the meantime, Hurricane Hazel swept through in 1954, and "a tent full of supplies blew away."

Trans-Canada Air Lines wasn't exactly sympathetic or accommodating. At one point, during renegotiations of its contract with Aero, the airline demanded the company take on responsibility not only for delivering food aboard its airplanes but also for collecting the dishes and utensils later. Aero agreed "under protest, pointing out that [its] equipment kept being pilfered by souvenir-hunting passengers."

Still, TCA kept demanding more and more, including, incredibly, nine-course meals featuring Jamaica turtle soup, to please the palates of passengers on its new futuristic Lockheed Super Constellation jets, which also boasted "unheard-of" refinements like air conditioning, reclining seats, even extra lavatories.

As a result, CRNCo.'s Aero subsidiary was facing an "unremitting financial squeeze" during the mid-1950s as demand for new and expanded flight kitchen facilities outstripped the company's capacity to develop them. Instead of confronting those issues head-on, "company minutes record an understandable display of cold feet, as the directors cast about for alternative means of raising cash."

At the same time, the company, which treasured its long-standing reputation as a benevolent employer, was also facing a looming mass retirement crisis. A generation of loyal but aging workers was heading into retirement without ever having considered there would come an end to their working days and without a company pension plan to fall back on. It was PJ who took on the task of studying the prospects for a company-wide pension plan and the feasibility of providing generous retirement allowances.

Paul James Phelan shouldn't have cared as much as he did. Theoretically, he wouldn't have been destined for a top leadership role. He was not his family's oldest child, or even its first son. He was the eighth of ten children born over the course of just fourteen years to Harry and Estelle Phelan.

Of his three older brothers, two had attracted headlines for all the wrong reasons: one tried to kill himself by shooting himself in the heart in Los Angeles over a nightclub bill he couldn't pay; another had been sentenced to die by a rebel firing squad in the lead-up to the Spanish Civil War. He was only saved by the personal intervention of Anthony Eden, the British foreign secretary. And PJ's two youngest brothers, of course, had already died in service early in the Second World War.

PJ's own beginnings had been anything but auspicious. "As a child, he stood last in school, was a stutterer, spent time in Latin class drawing yachts and airplanes." He attended De La Salle College in Toronto, a private Catholic school, "but left before earning a high school diploma." Instead, he parlayed a small family inheritance into a planned trip around the world. He got as far as Germany when the winds of war began blowing gusts, and he quickly headed home to Canada to enlist in the Royal Canadian Air Force.

At some point before the war—probably between leaving school and beginning his world travels—he did a stint as a lowly clerk at the family business. He was initially dispatched to Union Station where he was introduced to the inner workings of the operation, including observing a "strange and wonderful production line buttering several hundred slices of bread at once with the aid of a large paintbrush. He saw, in an adjoining office, a desk piled high with crumpled dollar bills—the instant feedback provided by a 'cash-only' business. He nodded hello to the somewhat Dickensian clerk dozing off at another desk, his head drooping lower and lower until at last a fresh ink spot adorned his startled nose. And, having absorbed these things, Paul Phelan headed for the company's North Bay, Ontario, station, where he commenced to look not to the past but to a future of his own."

By 1961, however, the future for the Canada Railway News Company looked to be further and further in the rear-view mirror. While the company continued to spend money faster than it could make it just to keep up with the exploding demand to service the airline industry, profits from its railway operations shrivelled to just $82,000 in 1960, and then to nothing at all in 1961.

To make matters worse, "in a classic rush to corporate judgement [*sic*]," the board made a $300,000 deal with a company called MealMaster Foods to supply Air Canada—the newly christened incarnation of Trans-Canada Air Lines—with futuristic flash-frozen meals for its passengers. Turkey dinners began flying off the assembly line "like a machine gun." The problem? The company lost three cents on every dinner it served. "We were losing our shirts," Paul would complain. It would take years for the company to extricate itself from that mess.

The only good news was that the CRNCo.'s corporate assets—"the gilt-edged balance sheet so beloved by TP"—were still worth three times the company's debt. That gave PJ, who took over as president in 1961, the room he needed to make his own corporate dream reality.

By then, there were 2,000 outstanding CRNCo. shares, "scattered from Halifax to Vancouver and held by almost 50 individuals and trusts." They had been trading at deflated prices within the family for years. Working at first with just a foolscap pad, and later "with a phalanx of auditors and lawyers," PJ devised a plan to buy back the outstanding shares for a generous $1,000 a share. That would require a total payout of $2 million.

PJ found the first million in CRNCo.'s own balance sheet, effectively buying back the shares with his shareholders' own money. "Then," according to *Cara: 100 Years*, "he offered them a debenture covering the remainder, geared to an interest rate equal to the dividend to which they'd grown accustomed. This he promised to pay off in ten years out of corporate earnings; in fact, it was paid off in five."

At that point—with total control of the company in his hands—PJ undertook a corporate restructuring, merging CRNCo. and Aero into a single entity he called Cara Operations Ltd.

Why Cara? Well, that seemed to depend. At times, PJ noted that Cara was an Irish word meaning "friend." But in 1992, he would tell a reporter for Canadian Press that the name Canada Railway News Company had simply seemed "old fashioned," so he had prosaically shortened it to Cara, the first two letters of the first two words of its former incarnation, "Canada Railway..."

At around the same time, PJ began a personal transition from being his company's entrepreneur-operator-everything to becoming its owner-overseer. Because he would now be supported by professional managers who could run the company on a day-to-day basis, PJ had the time to focus on future big-picture thinking.

Boyd Matchett became the key professional manager for PJ. By the time he officially joined Cara as its vice-president and general manager in 1962, he was already intimately familiar with the firm's operations. In 1961, PJ had hired Urwick Currie, a Canadian management consulting firm, to help him plot Cara's next steps. Matchett, who'd spent more than a decade as the Paris-based manager of Massey Harris, the Canadian tractor maker, before returning to Canada and joining Urwick, had co-authored its report on Cara, which "both pinpointed the firm's weaknesses and stressed its potential for reorganization and diversification."

PJ liked what he read. More than that, he liked Matchett. Though six years younger than PJ, Matchett was also a Second World War veteran—he'd been a sonar specialist aboard naval vessels escorting merchant convoys across the North Atlantic—as well as a sportsman who enjoyed tennis and skiing. They were both charter members of the Osler ski resort in Collingwood, Ontario.

With PJ's blessing and support, Matchett began upgrading Cara's flight kitchens and consolidating its retail operations in air terminals, railway stations, hotels, and shopping centres into one entity. Matchett became company president in 1969.

PJ had already taken another key step in Cara's evolution, taking the company public in 1968. The initial public offering represented approximately 29 per cent of the outstanding stock. PJ, through his family's Holdings company, still owned 52 per cent of the operating company, giving him ultimate control. Investors seemed more than happy with that, driving up the price of the stock by 55 per cent—from $13 to $20 a share—in its first three days on the market.

That may have been a reflection of some of the newly public company's ambitious expansion plans. According to a *Financial Post* article that summer, Cara was already planning a new chain of fast, self-service restaurants as well as more highway restaurants under a deal with Imperial Oil, and was even considering getting into the motor-inn business in collaboration with an American or Canadian chain.

None of those grand plans came to fruition. Instead, the deal that would ultimately transform Cara's future, which wasn't cemented until nearly a decade later, happened more by accident than design.

That's another story.

~

Bernie Syron hadn't intended to become the president of a fast-food franchisor. But he'd studied corporate financing at law school, and the first job he landed after graduation was as corporate counsel to Harvey's, then a ten-year-old Canadian hamburger chain.

Harvey's specialized in cooked-to-order charcoal-broiled burgers customized with a variety of toppings while the customer watched. The concept was the brainchild of a savvy Toronto-based Montreal native named Rick Mauran, then just twenty-five.

There was no Harvey. In truth, Mauran, who had been looking for a brand name that conveyed a sense of down-home friendliness, chose Harvey's after seeing an ad in a Toronto newspaper for John Harvey Motors, a local car dealership popularly known as Harvey's that was in the process of closing its doors. Originally intended to be a seasonal operation only, the first Harvey's restaurant opened in 1959 in Richmond Hill, a Toronto suburb. It was so successful Mauran kept it open year-round. (At the time, there was little competition in the burger business; the first McDonald's wouldn't open in Canada for another eight years, and its first Ontario franchise, in London, Ontario, didn't launch until 1968.)

Mauran soon opened an additional Harvey's at 238 Bloor Street, just a few metres from another Mauran chain culinary creation known as Swiss Chalet. Its decor—dark wood panelling and ceiling beams, and small fake windows with frilly cotton curtains—had been designed to recreate the appearance of a Swiss mountain hideaway, a nod to Mauran's Swiss ancestry. The restaurant's original menu featured comfort food—broiled chicken spit-roasted over an open flame accompanied by a baked potato or fresh-cut fries, coleslaw, dipping sauce, and half a hamburger bun, not to forget a water bowl with a lemon wedge to wash your fingers in after eating. The restaurant's limited menu was carefully priced to attract young working families seeking an affordable outing.

In the beginning, Syron's corporate focus was supposed to be expanding Mauran's other venture, the publicly traded Harvey's chain. But then, in 1969, just a year after he joined the company, the stock market "went to the dumpster, our stock went to nothing." He laughs. "So, I'm sitting there. The company's insolvent, the president has resigned, and Rick came to me and said, 'What do you think? Can we turn this around?'"

Syron, who'd been carefully analyzing the company's pluses and minuses, offered a straightforward response. "Well, I don't think there's any [new] problem because I can see all the problems," he told Mauran. "I told you about the problems, and you were not listening."

Mauran was listening now. There were too many distractions in the company that "don't count for really what you're doing," he told Mauran. Like that subsidiary company in Germany they needed to jettison. And too many "bad franchises." Not to forget those other franchises that needed to be refinanced.

Mauran agreed with Syron's assessment, so in 1969 the two men teamed up. Syron became the company president. "We spent four years cleaning up. I was on the road all the time." Eventually, they'd righted the corporate ship to the point where they were able to not only begin opening Harvey's outlets again but also bring Swiss Chalet under the Harvey's umbrella. In 1974, they renamed the whole operation as Foodcorp Limited.

Three years later, Syron was approached by a British Columbia entrepreneur who was interested in opening Harvey's outlets on the West Coast. At the time, Syron says, he was too busy expanding in Ontario, "so I said, 'Certainly.' I sold them a blanket franchise to open so many stores, a typical kind of deal." But the would-be franchisee soon ran into financial problems of his own. Rather than abandon the idea entirely, the would-be franchisee approached someone he knew at Cara to see if that company might be interested in partnering with him.

"And that," says Syron, "is when Paul Phelan arrives on the scene."

PJ wasn't interested in a partnership. "Paul does not take partners," Syron explains today with a laugh. Instead, he offered to buy not just the phantom British Columbia franchises but Foodcorp itself. "Paul was a very smart guy, and he understood the fast-food business was a growing business, and Cara needed to own a piece of it."

Cara had already tried, without great success, to grab a big bite of the burger business. The year before, Boyd Matchett, in what was described as a "base-broadening" move, had engineered the purchase of the fifty-five-restaurant Winco Steak N' Burger chain, a successful but relatively small-scale competitor in the fast-growing fast-food burger space. But Steak N' Burger with its Wild West theme—the walls were festooned with western memorabilia with wagon wheels for chandeliers and waitresses in Stetson hats—already seemed dated and out of step with an urbanizing cosmopolitan Toronto.

It didn't take PJ long to understand that, if he really wanted to become a serious fast-food player, Steak N' Burger wasn't the way to go. "So, he looked at us," Syron explains today, "and he said, 'How do I buy the company?'"

It wasn't that simple. Because Cara's existing business was primarily based on monthly contracts and leased land at airports and train stations, it didn't have significant stores of cash or capital assets of its own to use as collateral. "So, when Paul went to his bank for a loan, the bank turned him down." Instead, in an unusual arrangement, Cara purchased Foodcorp for $35.5 million, twice its book value, using Foodcorp's own assets and significant cash flow to secure the necessary loan.

Why didn't Foodcorp simply buy Cara instead?

There were a couple of reasons, Syron says now. For starters, Foodcorp wasn't interested in getting into the less glamorous airline-railway catering business that was Cara's stock-in-trade. Perhaps more importantly, Rick Mauran had already begun to lose interest in the fast-food business—he and two partners had launched Mackenzie, a mutual fund company, in 1967—and was ready to sell.

The Foodcorp deal not only added seventy-three Harvey's and fifteen Swiss Chalets to Cara's existing fast-food roster of Steak N' Burgers but also vaulted Cara into a pre-eminent position as Canada's largest public company in the hospitality industry with $300 million in annual sales.

But PJ's decision to buy Foodcorp and keep control rather than merge the two companies had been expensive. While he was happy to take credit for its success, noted journalist Ian Brown, PJ "berated" Boyd Matchett for months over the cost required to make it happen.[18]

Initially, Foodcorp operated as a subsidiary of Cara. Matchett, based in Cara's head office on York Street, continued to oversee the parent company and its four divisions—the airline services division, which operated in-flight catering and flight kitchens; the air terminal restaurant division; the retail stores division; and a relatively new high-end urban restaurant division. Meanwhile Bernie Syron and his original team ran Foodcorp—now including Winco—from a separate head office at 240 Bloor Street.

"What happened," Syron explains, "is that we're making a lot of money and they're [Matchett's group] not doing very much. So, Boyd wanted to amalgamate, and he wanted to take over everything. But we said, 'No, that's not going to work for us. We're building a big company here. We're doing well, we're successful, and we want to stay that way.'"

PJ Phelan had a critically important decision to make. But this time he would have help from a new source.

~

One of the side effects of PJ's decision to hire Boyd Matchett to run his company was that he had less and less Cara business to occupy his days. With the crucial, business-changing exception of masterminding the Foodcorp deal, PJ's day-to-day role in the company he had recreated had become increasingly marginalized. Business journalists, who used to call to ask PJ's opinion on Cara's stock prospects or the state of the hospitality business, now spoke to Boyd Matchett instead. PJ still attended board meetings and met almost daily with his presidents, Matchett and Syron, but he seemed content to let them operate his companies.

"Mostly I used him as a sounding board and a mentor," Syron explains. They'd usually meet late in the morning after PJ arrived at the office. "He'd always say, 'Let's go to lunch.' And I'd say, 'Let's have our meeting first.'" Syron's official explanation was that they shouldn't discuss business at the Toronto Club, PJ's favourite haunt, in case someone might overhear their conversation.

So, the meeting would happen first. PJ would invariably ask, "'What about Swiss Chalet? What about Harvey's? What are we doing here? What about over there?' And I'd bring him up to speed." Finally, after their business conversation wrapped up, they'd leave for lunch. "That was our ritual," Syron explains. "We never met in the afternoon. We always met in the morning when he came in."

Why was that? "Well," Syron explains coyly, "it was just a better time."

The reality was that PJ's boozy lunches at the Toronto Club, which was located conveniently near to Cara's York Street headquarters, often stretched late into the afternoon. If he wasn't at his club, "he'd go with his buddies sailing," Syron explains. Which was just fine by Syron. "In a way that worked perfectly from the company's point of view," he says, "because you were able to sort of manage the business without interference."

Thanks to their personal wealth, which grew in step with the seemingly inexorable growth of Cara, PJ and Helen had become in-demand Toronto socialites who attended events and fundraising dinners almost nightly.

When they weren't traversing the city's social circuit, they often entertained at home in their 8 Old Forest Hill Road mansion where their parties, sometimes for one hundred or more guests, were already legendary. "Sailing parties, neighbourhood parties, Christmas parties, parties for this event or that event," Rose, their youngest daughter, remembers. "There were lots of parties."

And travel. During the winters, PJ and Helen often vacationed at the Club at Windermere Island in Eleuthera, a string of islands on the Grand Bahama Bank. With a spectacular sandy beach running the island's entire

8-kilometre length, beachside villas, a pool, tennis courts, and a restaurant, the Windermere was one of the most private gated resorts on the planet. It offered what *Globe and Mail* travel writer Wallace Immen described as an "escape for people whose reality is too much inhabited by phones and flashbulbs, beepers and business, fans and frenzy. Little wonder then that the roster of guests attracted to the island becomes regular fodder for the social columns. Dukes, duchesses, barons and viscounts are members along with a cross-section of Toronto's business aristocracy ... Paul Phelan, who is chairman of Cara Corp., rubs shoulders here with the Astors, Kents and Waleses."[19]

Helen even brought her chauffeur along wherever she travelled. He'd originally worked for Helen's father, Percy. When Percy died, he "bequeathed" the chauffeur—and his salary for life—to his daughter. "She couldn't bear to get into a taxi with another driver," a family friend said. So, the chauffeur would accompany them when they travelled, rent a car when they landed, and be available, as needed, to ferry Helen and PJ wherever they wanted to go wherever they were.

When they weren't travelling internationally, PJ and Helen could pick and choose from getaway properties closer to home. In 1963, the year their eldest daughter, Gail, married, they[20] bought Braeburn, a 100-acre farm and rambling farmhouse near Collingwood, a tourist destination on the southern edge of Georgian Bay. PJ later acquired additional parcels of adjacent land until he ended up with about 350 acres.

"At first, it was because I was getting married," Gail remembers, "and then later, when they hoped that Paul would marry [his then-girlfriend] Liz, they wanted to have a centre, a family centre for us to be together as the Phelan family." The farm, which was conveniently located at the base of the "poshest" ski resort in the Blue Mountains, Osler Bluff Ski Club, became a hub for family ski vacations as well as another venue where the Phelans would entertain.

In 1970, the Phelans bought a more rustic 1-acre property at Pointe au Baril, a collection of islands on the eastern shore of Georgian Bay, 200 kilometres north of Collingwood. Gail's young family spent most of their summers in one of its four small cabins, while PJ and Helen came, usually in August, for the sailing.

None of that is to suggest PJ didn't continue to do business. He did. He owned several Toronto rental properties in and around Rosedale, including a forty-six-unit apartment building on St. Clair Avenue West, all of which he operated through Holdings. At one point or another, all his children would end up living in his buildings, as would PJ's sister, Estelle McPherson, and Sharon's daughter, Holiday, who lived in a two-unit building on Russell Hill Road.

For a time, PJ's personal passion project became the dowdy Hotel Victoria at 56 Yonge near King Street, which he bought in 1971 for just $10,000 cash and an agreement to assume responsibility for its growing debts. Built after the city's Great Fire of 1904, the eight-storey hotel, named in honour of Queen Victoria, had once been a downtown Toronto landmark. It served as everything from an emergency hospital during the 1918 flu pandemic to the home of the Churchill Club, which raised funds for the war effort during the Second World War.

By the late 1960s, however, the hotel—unrenovated since the war—had fallen on hard times. It came to be known, according to the *Toronto Star*, for its "cigar-chomping prospectors, ladies of the evening and beer-drinking Bay Street stockbrokers." When PJ bought it, the hotel was facing "foreclosure and, most likely, a hasty demolition in the name of progress."

Instead, PJ spent $2.5 million to return the Victoria to its "Edwardian glory days." According to a later history of the hotel, he "became personally involved in every detail of the renovation, 'picking up Victorian prints in London to hang on the walls, changing the upstairs bar into a port for sailing enthusiasts, and commissioned the Ken Cameron oil painting hanging over the lobby fireplace.'"[21]

The hotel returned to profitability during the 1970s and early 1980s, thanks largely to PJ's efforts. But when PJ learned he would have to spend millions more to upgrade the facilities to meet Toronto's new and tougher 1980s fire and safety codes, he decided to sell instead, pocketing $2.5 million from real estate developer Charles Goldsmith.

By then, PJ Phelan had another passion project into which to pour his time and his money.

~

As children, PJ and his brothers had learned to sail at the Royal Canadian Yacht Club on Toronto Island where their parents owned a house. Although PJ's father had been a prominent golfer and his grandfather a legendary horseman, sailing would become PJ's personal passion.

How passionate was he? Well, when he died in 2002, his obituary in the *Globe and Mail* began with this sailing-centred sentence: "Paul Phelan, a dashing yachtsman who took over a long-established family firm and later received the Order of Canada for his contributions to the sport of sailing, has died in Toronto..."

Such a description would not have displeased him.

Explained his daughter Gail: "He would say, 'I would go crazy if I couldn't sail.' He loved sailing, and he wanted people to share that experience."

Although PJ had been a competitive sailor himself and even raced internationally—as a young man after the Second World War in 14-foot dinghies and three-person dragon boats and, later, as the owner and sometime skipper of larger competitive yachts—he would ultimately become best known for his role as a sailing organizer, financier, and philanthropist.

In the early 1960s, he served as commodore of the Royal Canadian Yacht Club and president of the Canadian Yachting Association, a role he would reprise thirty years later. After others began managing Cara on a day-to-day basis in the '70s, PJ volunteered for the role of Canadian representative on the International Yacht Racing Union, the sailing world's governing body, which PJ described as the "world parliament of yachting." By that point, his sailing interests extended well beyond Canada, and he began to believe that his contribution to the sport of sailing, even more than his successes at Cara, would be his true legacy.

It was no surprise then that the focus of PJ's attention—and passion—became the America's Cup. It's reputed to be the world's oldest continuing international sporting competition, not to mention sailing's most coveted prize. The Auld Mug, as it is informally known, is awarded to the winner of a series of races between a vessel representing the yacht club that currently holds the Cup and a yacht from a challenging club. It is, depending on your choice of metaphor, sailing's equivalent of a world championship boxing match, soccer's World Cup, scaling Mount Everest, or even the Holy Grail. Among sailors, it is a big deal.

The first America's Cup—a race around the Isle of Wight between yachts from the British Royal Yacht Squadron and the New York Yacht Club—took place in 1851. The Americans won. And won. And won. Over the next 132 years, the NYYC successfully defended its title twenty-four times against all comers.

Over time, thanks to the event's growing international prestige and the tourism and economic windfall awaiting any country that could claim America's Cup bragging rights, plenty of well-heeled yachting enthusiasts were eager to ante up multiple millions of dollars to purpose-build ever sleeker, ever swifter 12-metre yachts simply to challenge for the prize. By 1970, so many challengers clamoured for the opportunity to take on the Americans that the would-be challengers had to first compete against one another in a gruelling series of fifty or more round-robin preliminary races to earn the right to be the last yacht left sailing to compete against the reigning champion.

Canada was late to this modern competition. A Canadian yacht had not competed for the Cup since 1881, when it had lost.

But then, in mid-1980, a Calgary lawyer, sailing enthusiast, and Canadian nationalist named Marvin McDill registered the semi-mythical Secret Cove Yacht Club at a dock and crumbling shack on Halfmoon Bay north of Vancouver and fired off a cheeky, I-challenge-you letter to the denizens of the New York Yacht Club demanding the opportunity to compete for the 1983 America's Cup.

Four months later, the Americans "deigned" to accept the challenge, not only from McDill's Canadian entry but also from other well-funded would-be challengers from Australia, Britain, France, and Italy. All would first have to fight it out for the right to take on NYYC.

The economic and logistical challenges simply to get to the starting line of the first challenge race were daunting.

By the time the NYYC accepted the Canadian challenge in late 1980, for example, *Canada I*, the designated name for Canada's entry, had yet to be designed let alone built.

McDill's campaign to raise the $5 million needed to mount even a modest challenge had barely begun when some expected sponsors backed out. "Most company treasurers spun their wheels," wrote Peter C. Newman in *Maclean's*, "citing the tough economic climate, and primly raised their eyes heavenward while invoking responsibility to shareholders."[22]

McDill initially tried to raise the cash he needed regionally but, as Newman wrote, that "strained the fiscal resources of western Canadians, not usually noted for their philanthropic impulses." Too late, McDill turned to key members of the eastern Canadian yachting fraternity, including PJ.

Though he believed McDill "didn't know what he was doing, that he was biting off more than he could chew," PJ found himself attracted by McDill's patriotic pride. "Canada is a strange country," he told *Canadian Yachting*'s Doug Hunter. "I think I know the country well. We don't know how to pull it together.[23]

At first, PJ simply dipped his toe in the funding waters. In late 1981, at the urging of his twenty-six-year-old cousin Terry McLaughlin, who'd been tapped to skipper McDill's entry, PJ purchased *Intrepid*, the yacht that had won the Canada's Cup sailing prize in 1967 and 1970. He leased it to McDill's group for $1 as a crew training platform. Later, after McDill ran into more serious financial problems, PJ not only agreed to hold a $291,000 mortgage that would allow McDill to complete construction of *Canada I* but also promised to make an additional $100,000 gift to the organization if the balance was ever paid off. Helen also wrote a cheque for $10,000.

It wasn't nearly enough.

Most of Canada's rivals were underwritten by wealthy patrons like Karim El Husseini Shah, the spiritual leader of fifteen million Ismaili Muslims and one of the world's richest men. According to *Maclean's*, El Husseini Shah "spent only an hour on the phone to enlist the financial support of 17 of Italy's leading corporations for the nation's $5-million investment." The British entry boasted $8 million in financing organized by an English merchant banker.[24]

Still, *Canada I*, skippered by McLaughlin, did manage to make it as far as the semifinals in the elimination races off Newport, Rhode Island, in August 1983. During the round-robin semifinals, however, *Canada I* figuratively ran aground, losing every one of its races, including to Britain's *Victory 83*, Italy's *Azzurra*, and the eventual winner of that year's America's Cup, *Australia II*. "The brutal truth," noted Maclean's, "was that *Canada I* was just not fast enough."

Undaunted, McDill promised he would return. "Of course, we'll be there," he told reporters. "We've already begun to put the pieces together for another shot."

PJ Phelan wanted to be part of that next shot too. Actually, he wanted to be more than just part of it. He had been "outspoken," *Maclean's* reported, "about his ambition to run the next Canadian America's Cup challenge."

But now, PJ wasn't the only one who wanted the Canadian helm.

Australia II's victory in 1983, reported the *National Post*, had already served as its country's "calling card to the rest of the world. Australia has quickly, cleverly and aggressively used the victory to help launch an intensive public relations effort which will translate into more than a billion dollars' worth of tourist revenue and inestimable goodwill worldwide." By the time of the first preliminary races in Fremantle, the site for the Cup races, Australia was expecting to welcome a million tourists.

What might a Canadian victory mean for this country?

By 1985, there were two Canadian groups challenging to challenge for the prize—McDill's group with its plans for an updated *Canada I* called *Canada II*, and an eastern Canadian group spearheaded by Donald Green, chairman and chief executive officer of Tridon, a Hamilton, Ontario, auto parts manufacturer. Its *True North* entry even had seed money from the tourist-hungry Government of Nova Scotia, which had put up $1.5 million in exchange for the group's promise to build its yacht at a dock in Halifax Harbour.

By then, however, $1.5 million was chump change.

In the summer of 1985, Green confessed to reporters that the true cost for *True North*—which he'd estimated a year earlier at $10–12 million—had now ballooned past $16.3 million. McDill's budget was a smaller but still not inconsiderable $7 million. The fact that they were each looking in the same places for significant financial contributions, Green allowed, made it easy for potential corporate sponsors to just say no. And they did.

In addition to the costs of designing and constructing their vessels, each group had to contract in advance for its own separate dock space in Fremantle and had to plunk down huge deposits to reserve space for their own sail lofts, crew accommodation, and management offices in the Australian port city. Just in case...

McDill and Green each faced severe cash flow problems. By the end of 1985, *Canada II* had spent $3 million and was $400,000 in debt. *True North*, which had already spent $8 million—much of which it didn't have—was being hit daily with new bills from Fremantle. Green was personally liable for a significant portion of *True North*'s budget.

What if the two groups put their money—and their minds—together to develop a single Canadian challenger?

While McDill and Green recognized, at a theoretical level, that one Canadian entry made the most economic and political sense, neither was prepared to concede to the other. Green claimed "philosophical differences" kept them from combining forces. But those differences were probably pettier and more personal than philosophical. Green had publicly claimed McDill's group had "no chance" of winning; McDill countered that Green was "trying to belittle our effort."

In December 1985, in what was billed as a last-ditch effort to find common ground, Nova Scotia Conservative Senator Finlay MacDonald, himself a *True North* board member, orchestrated a meeting in Ottawa between the two men and Minister of State for Fitness and Amateur Sport Otto Jelinek. It didn't go well. All Jelinek offered was moral support. McDill and Green didn't need the government's good wishes. They needed cash to pay off their ever-escalating debts.

Which is when PJ—"considered by the sailing community to be the godfather of yacht racing in Canada"—stepped in to save the day. He already knew the players, having contributed to McDill's first effort, and he had become a co-founder and member of the fundraising executive council for the *True North*.

He wished he hadn't joined Green's board. "I should have stayed above the fray," he confessed. He worried that Green, trained as an engineer, missed the big picture. But then, so did McDill. "How can a man like Don Green or McDill, successful businesspeople, start into these world-challenging situations if indeed they can't see the woods for the trees?" he wrote in his diary in February 1986.[25]

PJ could see both the woods and the trees, and he knew what needed to be done. In April 1986, he invited Green and McDill to join him at Cara's headquarters in Toronto for a series of intense, weekend-long sessions. PJ understood he was dealing with two men whose egos were bigger than their war chests, so he alternately flattered, browbeat, cajoled, enticed, and finally bribed McDill and Green into joining forces.

"It was too sad to see this thing go down the drain," he explained to the *National Post*. "I wanted to be the catalyst for keeping it alive, but at the same time I won't put up with any backbiting. They'll pull together for Canada."

To forge what was described as "an uneasy, desperate marriage," PJ agreed to pay off $3 million in outstanding debts the two groups had already rung up, as well as buy their three yachts—*Canada II*, *True North One*, and a still-under-construction *True North Two*—for far more than they were worth.

As Citicom chair David Howard, a former Canadian Olympic sailor and commodore of the Royal Canadian Yacht Club—whom PJ had convinced to become chair of the combined venture—put it ruefully: "If you offered [the yachts] through the pages of the *Financial Post*, I suppose they would fetch a fraction of what we paid."

At a May 1 press conference in Toronto, PJ announced the establishment of a new umbrella organization, Canada's Challenge for America's Cup Inc., merging the two competing groups into one. McDill and Green—now nominal vice-presidents of CCAC—switched ties and mugged for the cameras. Neither was happy, of course, but neither man had had much choice.

PJ, who had effectively agreed to underwrite the new unified effort until it could attract sufficient sponsorship on its own, called the shots. "I am underwriting them," Phelan told reporters, "but I don't want the public to think that we don't need support." With that, PJ—the mastermind of it all—slipped off the stage. "It is my wish," he said, "to slip into the background as an honorary chairman."

PJ's efforts salvaged Canada's challenge, but he couldn't change the ultimate outcome in Fremantle. *Canada II*, which had become Canada's entry, did manage to defeat France's *French Kiss*, an eventual semifinalist, and the United States' *Stars & Stripes*, the winner of the 1987 America's Cup, in single races, but as in 1983, Canada was eliminated in the elimination rounds. Canada still wasn't fast enough.

Despite the outcome, PJ's efforts to keep "the various incarnations of Canada's modern Cup aspirations alive" earned him recognition as Canada's Yachtsman of the Year. Three years later, he was named to the Order of Canada, the country's highest civilian honour, "for financially salvaging Canada's challenge for the 1986 America's Cup as well as for providing opportunities to foster international youth competition. His philanthropic contributions towards the development of the sport have helped bring worldwide recognition and distinction to Canadian sailing."[26]

While PJ's generosity won him public plaudits, they raised private concerns within his family and around the boardroom table at Holdings. Without consulting members of the family, he had committed Holdings to selling Cara stock that was supposed to help underwrite future Phelan generations.

There were pluses, of course, but also minuses. Too many minuses, Paul David suggested.

It was the late fall of 1983 and PJ Phelan, his son, Paul David, thirty-two, and his daughter, Gail Regan, thirty-nine, had gathered in PJ's office at Cara headquarters on York Street in Toronto. "Dad was on the sofa and Paul was on the chair," Gail recalls. Gail, ever the precise MBA graduate, used a foolscap pad left over from that day's Cara board meeting to make notes and acted as the meeting's facilitator.

The topic: Boyd Matchett's performance versus Bernie Syron's promise.

In the immediate aftermath of 1977's PJ-engineered acquisition of Foodcorp, Cara's future had never seemed brighter. In 1978, one analyst described Cara as "the jewel of the fast-food stocks." Patrick Fellows, the *Toronto Star*'s "Your Money" columnist, quoted the analyst and topped his praise with a ribbon and bow: "We can find no substantial cause to argue" with the analyst's conclusion, he wrote.[27]

By the summer of 1981, Cara—"Canada's largest public company in the hospitality industry"—was reporting annual sales of more than $300 million and a compound earnings growth rate of more than 22 per cent through its previous eight years of rapid expansion. "Food Giant Has Growth on the Menu," headlined a *Financial Times* news service report.[28]

But there was already trouble nipping at its heels. Cara had dramatically added to its debt with the acquisitions of both Winco and Foodcorp. In 1981, interest rates skyrocketed to their highest levels in modern history. Since much of Cara's $70-million debt was pegged to the prime interest rate, Cara's interest charges in 1981 were projected to be $16 million higher than they'd been in 1980. That would be on top of the $13 million more in interest payments the company shelled out in 1980 compared to 1979.

To make matters worse, Winco—which Bernie Syron would later describe as "a good chain but a bad deal"—was looking even more dated. Matchett, who'd promoted its acquisition, had finally publicly acknowledged its "tired" image.

But that raised a question. Should the company modernize the chain—or find a buyer for it and move on?

To complicate matters, Foodcorp's own much-touted three-year, $20-million expansion into the Quebec market had gone badly. After what seemed like a successful pilot venture in Dollard des Ormeaux, a Montreal suburb on the edge of an English-speaking area, the company moved quickly, committing $5 million to add three more Chalet Suisse Bar-B-Q outlets, this time in predominantly francophone neighbourhoods. Those didn't do nearly as well. Post-mortems suggested that Foodcorp had miscalculated, that the pilot project had been popular with English-speaking residents, in large part because they were already familiar with Swiss Chalet, and that the company would now have to commit to an expensive advertising campaign to convince their French-speaking neighbours to embrace the concept too. Oh, and then there was an added wrinkle. Thanks to its research, Cara had discovered French-speaking Quebecers preferred dark meat over white meat in their chicken.

At the same time, other Swiss Chalet expansion schemes—into South Florida and Ohio—failed to establish hoped-for beachheads in the United States market.

And then, all that worse suddenly became much worse. In June 1982, a previously unknown company—Omi Equities Ltd., a company jointly owned by a Buddhist minister and his sixty-member Calgary Buddhist Temple congregation—won an eight-year contract worth $2 million a year to provide food services in a large dining room and two licensed lounges at Edmonton International Airport.

N. K. Ikuta, the fifty-six-year-old Buddhist minister who headed Omi, compared his Calgary-based company's success to a "David and Goliath situation" with his staff of 160 competing against Cara's 12,000 employees. And winning.

The deal was just one airport contract, of course, and Cara still controlled all food services at airports in Vancouver, Calgary, Regina, Saskatoon, Winnipeg, Toronto, Montreal, Halifax, and Gander, Newfoundland.

But the portents were ominous. Bill Campbell, Transport Canada's western regional superintendent of marketing and properties, told Canadian Press that Cara had won airport agreements "for so long that many potential competitors stopped bothering to bid." Now, he predicted there'd be renewed competition, including for the lucrative contract at Toronto International Airport slated for renewal in 1984. And he suggested Transport Canada officials there were thinking of following their Edmonton colleagues by "splitting up the food services contract and abandoning a complex bidding procedure that traditionally has favoured Cara because of its familiarity with the details involved."

In October 1983, Campbell's prediction came true. A company called York County Quality Foods bid $65 million and won the food concession leases at Toronto International Airport, a contract that Cara had owned for more than twenty years. The year before, Cara had reported sales of $14 million worth of food and beverages at the airport.

No wonder, then, that by 1983, Cara had experienced five consecutive quarters of earnings decline.

None of it was good, and it was all happening on Boyd Matchett's watch.

Despite all that, Bernie Syron's Foodcorp group was aggressively pushing ahead with its English-Canadian expansion plans—to open 25 new Swiss Chalets and 70 new Harvey's within three years, giving them a national network of 70 Swiss Chalets and 178 Harvey's, all with expanded menus.

Swiss Chalet and Harvey's, everyone agreed, were now key to Cara's future. "We wanted Swiss Chalet and Harvey's to be bigger, to thrive," recalls Gail. "We didn't want its resources drained by one-offs."

The one-offs she worried most about were within the purview of Daniel Phelan, a son of PJ's oldest brother, Darragh. Daniel himself was well qualified. He'd earned a degree in hotel administration from Cornell University and had worked his way up the ladder in the hotel industry, eventually serving as the general manager of Skyline Hotels Canada before joining Cara in 1965. After a stint as the general manager of Cara's central region, he'd been appointed vice-president of a new forward-looking division, Urban Restaurant/Inns. There, Daniel reported to Boyd, not Bernie.

During the early 1970s, Daniel launched a collection of one-off restaurants in Toronto's Commerce Court complex. They included Wellingtons, a high-end dining room featuring "international cuisine with an emphasis on fine wine"; The Teller's Cage, a restaurant with "contemporary entertainment"; and Café Galleria, "a Mediterranean-style café."

All were interesting, all were ambitious, but all would be hard to replicate across the country in the style of a Swiss Chalet or a Harvey's. Those were the company's modern models for success. So why, then, was Cara continuing to invest in Daniel's ambitions?

Gail liked Boyd. "I thought he was very professional." But she worried too. "I didn't think Boyd was controlling my cousin Danny." Paul David agreed. In fact, it was an offhand remark by PD during a visit that summer to Pointe au Baril, the Phelan family cottage compound on Georgian Bay, that had been the catalyst for this meeting. "I'm concerned about the leadership," he'd said.

"That perked my ears up," Gail says today, "so I started thinking about the leadership too." The more she thought, the more concerned she became.

The Phelan siblings had undefined, uneasy roles inside Cara.

PJ had encouraged Gail to sidetrack her own academic ambitions and get her MBA. She'd joined Cara Operations' board in 1979 and moved into an office at Holdings in 1982, but PJ offered her no clear role in the company and no obvious path forward.

Paul David's upward trajectory, by contrast, should have been straightforward. He was the family's only son, and his father had often half-jokingly referred to him as "The Prince" or the "Designated Heir." Since his childhood, PD himself had assumed he would one day be King, taking his father's throne as both the head of the family and the head of the family business.

And yet PD was diffident, almost noncommittal. Like his father, his first love was sailing, and he spent much of his time competing internationally. He was fascinated with computers, and his primary business focus became the stock market world favoured by the Gardiner side of his family. Although he was also on Cara Operations' board for a time and later had an office at Holdings, he occupied most of his days there trading commodities. Perhaps because of that apparent disinterest, or perhaps because of his own occasionally erratic behaviour, PD's inexorable journey to the top seemed to have stalled.

But perhaps the real reason for that was none of the above. Perhaps—and this is most likely—his father simply wasn't ready or willing to let go. PJ kept a framed cartoon on his office wall, Rose would remember. It showed an old man seated behind a desk. The caption, a riff on William Shakespeare's poem "Seven Ages of Man," read: "Sans eyes, sans teeth, but 51 percent in control."

For PJ, part of exercising control involved creating uncertainty and sowing dissension. By encouraging Gail to join the company, PJ had signalled to his son that he might not be the heir apparent after all. But, at the same time, by failing to create a plan to integrate Gail into the company, he'd left her dangling too. And, of course, simply by bringing Gail in at all, PJ had created a rivalry between his children, whether they'd sought it or not.

Gail says she hadn't. She still presumed Paul would ultimately become chair of Cara Operations and she—using the skills she'd gained during her MBA—"would be kind of quietly in the office looking at the books. There is an enormous amount of analytic work that needs to be done in corporations, and that's what I saw myself doing. I saw Paul and I having meetings and developing strategy, and I would participate in that. But I thought that Paul would succeed my father."

Parsing PJ's larger schemes and longer-term dreams was a fool's game. Helen, according to an October 1984 article in *Quest*, believed that PJ's "vision" was that "one day their four children, heirs to Cara and Swiss Chalet and also to a crucial chunk of [the Gardiner family's] Scott's [Hospitality] would join forces with [brother-in-law] George [Gardiner's] son, Michael, and run the Biggest Chicken Empire in the World."

The problem with that, as Helen herself confided to writer Ian Brown, was "professional jealousy" between her husband and her brother. "I don't think either would want the one to outdo the other."[29]

The alternative to a marriage of the family businesses seemed to have become an ongoing, never-ending competition between Cara and Scott's. Cara went public successfully in 1968. Scott's followed suit a year later.

Swiss Chalet opened takeout counters to counter Kentucky Fried's dominance in the grab-it-and-go fast-food world. So, Kentucky Fried added salad bars and sit-down sections to its takeouts to challenge Swiss Chalet's dominance in the family restaurant sector. They even sparred over which company's chicken was better for its customers. Bernie Syron "began touting the nutritional value of Swiss Chalet barbecued chicken over (by implication) the grotesque, fattening blechiness of the Colonel's."

According to Brown, competition with his Gardiner neighbour kin was one of PJ's key motivations. "What did Paul Phelan see when he looked across the garden at home in Forest Hill. He saw George Gardiner and his son Michael, the Harvard graduate, running a hugely successful restaurant chain of their own making. Phelan's own children, by contrast ... had wandered, as only the young of the massively wealthy can, trying, as one put it, 'to be our own persons, to be nameless, to work things out.'"

PJ had alienated his own children with his behaviour, confused them about what he really wanted from them, raising the spectre that none of them would be ready—or willing—to take their rightful place as the fourth-generation leader of their one-hundred-year-old family business.

To complicate matters, Brown wrote, PJ's decision a decade earlier to turn day-to-day management of the business over to Boyd Matchett, the management consultant he had put in charge of his company, had also left him alienated from the company he had built. "If he thought about it long enough, he couldn't have been blamed for feeling left out of his own company," Brown concluded.

That was the situation in the fall of 1983 when Paul David and Gail met their father in his office to try to convince him to replace Matchett with Bernie Syron, the more dynamic head of his Foodcorp subsidiary.

"It wasn't that hard," Gail acknowledges today. "Dad liked to win." Twenty years before, he had worked "so hard, and at the expense of his health," to win a twenty-year airport contract at Malton. Losing that contract, she says, "was personal for him." He blamed Matchett for its loss.

Worse, PJ then had one of his "revelations." He began to believe Matchett—who'd already become a wealthy man with $10 million in Cara stock—"was trying to take the company away from the family," he told Brown. "I think Mr. Matchett's management approach to the administration of the business prevented my children from learning more about the business. If a family business is to survive, the younger members of the family have to be knowledgeable."

So, PJ accepted Gail's and Paul David's advice. Matchett, to whom PJ had dedicated *Cara: 100 Years*—"To J. Boyd Matchett who made the modern dream come true"—was out. Bernie Syron was in. To ease the blow, PJ named Matchett Cara's vice-chairman.

In many ways, jokes Bernie Syron today, the most "cataclysmic" knock-on decision from the management shakeup involved closing Cara's long-time York Street head office and consolidating corporate operations at Foodcorp's headquarters on Bloor Street. The unspoken issue was that PJ lunched almost every day at the Toronto Club, just down the street from Cara. Where would he eat now?

"How did I get around that?" chuckles Syron. "Enter the York Club. It's on St. George Street, just a block away [from Foodcorp's Bloor Street headquarters] and even more convenient than the Toronto Club. So, I sold him on that."

Cara had made another important transition. Paul David and Gail, working together, had helped make it happen.

It would be one of the last times they would be on the same side of any discussion, family or business.

Generation Last?

~

One of Gail Regan's earliest memories bubbles up from when she was just four years old. Gail is listening to her mother blame her for the fact her brother Philip was never born. "Because I walked late," as Gail explains matter-of-factly today.

"If you hadn't walked late," she remembers her mother telling her, "I wouldn't have had to bend over and pick you up so much, and maybe little Philip's cord wouldn't have gotten wrapped around his neck, and he would have lived."

Instead, little Philip died before he could be born. If he'd lived, of course, he would have been the Phelans' first male child and therefore—by the then widely accepted logic of primogeniture—heir to the reins of the family's incredibly successful business empire. What would his existence have meant for Paul David? For PD's career? His life? Would PD have even been born? On the other hand, if Philip lived, might he have inherited, along with primacy among the Phelan children, the mental health issues that plagued

Sharon to her grave. But, of course, if Philip had lived—and his arrival had created the then-idealized one-boy, one-girl "million-dollar family"—would there have been a Sharon? What about Rose?

But there'd been no little Philip, and for that, Gail was to blame.

Gail sighs. "She told me that more than once. I mean that's something that, as a mother, you just don't say to a little child. 'You killed your brother.'"

Helen Doris Gardiner Phelan, needless to say, wasn't cut out to be a mother, at least not one cut from the 1950s June Cleaver *Leave It to Beaver* cloth.

It is an unseasonably cool spring day in late April 2022. Gail and her youngest sister, Rose, her only surviving sibling, have gathered at Gail's comfortable old house in Toronto's comfortable old Rosedale neighbourhood to rummage through musty banker's boxes full of intermingled, interconnected family and business histories and reminisce, trying to make sense of what happened in the fourth generation of the Phelan family business dynasty.

It's complicated.

For starters, the members of this fourth generation don't form one continuous family line so much as a series of concentric only-child circles, each shaped by changing family circumstances and by the seismic social shifts shaking their larger worlds.

That's why it makes sense to begin any exploration of the fourth generation of the Phelan family by considering each child individually.

If you're going to understand Gail, for example, it will help to know something even Gail didn't know officially until she was in her mid-fifties. She is mildly autistic. She is high functioning, smarter than most when it comes to matters of the mind—she skipped two grades in school and has a PhD—but with a sometimes less than finely tuned set of social skills.

"I think of 'Gailey' as a wee bit eccentric, imaginative and creative," was the way the late James Gillies, a Phelan family friend and the founding dean of York University's School of Business, described her to *Canadian Business* in 2004.

Gail says what she thinks, sometimes without fully comprehending how others might hear her bluntness. Occasionally that is to her own detriment. She occasionally wonders today if her directness could have been a trigger for what eventually went so wrong in her adult relationship with her brother, Paul.

We'll come back to that.

Gail, the Phelans' eldest child, was the over-achieving dutiful daughter who came of age in the *Father Knows Best* 1950s. She was born in the summer of 1944 at the tail end of the Second World War. After PJ was released from military service in the fall of 1945, the family settled in Toronto. Although he was now officially a shareholder and director of the family business, the family lived in what Gail remembers as "a cute little house in North Toronto." There were no servants.

Her grandparents on her mother's side, Percy and Gertrude Gardiner—Baba and Nana—were the ones with the servants. The Gardiners lived on Old Forest Hill Road—where Helen and PJ and family would eventually settle—and every Sunday hosted the family, including Helen's brother George and his family, for formal dinner at noon. Even the seating arrangements were formal. "I would sit at a certain spot beside my cousin, who was six months older than me," Gail explains. The appetizers were shrimp and cream cheese on celery topped with paprika. "I love that to this day," she jokes.

As a preschooler, Gail attended "a free form" nursery school, "sort of a just play ... an unstructured environment. I hated it." The following year, her parents sent her to junior kindergarten at the Catholic-run Ursuline School. "I loved it." Why? "The nuns wore whips around their waists. They would smack children for talking. I loved the quiet of this. Stimulation and over-stimulation have always been big issues for me."

Gail recalls little about her siblings as children. She and Sharon, who was three years younger, would sometimes play, she says, "cuddle and watch

TV together. We had a particular snack that we liked. But then Sharon got a friend, the girl next door, Grace. I would sometimes play hide and seek with them. I preferred to be the seeker, not the hider. I was sort of bossy as a kid."

Gail remembers Paul, nearly seven years her junior, "in his playpen looking out the window. I adored him. He was very good-natured and plump." But Paul changed the family dynamics. Their mother hired a Scottish woman named Betty Brown to serve as his nanny, and Gail was left to her own devices. "I don't have a sense of an adult bringing me up," she says now. "Mom was there only sometimes." Later, when she was in university and Paul was in grade school, Gail remembers seeing him arriving home from school at nearby Upper Canada College dressed in his uniform short pants. "He looked so cute."

Rose's arrival, at a time when Gail was almost a teenager, changed the family dynamic even more dramatically. "I was older and more aware," Gail recalls. "Rosemary had colic, which is noisy, so that would have disturbed me because of the autism. But I worried about Rose too."

When Gail was in grade 5, her mother pulled her out of the Ursuline School she'd adored and enrolled her at nearby Bishop Strachan School instead. BSS, which bills itself as "Canada's oldest day and boarding school for girls," is also one of its most prestigious. That was one of the reasons her mother chose it. "It was also closer, just down the street, so I could walk and there wasn't the hassle of transporting me. But the other thing is, BSS had some [new student openings], and Mom wanted to be sure to get me in."

Gail remembers Bishop Strachan, where she would spend the next six years, "as a very undisciplined place, almost like *The Belles of St. Trinian's*," the 1954 British comedy film in which its schoolgirls "are more interested in racing forms than books."

By the time she reached high school, Gail says, "I just could not sit for a minute because of the noise and the unruliness and the sheer 'wiggliness' of the girls. So, I just said, 'Mom, I am so bored, and my classmates do not concentrate. I can't learn anything here.'"

She ended up taking her final year of high school at Thornton Hall, another Toronto private school, but one with a focus on academic excellence, individual attention, and a very low student-to-teacher ratio.

Having skipped two grades in school, Gail was barely seventeen when she arrived at Toronto's University College with a plan to study sociology. "Sociology," she points out now, "has to do with organizations. And I thought it would be practical for understanding organizations, understanding business. Because I knew I'd be involved in business, if not working there but involved in the business somehow."

Two years later, in June 1963, just a month before she turned nineteen, Gail married Tim Regan, a retail manager at Swift Foods, a well-known processor and canned meat products company. He was six years her senior. They'd met at a party at a friend's apartment. Her friend "had asked some guys over, and he was one of them." Gail hosted the next party. "He came to my party, and after that, we started dating."

She married quickly, she says now, "because I was in love and because Tim adored me. But, also, because I wanted out of that house."

In part, that was because of her younger sister Sharon. By the time Sharon was in her mid-teens, she had begun acting out her personal demons. She was out of control, skipping school, drinking, doing drugs.

But Gail also wanted out of the family home, she says now, because of her parents—and what she saw as their lack of parenting. She wanted to show her siblings—by her own example—that families didn't have to be raised the way their parents had raised them.

Although PJ and Helen "seemed very devoted to each other, very loving," Gail remembers, neither was much of a parent to any of their children. They left that to "the help," the live-in cook and nanny. "On the nanny's day off, my mother looked after the kids. On the cook's day off, my mother cooked." Helen wasn't especially interested in either.

There is a famous family story from much later when they would spend summer vacations at their cottage compound on Georgian Bay. Although Gail usually made dinners for the family at the cottage, she recalled a day when her mother volunteered. "No, let me do it. I'm going to make a vegetable casserole." Helen spent the entire afternoon preparing that one dish, Gail says. It was ultimately served as one among many other dishes supplied by family members. But later, her mother would recount the story of how she'd spent an entire afternoon preparing her casserole, then add plaintively, "What if they'd asked me to make the whole dinner?"

It wasn't that her mother wasn't busy; it was simply that she preferred to occupy her time with more compelling matters than domestic chores or child-rearing. Helen and PJ entertained for business and pleasure most weekends and filled their weeknights attending concerts, and business and charity events. Helen had her own community interests too. She was active with the Junior League and served on the board of Women's College Hospital. "And, of course, Baba would take quite a lot of her time."

After Gail's grandmother died in 1956, Percy Gardiner would call his daughter, Helen, every morning. They would chat for an hour about his business deals or gossip about Toronto's broader business world. Helen served on the board of Scott's Hospitality, the Gardiner family's restaurant wing, and controlled her family's Langar Foundation, which took its name from the last syllable of Phelan and the first syllable of Gardiner. Helen was astute about business, in many ways, a woman ahead of her time. But when she was growing up, Helen's relationship with her father had been at least as fraught and complicated as the one her daughter Gail would later have with her own father.

In 1993 in a *Toronto Sun* feature marking the 30th anniversary of the publication of Betty Friedan's iconic book, *The Feminine Mystique*, Helen explained to the reporter that she'd become a feminist as a young woman after winning a scholarship to do post-graduate work in the United States. Her father said no, though he later supported Helen's brother's decision to study at Harvard. "Women back then were channelled into domesticity," she noted with some bitterness.

There is, of course, an irony in this. While Helen would be supportive of her oldest daughter's academic ambitions and even mentored her on the intricacies of businesses and boards, she still considered Paul David, the family's third child and first son, to be the only logical successor as head of the Cara family business.

After earning her BA in 1965, Gail had continued her studies at the Ontario College of Education and then landed a part-time teaching position—"I had two kids by then, so I didn't want to be overwhelmed by a full-time teaching job"—at Loretto College School, a private Roman Catholic high school in Toronto. Two years in the classroom convinced Gail that teaching high school was "very rigid and not for me. But I loved education." So, she returned to school, this time the Ontario Institute for Studies in Education (OISE). She earned her PhD in 1973 and began what she expected would be a lifetime career as a professor in the University of Toronto's Faculty of Education.

But four years later, her parents sidetracked that plan. "Mom and Dad came to me and said, 'Even if you're interested in academia, we want you to do an MBA. You're scholarly; you will learn business most efficiently by doing an MBA. And we're going to need you on the financial side of both businesses, whether you actually work for these businesses or not.'"

Both businesses meant Cara and also Scott's Hospitality, the Gardiner family umbrella that owned hotels, the Blacks chain of photo shops, a fleet of school buses, the Manchu Wok fast-food franchise, and, oh, yes, over a hundred revenue-generating Scott's Chicken Villa restaurants in Ontario, all featuring Colonel Sanders's finger lickin' good Kentucky Fried Chicken.

"Growing up," Gail says today, "I regarded us as having two businesses, Scott's and Cara, and Scott's was bigger, more successful, steadier, and solid ... Now, why did I go to Cara and not to Scott's?" she asks herself. "Well, it could have been that George [Helen's brother] was comfortable with Mom on the board of Scott's but wasn't comfortable with me." Or, she suggests, it could have been that George and her mother already knew they planned to sell Scott's rather than pass the company on to the next generation.[30] "Scott's would've been a dead end for me," Gail says now.

But, perhaps even more importantly, she adds today, "it seemed that Cara needed me more than Scott's. Dad was getting fragile and my brother, Paul, would come in, do a training program at Cara, and then he would leave. He had his own business, trading commodities, so it didn't seem to me that he was really stepping up, that he was engaging."

After earning her MBA in 1978, Gail tentatively dipped her toe into Cara's business operation. "By then, I had four kids, so I went on the board of the business, but I didn't get a job at the business in the beginning."

Soon, however, she "talked the family into" letting her run the company's Rib of Beef Restaurant and the Cork Room Tavern near what was then the Toronto Stock Exchange building on Bay Street. "I said, 'I need to get my feet wet. So, please let me do this.'"

She says she learned a lot. "I developed an appreciation for how smart you have to be in the restaurant business because when you lease property, you're betting that that concept will last for twenty years." And that the environment around it will continue as it had. It didn't.

"The stock exchange moved, so then the bar was absolutely deserted. It hadn't been kept up. So, we closed the bar and then I managed to lease the space." She leased the bar to Gardiner-owned Scott's for one of its restaurants and worked with a consultant to transform the steak house into an Asian-themed restaurant. "That worked a little better," she says, but adds that the best news was that the building's owners eventually decided to renovate the building and all the leases, including Cara's twenty-year lease, were terminated. "We got out a little earlier than I'd expected."

By then, Gail had joined Holdings Ltd. and begun to better understand both the workings and weaknesses of the company, as well as the urgent need to plan for generational succession.

That would soon change everything about everything for Cara. And for the Phelans.

"I'm not taking her back," Betty Brown declared flatly. Sharon Gertrude Phelan was barely a teenager. Her parents were away. Still. Again. And Betty, the nanny, had had more than enough.

Two nights earlier, when Sharon passed out from drinking with no parents around to take charge, Betty had rushed her to the emergency department at St. Michael's Hospital, then spent the night with her, "drying her out."

Now, the girl had done it again. "I'm not taking her back," Betty repeated.

"So, Betty got salt and water and made me force it down Sharon's throat so she would throw up," Gail remembers. "I thought it was so intrusive, but what else could I do? I had to save her life." She pauses. "But that was the night that I resolved to get out of that house. It was too much responsibility." Gail was only sixteen herself.

None of her siblings seemed to know exactly what was wrong with Sharon, Helen and PJ's second daughter. "She had a mental illness," Gail says today, "but that illness was never defined for us." From Gail's point of view, Sharon had simply gone from being a "beautiful and charming and full of life" child to an off-the-rails teenager. "Delinquency, drinking, drugs, mood imbalances..."

Mental illness was not unknown in the Phelan family. In 1934, one of PJ's older brothers, Thomas Patrick Phelan, had tried to kill himself by shooting himself in the chest at the popular Cocoanut Grove nightclub in Los Angeles. After consuming two quarts of champagne, Phelan told his server he had no money to pay his bill. According to a newspaper account of the incident, the twenty-seven-year-old was then escorted to an office adjoining the club's dancing pavilion where he "suddenly whipped out a revolver and shouted, 'You'll never take me out of here alive.'" He then shot himself "near the heart." It appears not to have been a spur-of-the-moment decision. He left a note for his father. "Dad: This is going to solve a lot of difficulties. Give my love to mother, yourself and the gang." But surgeons were able to remove the bullet, and Thomas lived another forty-three years.

Then there was the even more troubling case of Warde Phelan, another of PJ's older brothers. Warde had served as a flying officer in the Royal Air Force during the First World War but had been kicked out for "showing off." He'd violated air force rules against low-altitude dives. One day, after performing what was known as a "terminal velocity dive" from 10,000 feet, Warde "swung down to tree level and did a bit of hedge hopping. They canned me because I thumbed my nose at the boss."

There followed a series of wild misadventures across Europe, which Warde later documented in a rambling 1937 interview with legendary *Toronto Star* journalist Gordon Sinclair. Warde eventually ended up in Spain where he served briefly as a pilot for Franco's republican forces during the first year of the Spanish Civil War. Captured in 1936 and convicted of espionage, Warde was sentenced to die at the hands of a rebel firing squad. He was only saved by the last-minute intervention of British foreign secretary Anthony Eden. Freed, he made his way back to North America.

"Today," Sinclair reported on February 24, 1937, "18 hours after dropping off a ship in New York harbour, [Warde Phelan] wandered into *The Star* office, large as life and full of the old zing."

It didn't last. Warde would eventually suffer a breakdown that ended with him, quite literally, up in a tree, swinging a sword, and threatening anyone who came near him. Carted off to the province's mental health facility at 999 Queen Street West, which was popularly known at the time as "the lunatic asylum," Warde became one of the first patients in Ontario to be lobotomized.

Finally released from the hospital but damaged by his experiences and suffering what we might now describe as PTSD, Warde lived out his life quietly with a caregiver, paid for by PJ.

Liz Smythe, who would become Paul David's high school girlfriend, remembers Warde as a regular guest at Phelan family Christmas dinners. "He used to write cheques to the children for these huge amounts—forty-five thousand dollars—in this beautiful old script with his flourishing signature. And then, on the back, it would say, 'see my agent, So-and-So, in Montreal.' The kids would all say, 'Gee, thanks, Uncle Warde.'" Suggests Smythe, "There was always that fear within the family of what they used to call insanity."

And then along came Sharon. While still a teenager, Sharon left home and moved to Greenwich Village in New York where she began experimenting with ever more dangerous drugs. "She saw this ad in the health food store to join the League of Spiritual Discovery," Smythe remembers. "She thought, 'Well, that sounds interesting. I'll go down there.' And it was a euphemism for LSD. She had a terrible rocky road there."

Finally, in desperation, PJ and Helen recognized that what seemed to make Sharon happiest were horses, a love of which she'd seemingly inherited from her great-grandfather. So, her parents bought her a 500-acre horse ranch in the redwoods near Mendocino, California, north of San Francisco. There, Sharon would marry briefly, have a daughter she named Holiday—after the singer Billie Holiday—and operate her horse farm.

Sharon's parents seemed happy to support her, happier still to know she was living somewhere other than with them in Toronto.

~

It had been the best night of Liz Smythe's brief sixteen-year life. Except, of course, for those few dark, out-of-nowhere moments the night before that still seemed so inexplicable to her.

And now this latest one, unfolding in front of her this morning.

Liz and her boyfriend, Paul Phelan, were seated at a dining table on the terrace at 8 Old Forest Hill Road waiting for Betty, the Phelans' beloved nanny, doubling today as cook on the cook's day off, to serve them their morning-after steak, eggs, and potatoes breakfast. This morning's breakfast followed last night's Battalion Ball. Liz had been Paul's date for the formal, one of the oldest traditions at Upper Canada College dating back to 1887, and considered the most prestigious event on UCC's student social calendar.

PJ and Helen Phelan had already left this morning for a luncheon at the yacht club. No surprise there, Liz knew. Paul's parents always seemed to be somewhere else, always socializing, rarely present with their children. Not that she was complaining.

Betty placed their trays on the table. Liz picked up a teacup from hers, then "shamelessly" turned it over to check the stamp on the bottom. "Minton." Of course. Minton was Europe's leading ceramic factory, supplier of tiles to the British Houses of Parliament and the United States Capitol, not to forget providers of exquisite and expensive bone china to grace the dining tables of European and North American aristocracy, folks exactly like the Phelans. The Phelans, Liz thought to herself, "did not even own *everyday* china."

As she examined the markings on the bottom of the cup, she sensed a rising tension in the conversation between Paul and the nanny.

"Where's the ice for my Coke?" Paul demanded.

"I forgot it," Betty said.

"That was the first thing I said when I came into the kitchen." Paul sounded threatening now. "I told you not to forget the ice."

"You shouldn't be having Coke for breakfast," Betty replied coolly, adding: "And you'll not be speaking to me that way, Mr. Too-Big-for-His-Britches."

At which point, Paul suddenly picked up his breakfast tray and pitched it—steak, potatoes, eggs, expensive china, the glass of Coke with no ice—at a wall.

Shocked, wanting to make things right, Liz bustled out of her seat and rushed over to pick up the pieces.

"Sit!" Paul shouted at her.

She sat.

In the strained silence that followed, Betty silently returned with a replacement tray. Steak, eggs, potatoes, more Minton china, a glass of Coke, this time *with* ice. The shattered remnants of Paul's rage lay scattered on the floor of the terrace, unmentioned and unremoved.

Paul and Liz ate in silence. What to do to break the tension, she wondered, to get back the lovely, loving feelings from the night before? From even just a few short moments ago? Liz thought about what her mother—"the consummate sweep-things-under-the-rug person"—would do. She smiled at Paul. "The buds are coming out on the trees," she said.

The scowl, she would recall years later, disappeared, and Paul agreed amiably. "Spring is just about here," he said, as if the last few minutes had never happened. "Are the Leafs going to win the Cup again, do you think?"

And all was right with the world again.

Liz Smythe was far from the first to witness one of Paul's outbursts.

John Brooke, one of his best friends at Upper Canada College, remembers a day in high school when they were fooling around at the hockey rink. He doesn't remember what triggered Paul's anger, "but I did something he didn't like, and he grabbed my hockey stick and cracked it over his knee. I was astounded that he would do that." As was the case with the breakfast tray, Paul's anger flashed hot, and then was gone as if it had never been. "He would get angry like that sometimes in high school, and it would surprise me in a personal way," Brooke recalls today. "And then he was done with it." Brooke laughs. Brooke wasn't quite done. "To Paul, it was just a hockey stick. To me it was a hockey stick that cost twenty-five bucks."

Gail's memories, of course, go back further. She remembers when Paul was a rambunctious two-year-old. The Phelans had the first television set in their neighbourhood, and children from nearby houses used to gather in the late afternoon to watch *Howdy Doody* and a western. The problem, remembers Gail—she who couldn't cope with noise and commotion—was that the youngest children were "hopeless because they weren't interested in TV. They were interested in the other children. They would climb around and interrupt." Finally, Gail, the eight-year-old "boss" of these gatherings, issued an edict: no children under three: "Paul got very angry. He had a temper tantrum. So, I was punished for not letting him in. I was pulled out and wasn't allowed to watch with the group for a week."

Whatever the merits of that particular crime and punishment, it illustrates a reality. Paul rarely suffered consequences for his own behaviour. Paul was barely a teenager, to note another example, when teachers discovered beer in his locker at Upper Canada College. School officials were concerned enough about his overall behaviour to call his parents in for a conversation and urge them to "find Paul a psychologist or counsellor."

His father's response: "You're the expert in boys," he told them. "Make him a steward, get him into sports. I'm relying on you to handle him." And that was the end of that.

The first time John Brooke got drunk was with Paul "when we were fifteen or sixteen." Paul had just returned from a family Easter vacation in Bermuda where he had learned a thing or two about making a complicated mixed drink featuring gin, Grand Marnier, cherry liqueur, Bénédictine, pineapple juice, lime, bitters, and club soda—and was ready to try out his newfound expertise on his friend. "Phelan got me drunk on Singapore slings—really, really rolling in the dirt drunk," Brooke remembers. "I just thought it was lemonade with gin in it, but he was chuckling away and feeding me more and more. But he was bigger than me, so he could hold it way better."

PJ looked on with amusement. "He kind of let Paul do whatever he wanted," Brooke says.

Liz Smythe recalls her own first experience with PJ's laissez-faire parenting style when it came to alcohol. On one of their first dates, she and Paul had gone to a drive-in movie with some of Paul's friends. "They had a case of beer in the trunk and had downed several," she says. "After the movie, I asked Paul if he was okay to drive home, and he said he was. But he forgot to turn the headlights on and we were stopped by the police right outside the drive-in." Paul failed a sobriety test, and the police carted him off to jail.

The other boys drove her back to 8 Old Forest Hill Road where she was supposed to spend the night. "I barely knew Helen and PJ at this point," she recalls. After blurting out the story of the drive-in and Paul's arrest, PJ sent her to the kitchen while he shouted up to Helen with the news.

"Was anyone hurt?" Helen wanted to know.

"No," PJ replied. "It is the usual goddamn bore. Paul David is in jail."

"I was stunned," Liz remembers, thinking, "'Who were these people?' PJ then came back to the kitchen and poured me a glass of milk."

"You need to keep Paul on a very short leash," he told her. "Do you understand what I am saying? A tight leash. Can you do it?"

"I think so."

"Good."

That was the end of that conversation too. Paul returned from jail in the morning, and "nothing further was said."

There were, of course, softer sides to the often rough-edged, sandpapery relationship between father and son.

John Brooke says PJ—who often referred to his son as "Paulie"—could be "very affectionate" and often playful with PD. He recalls one "bizarre little moment" on a Saturday afternoon when the boys were in junior high school. Brooke's family lived in Lawrence Park, another affluent Toronto neighbourhood but one that wasn't quite as old moneyed as Forest Hill. "In our neighbourhood, there would be ball hockey games on Saturday afternoons," he says of the distinction. "There were no ball hockey games on Old Forest Hill Road."

At the time, PJ owned a usually chauffeur-driven Cadillac limousine with a personalized rabbit's frontispiece, like the Spirit of Ecstasy angel hood ornament on a Rolls-Royce. "I think it was supposed to indicate fecundity," Brooke suggests. He and his neighbourhood friends "were getting ready for the game when this big limo with the rabbit on the front comes around the corner. Mr. Phelan was driving it with the chauffeur's cap on, and [Paul's] in the back seat with his hockey stick and Timmy, the Phelans' poodle. Paul got out and played street hockey with us ... Mr. Phelan was loving it."

There was, for good and ill, a sense of entitlement that came with being the son of a Phelan.

Two years after Paul's arrest for drinking and driving, Liz remembers another incident in which she saw what seemed to her to be more consequences of the lack of consequences in Paul's upbringing.

While competing in the Pan American Summer Games in Colombia, Paul had gotten into trouble with his coach and was kicked off the team after he was caught smoking pot with the coach's daughter.

"Back in Toronto, he obsessed about the unfairness of it all," Liz recalls. "He kept writing letters and reading them to me, asking for my opinion. I kept telling him he sounded like a stupid ass and that all his threats about getting the commodore or someone else to get the coach removed were pathetic. I kept advising him to admit he did something wrong and to accept responsibility. Quoting my grandfather, I said, 'You've got to take your licks.' But he remained defiant."

By the time Paul David had come along, it seemed clear that PJ and Helen had given up even attempting to act like conventional parents, if that had ever been a goal.

Paul's own explanation at the time was that his parents' experiences with Sharon—"They went through hell with her," he once told Liz. "Doctors, psychiatrists, you name it."—had disabused them of any notion that they could or should even try to parent. "They concluded they were utter flops as parents and decided the rest of us should just raise ourselves," Paul David told Liz.

By the time of his senior year in high school, Paul David, though only a "moderate" student academically, had become a multi-sport athletic "big man" on the UCC campus. In part, that was because of his natural athletic gifts. "He was a big strong boy," says a fellow student who played football with him and didn't try to tackle him, even in practice, "because his legs were huge. He'd run right through you."

Paul David was a star fullback on a 1969 UCC senior varsity football squad that not only won its league championship but also boasted future Canadian Football League stars Stu Lang and Dave Hadden. "Paul would have been the third star on what was a very impressive team," recalls fellow team member Andrew Hunter.

That winter, Paul David also starred as a power forward on the college's senior varsity hockey team, the Blues. In between hockey practices and games, he skied competitively.

Hunter, also a member of the hockey team, remembers that after they'd won the championship, PJ and his own father had showed up with celebratory bottles of "champers" for the boys. "That was a no-no because the principal was there, and it was against the rules. They brought it into the locker room, and we drank it anyway."

Paul David completed his senior year athletic trifecta that spring as a star bowler on the school's cricket team, which won its championship too. He was such a good bowler—similar to a pitcher in baseball—"he was pitching the equivalent of a no-hitter every time he went out," marvels Hunter.

At the end of the season, he was chosen to be part of an all-Canadian under-19 cricket team that toured England. During the summer's tour, however, Paul refused to travel on the bus with the rest of the team. Instead, he rented a Volkswagen van, and he and Hunter, who was also a member of the Canadian team, followed behind. "We were told to travel in the team bus," Hunter says, "so we broke the rules." That gave them the chance to veer off the prescribed route from time to time. They went skating at the Bristol Ice Rink after drinking too many bottles of baby champagne, and made occasional forays here and there, hoping to pick up girls. "But this is what I loved about PD," notes Hunter. "He loved breaking the rules." Like father, like son.

When Liz Smythe's father first asked her about her new boyfriend, Liz had triumphantly explained that Paul Phelan was "first string in football, first in hockey, first in cricket, and he races in skiing and sailing." Her father—himself a product of that same Upper Canada College, which Liz describes as "the very male, brutally male, incredibly fierce, competitive centre of the establishment of Canada"—was suitably impressed.

Liz's father was Stafford Smythe, her grandfather Conn Smythe. They were members of an even more famous, if not more financially successful, branch of Toronto's Irish aristocracy. Like Paul David, Smythe father and son had also attended Upper Canada College. So had Liz's paternal great-grandfather. Good Canadian Irish Protestant bloodlines.

In the 1920s, Conn Smythe—who owned a Toronto sand and gravel company with the company slogan, "C. Smythe for Sand," painted on its trucks—had joined a consortium of businessmen who bought the Toronto St. Pats NHL hockey team. After changing its name to the Maple Leafs, overseeing the building of Maple Leaf Gardens, and laying the groundwork for what would become one of the most valuable sports franchises in North America, Conn Smythe engineered a deal in 1947 to make himself majority owner of the Maple Leafs—with the help, it should be noted, of a $300,000 loan from Helen Phelan's Irish Protestant stockbroker father, Percy Gardiner.

By the time Conn's granddaughter, Liz, met Percy's grandson, Paul, the struggle over who should succeed Conn Smythe—a familiar issue of family business succession that would soon rip the Phelan family apart—had already done its worst to the Smythes.

In the mid-1950s, Conn had named his then-thirty-something son Stafford to head up a seven-member Maple Leafs operations committee. It immediately became known derisively as the "Silver Seven" because all its members—including Stafford and Percy Gardiner's son, George—had been born with silver spoons in their mouths.

Despite having theoretically changed the management structure, however, Conn Smythe refused to cede control of his enterprise. He and Stafford bickered constantly until Stafford abruptly resigned in 1961, threatening to leave hockey entirely unless his father agreed to sell him control and retire himself. Conn reluctantly agreed. Five years later, Conn Smythe severed all ties with the Gardens to protest his son's decision to stage the controversial Muhammad Ali–Ernie Terrell world heavyweight boxing championship. At the time, no US venue would host the fight because of Ali's refusal to be drafted into the US military. Conn publicly accused his son of "putting cash ahead of class."

"My grandfather was a great friend of your grandfather," was the way in which eighteen-year-old Paul Phelan had introduced himself to fifteen-year-old Liz Smythe. "He backed his bid to become majority shareholder."

"We owe everything we have to you, then?" she teased him.

"Well, I wouldn't go so far as to say that," he replied. "I do know they had a mutual admiration for one another."

And it was clear, in that instant, that there was a mutual spark between their grandchildren too.

It was the early winter of 1968. Liz had been invited to spend the weekend skiing with a school friend at her family's chalet in Collingwood. It so happened her friend had a Saturday night date with a senior from Upper Canada

College and invited Liz to tag along to the party, which was being held at the Phelan family farm just up the road.

Paul David Phelan's parties in Collingwood and Toronto were legendary—famous among his schoolmates, often infamous among their parents. Because 8 Old Forest Hill Road was just a few blocks from Upper Canada College, whispers of "a party at Phelan's this weekend" would quickly spread through the college grapevine and "a hundred, two hundred people would just show up," remembers John Brooke.

PJ and Helen would often be absent during Paul David's impromptu house parties, perhaps attending a party or social event of their own somewhere else, leaving the teenagers—happily—to their own devices.

Occasionally, one of Paul David's parties downstairs would coincide with a PJ and Helen event on the main floor. No problem. The good news was that there was lots of room in and around the mansion for everyone. Mix and mingle.

Sometimes, Paul David's parties were elaborate affairs. Andrew Hunter remembers one night coming down the stairs past the statue of a knight in armour in its usual perch on the landing when he looked up, "and I'll never forget. There were joints hanging down from the ceiling. Seriously! I thought, 'Oh my God, does Helen know about this? Or does Paul Sr. know about it?' Then I thought, 'Well, they're kind of absent in the moment because they're busy.' And then I thought, 'Well, what a great party!'"

Many attendees at Paul David's Old Forest Hill parties remember that, as the parties wound down in the wee hours of the morning, PJ himself would hold court in the kitchen, cooking his famous "egg in the hole"—a slice of bread with a two-inch hole cut in the centre that was cooked in bacon fat until lightly toasted, flipped, an egg cracked into the hole, and then cooked some more—for the young people who'd stuck around.

Paul David's parties in the basement of the Phelan farmhouse in Collingwood, which was conveniently located cheek by jowl to the Osler Ski Resort, were equally memorable.

Paul's basement lair boasted bunk beds for guests, even its own sauna. During his mid-teens, John Brooke remembers "spending every weekend there." Paul's parents were often upstairs, "but they didn't come down. What was fun for us was that they allowed things to happen that probably wouldn't have been allowed at my house ... or at most parents'."

At the time Liz attended her first party at the Phelan farm, Paul was *persona non grata* among many parents of Collingwood's teens for having hosted a parent-free party the month before during which a lot of underage girls got drunk and sick. "But don't worry," her friend told Liz. Paul's parents would be home tonight. They weren't.

Liz's knowledge of the Phelans and what they did was second-hand and teenage vague. They were into "liquor," her friend had told her. "They import wine and own tons of restaurants and god knows what else." And Paul? He was, her friend said, "gorgeous, flat-out handsome, very, very rich, and completely intimidating."

When they were finally introduced that night, Liz couldn't disagree. "My first impression of Paul lived up to everything I heard earlier," she wrote in a fictionalized memoir years later.[31] "As handsome as all get out, his grip strong and warm, his smile just beautiful." He had thick Irish hair and eyes that were "blue and sort of green and so gorgeous ... I went weak in the knees."

She couldn't help but remember her own Irish maternal grandmother's admonition. "Whenever she was serving a hot cup of tea, she'd say, 'Be careful, that's as hot as Irish love.' So, one day I said, 'Well, what is Irish love?' And she said, 'Don't go anywhere near it.'" Too late. Liz was already smitten.

Oh, and there was something else her friend told her that night. Paul was one of the leaders of an in-group of older boys at UCC who'd made a collective decision that winter to date only the grade 10s from Havergal, the nearby private girls' school Liz attended. In part, she says now, they'd decided to date younger girls like her "because we wouldn't know what we were doing," but also, in part, because, for reasons unknown, they wanted to make Havergal's senior girls angry. "It worked," she laughs.

She and Paul spent much of that weekend in a 1960s teenaged mating ritual. She flirted, he pressed his luck. She teased, he pushed further. At various points, she kneed him in the groin, slapped his face, slugged him. He would say he was sorry. She would say he wasn't. He would smile and concede. And then he would try again.

By the end of the weekend, during the two-hour drive with him back to Toronto, she had—as she would write later—the opportunity "to gaze into his eyes, marvel at the length of his eyelashes, be impressed with his intellect, fall in love with his laugh. Wait. *Love*?"

By the evening of the Battalion Ball just over a year later in March 1970, they had become inseparable. And not just as a couple. Liz had become part of the Phelan family, invited to spend weekends at their Collingwood farm, vacation with them in the Caribbean, join the family for dinners at Old Forest Hill.

Whatever Helen Phelan's more complicated inside-8-Old-Forest-Hill relationships with her own daughters, she publicly exuded an aura of the society woman who had it all, which dazzled many younger women and girls, including Liz Smythe. "She not only was on the board of a hospital but also had her own business interests"—Liz remembers thinking at the time that "she seemed a woman ahead of her time."

Liz quickly decided to "do everything in my power to be her friend, and Helen, in turn, mentored and groomed me for the role of corporate wife." Liz was, at that point, still barely sixteen.

One important piece of advice Helen imparted to the young woman, who she already appeared to assume would become her daughter-in-law: "'Cute will only get you so far. Cute wears off. If you want men to respect you, you have to accomplish something. You can't just think you can go around smiling and being charming. It's not enough.' It was the best advice I've ever had in my life," Elizabeth Smythe Brinton says today.

Liz had come to understand Paul's place—and therefore her own—in the Phelan firmament. "He absolutely was given free rein as far as his parents were concerned. They never criticized him, chastised him. I remember PJ used to walk around the front hall of Number 8, going on about Paul: 'You are a prince, you are a prince, and one day you'll be a king.' Paul was absolutely groomed, trained from day one that he was going to head Cara."

And Liz Smythe? She was going to be his queen. She was invited to stay overnight whenever the Phelans gave a party. Helen would insist "I stand beside her in the receiving line ... I pictured my future self as a great hostess," just like Helen Phelan, Liz would write. "I would have married, right then and there, if permitted."

In fact, on the night of the UCC ball, she and Paul had hosted a pre-formal dinner and reception at the Phelans. "We will be out, so I'm turning the hostess duties over to you," Helen told Liz. "Make sure you get lots of food into the men. Don't let them get too drunk before the receiving line either."

At the ball that evening, there was a formal receiving line. Each arriving couple had to be introduced to the headmaster and his wife, and their names then announced in a loud voice to the rest of the room. Paul, UCC's cadet regimental sergeant major, "was supposed to keep every name straight, but he kept getting them all mixed up," Liz remembers. Finally, she stepped in, whispering the names for him to announce to the room. "He waited for my cue before he said anything. Once the introductions were over, I heaved a huge sigh of relief. We were finally free to dance the night away."

Paul's group had booked rooms for the night at the Royal York, Toronto's most prestigious hotel. "Anxious to get to phase three, the groping," she jokes today, the boys soon ushered their dates into cars for the drive to the hotel. But soon after they'd arrived there, Paul surprised Liz by asking if she wanted to return to the Phelan house instead. She did.

In the car, however, "Paul's face took a dark turn. We got to the front step, and I asked him to kiss me. He said no."

This mood swing, she soon discovered, had been triggered because one of his friends had unexpectedly kissed her as they were preparing to leave the hotel. "You enjoyed it," he accused her. She managed to placate Paul's anger.

Eventually, she found herself in the guest room and settled into bed "in the softest sheets I have ever touched in my entire life."

Her rest was brief. It was Paul. "Get out," she shouted.

"I just want to cuddle," he said. In bed, he apologized. "I wasn't very nice to you when you said you loved me. Did you mean it?"

She told him she did.

"I think I love you too. Let's go to sleep."

They did, but soon, the door opened again. A man entered, lurched around in the darkness, his arms in front of him, sleepwalking, or pretending to. He stopped when he saw them, mumbling, "Have I made a mistake? I made a mistake." And left.

"Who was that?" Liz asked.

"My dad."

"What was he doing?"

"Go to sleep. He's drunk."

That evening, when Liz told her older sister Mary about the incident on the terrace when Paul tossed the tray against the wall, she was appalled.

"What if that were your precious Limoges going into the wall?" she said. "He has a temper, and he is used to getting his way, evidently."

"Dad has a temper," Liz countered. She had once watched her father throw all his tools in a lake.

"He was mad at himself then," Mary told her. "There's a difference. He would never treat someone working for us like that, especially a woman."

Liz wasn't ready to concede. She was in love. "You have to make allowances when you are in love," she insisted. "You have to overlook some things."

For Liz, that would mean overlooking Paul David's many outbursts and jealousies over the next four years.

"I am an outgoing, naturally flirtatious person," Elizabeth Smythe Brinton tells me today, more than fifty years later. "But I quickly learned, 'Oh, boy, I better not do anything.'" Still, occasionally, she would say or do something and Paul "would flare up." Once, on a holiday with the Phelan family at an exclusive Bahamian resort originally built for British royalty because of its remoteness, she recalls an incident involving a teenaged son of the legendary—and legendarily well-to-do—American du Pont family. "He came to the table and asked me to dance. I accepted—and, ooh, that was an incident..."

Though Paul threw plenty of objects during their five years together, she says now, he was never physically violent with her. She wasn't afraid. "I would call him a stupid ass and tell him to get it together. But he knew he could not [be violent with me] or I would immediately leave. He knew that."

Liz's comfortable, cosseted teenaged life imploded just two years later at 11 a.m. on June 17, 1971, when three Toronto fraud squad detectives swept into her father's Maple Leaf Gardens office and unceremoniously arrested him, bundled him into a police cruiser in front of waiting news cameras, and whisked him off to police headquarters to be photographed and fingerprinted.

Stafford Smythe, the president of Maple Leaf Gardens, and Harold Ballard, his vice-president and fellow board member, had been jointly charged with theft and fraud for having illegally funnelled hundreds of thousands of dollars from Maple Leaf Gardens' coffers into their own pockets to pay for renovations to their houses and cover other personal expenses. At Smythe's bail appearance later that day, the *Globe* described him as "pale and silent."

The whole messy business had begun two years earlier in the summer of 1969 as a seemingly trifling matter, a summary offence of income tax evasion that might have resulted in a fine of as little as $25 with no mandatory jail time. But the cavalier mixing of business and personal, not to forget Smythe's and Ballard's controversial high profiles in a Maple Leafs–obsessed city, had made such rug-sweeping impossible.

In November 1969, after a county court judge pre-emptively dismissed the charges against the two men, Dalton Wells, chief justice of the Ontario Supreme Court, overruled that initial slap-on-the-wrist decision and ordered a trial.

Prominent lawyer Clay Powell was named a special prosecutor and the Toronto Metropolitan Police assigned three senior detectives to rummage through Smythe's and Ballard's lives and accounts, interviewing more than 180 people during their lengthy investigation. The Crown eventually decided to proceed by indictment—federal justice minister John Turner himself signed off on the decision—meaning the two men now faced fines of up to $10,000 and, worse, jail terms of up to five years on each of the five counts if they were found guilty. Although both men were major shareholders in Maple Leaf Gardens, the Gardens board soon fired them.

In the beginning, the Phelans had been supportive of Liz, seeing the allegations against her father as a "legal problem to be sorted out by lawyers." PJ told her on more than one occasion that what her father really needed was to have someone "running front" for him. "I remember wondering if they all had some fall guy in these big companies, or did he mean he should have been consulting a lawyer every step of the way?" In any event, Helen and PJ seemed convinced—and tried to convince Liz—that her father's case could be won in court, and that "the threat of jail was never going to come to fruition." That, at least, was encouraging.

So was the continuing presence of Paul. "He was my knight in shining armour, a great source of comfort." But in September 1969, soon after the scandal broke, Paul left Toronto to study English and film studies at the University of Western Ontario in London, a two-and-a-half-hour drive down Highway 403. "You might find someone else," she told him plaintively when he left, "but she'll never love you more than I do."

Liz had watched helplessly as her family splintered and her father spiralled deeper into despair and alcohol. To complicate matters, Liz herself became ill with both hepatitis and then mononucleosis that spring. "I was told to refrain from kissing," she remembers, but "explaining this to Paul, who came down to visit, did not deter him one bit."

By the spring of 1970, the public clamour over the accusations against her father had not subsided, and Liz was eagerly looking forward to spending a full month that summer escaping the news and the noise. She was scheduled to join a group of fellow summer campers paddling Northern Ontario's ancient canoe routes, "retracing the footsteps of the voyageurs."

But because she still did not have "the right white cell count" by early summer, her family doctor refused to sign off on her participation.

"Paul came to my rescue," Liz says now. "He asked his mother if I could accompany them to Ireland instead." Paul was scheduled to compete in a sailing regatta at Dun Laoghaire that summer. Liz could fly with the Phelans to Ireland, Paul suggested, then Liz and Rose—"for the sake of propriety"—could travel north together by train and meet up with Paul.

Paul's mother contacted Liz's father. "She insisted I travel as their guest," Liz recalls. "Dad insisted on paying my way. That went back and forth until my father said I couldn't go unless he paid. Helen was not used to someone taking such a stand," Liz says now, "and she was impressed by that. I was always appreciative of my father's insistence on my being on equal footing."

But that said, something subtle—or perhaps not so subtle—seemed to have changed in Liz's relationship with Paul's parents. "They were very clear from day one that they wanted their son to be with someone who had her own money." In the beginning, she had it. Now ... perhaps not so much. She—and the Smythes—had become supplicants. But that realization would only become clearer to her later.

Ireland turned out to be a welcome tonic for all the problems that had plagued her back home. "When the taxi from the station came down York

Road and neared the water, I saw him down by the pier. Paul, in yellow boots, a heavy, sodden vest, and with hair blown back by the wind, looked like a wild, Irish sailor. Rolling down the window, I yelled for him, waving my arms frantically. He ran up the street and jumped into the moving car. It was as if he came from the sea, came for me, as a gift from God. I couldn't fathom how I could love a man so much, so I contented myself with telling him every two seconds."

Paul wasn't just "incredibly handsome," she had long since decided. "He was gifted in so many ways. He was a wonderful musician. He loved music, we both loved music. And then he had this ambition to be on the Canadian Olympic sailing team. Paul raced Finns, a class that was all sail and very little boat. It required a great amount of strength to manage. He aimed to make the Canadian Olympic team. A legendary bowler in cricket, he was slated to represent Canada in two disciplines."

Ireland—with Paul—was a glorious respite.

Back home in Toronto, however, life was about to get much worse.

On October 13, 1971, the roller-coaster ride that had been Stafford Smythe's calamitous fall from grace came to an abrupt, devastating, skittering, inconclusive end.

Although Smythe and Ballard had recently staged a successful counter-coup, regaining control of the Maple Leaf Gardens board in the middle of the criminal investigation, their victory was both pyrrhic and short-lived. Arrested and charged, they faced a trial that was scheduled to begin on October 25, 1971.[32]

In early October, Stafford was admitted to Wellesley Hospital after being diagnosed with a bleeding ulcer. His condition quickly deteriorated. "When we started to think he may not carry the day," Liz recalls, she stopped by the Phelans, uninvited, to seek advice and solace. "It was wrong to show up without an appointment," she acknowledges, "but it was morning and I thought I could catch them, or at least Helen. When Betty ushered me in, there was a meeting of some kind underway, and PJ asked an employee to take me outside. I left feeling that I shouldn't have gone there."

Just a few days later, on the night of October 13, Stafford Smythe died of complications during a second emergency surgery. He was only fifty years old.

Liz telephoned Paul at university in London. She woke him up. He told her he'd jump in the car and be there as soon as he could.

"You have school, though," she said.

"Forget it. I want to be with you."

And he was.

Paul's parents? Not so much. "I looked for Helen and PJ at the funeral, which filled St. Paul's Basilica, but they did not attend." She was surprised. "They had been acquaintances, and Helen always liked Dad, calling him 'devastatingly attractive.'"

A few days after the funeral, she and Paul had dinner with the Phelans.

"They grilled me up and down about the money, about what portion [of her father's estate] would be mine. I detected a cold look, passing back and forth between them."

Liz also confided to Helen and PJ about the conversation she'd had with her mother in the car on the way to the funeral. Liz's mother's relationship with her husband had become increasingly fractious during the previous few years, partly because of his history of philandering, but also complicated now by his depression and increased drinking. Even before his death, it seemed, she had begun thinking of her own future. Suddenly, "a steady stream of suitors and predators were at our door," Liz remembers. "Mom was looking to remarry, and I was the brunt of a lot of bitterness. It was just plain awful."

Although Liz had been planning to attend an American college after her high school graduation, she promised her mother in the car that day she wouldn't leave her but would continue to live at home instead. "I half expected her to object," Liz told the Phelans, "but she said it would be better for her if I didn't go. 'I feel like I owe that to her,'" she suggested to the Phelans.

Helen and PJ, however, were dismissive. "This sacrifice you seem to be making for your mother is very misguided," said Helen, the champion of education for young women. "You don't owe her anything."

That seemed, Liz says now, "the most mind-boggling concept I had ever heard."

But it got worse. PJ chimed in that Liz's mother, a Quebec Irish Catholic, was "limited. She's going to do what she will, regardless of all the help in the world."

Helen then returned to the inevitable subject of her future with Paul. "You need to think of your future," she said. "When Paul graduates, we plan to move him into the family business. He's talked about marriage."

"I'm still in high school," Liz countered.

"Yes, finish high school, and then get married," Helen agreed. "You can continue your schooling in Toronto if you like, or maybe you'll want to have children."

"I do want children, but I have to find myself first."

"Oh, all these feelings seem important now," Helen replied, shutting down the conversation, "but in the grand scheme of things, they don't mean anything."

Liz had begun to feel as if she was simply a pawn in a larger social and business game the Phelans were playing.

After Christmas dinner at the Phelans two months later, the pressure to marry intensified—as did Liz's sense of being seen as someone whose future was now subject to others' whims. "I was sitting on the stairs and PJ came by and sat beside me. He said, 'You'll never go hungry.' I was so profoundly insulted by that. I was not going to be treated like a poor relation. And I wasn't going to be controlled because my family had crashed. I wasn't going to have digs and references to that for the rest of my life. I thought I would rather starve than have that fate, frankly."

The only good news was that Paul had remained steadfast. "He wanted to help." And yet ... they had been through so much in such a short time. "We were not the same pair anymore," she thought to herself. "We were not birds of a feather. I seemed to have changed colour and moulted."

"Well, what kind of wedding would you like?"

It was September 1973. Paul and Liz had just returned from a spectacular summer of travelling and sailing around Europe. They'd picked up a VW bus in Hamburg and—towing Paul's sailboat, the van jammed with sails—drove to Brest, France, for the world sailing championships. They'd camped on the beach with other sailors from around the globe. At one point, Rose joined them. Then Paul and Liz made their way to Sweden—"just the two of us"—for another set of races, and then back to Paris where they rejoined Rose "and had great fun."

Now they were all back in Toronto, and the pressure to nail down plans for the nuptials everyone agreed were impending had become much more intense. The goal of today's meeting with Helen and Gail at 8 Old Forest Hill was to make some decisions.

What kind of wedding would it be?

When Liz explained that she wanted to be married in Muskoka where the Smythe summer home was located, Helen was dismissive. It was a two-and-a-half-hour drive from Toronto. "That's the kind of wedding where you send a gift and don't go. I want the wedding to take place here in the backyard." She was already planning for four hundred guests.

Gail was quick to add that the Phelans would pay for everything.

While Gail no doubt intended that to be reassuring, Liz saw it as one more assault on her own family's straitened circumstances. She says she objected, but "they both chimed in very firmly that they would pay and that it had already been budgeted. The wedding would be in the Phelan backyard. I left feeling humiliated with my Irish pride in ruins."

By this point, Paul had graduated from university and was back living in Toronto in one of his father's apartments a few blocks from his parents. Gail had been led to believe he was attending the University of Toronto School of Management. He wasn't. He had decided to take the year off and "become a writer." But it wasn't going well. Liz, who was then in second year of university, would often stop by after her classes. She'd inevitably find Paul and his roommate, a young man who was "going to become an artist," playing table hockey.

"Did you guys get one thing done?" she would admonish them.

"Oh, we're going to," they'd reply. "We're going to. We're just ... Two out of three! Two out of three!" She laughs. "They were just addicted to that."

What Paul really wanted was for Liz to move in with him. She usually did spend weekends and occasional overnights at his apartment and probably would have moved in with him, except...

One day in her English class, a professor, trying to teach his students the "difference between a sad or unfortunate set of circumstances and a tragedy," had used her own father's death, probably unknowingly, as his measuring stick. "Throwing up at a smart dinner party and making a fool of oneself is not a tragedy," he explained. "What happened to Stafford Smythe ... That was a tragedy."

"Smarting and stinging" from what felt like yet another attack on her family, Liz ended up at Paul's apartment looking for comfort. "He answered the door soaking wet with a small towel held by one hand." There was a young woman Liz knew in the apartment who "sat on the couch. Her hair, like his, hung in wet shanks."

"Did you guys go swimming?" Liz asked.

They both laughed. "We did," Paul said.

"Where?"

"The Granite Club," the young woman answered.

Liz knew that neither Paul nor the young woman was a member of the members-only club. "What kind of idiot would not see the writing on the wall? I didn't even have the presence of mind to turn around and leave." And she didn't call Paul on what he'd done either. Instead, she stayed and had dinner with the two of them. "I was too proud and too crushed to even say anything about it."

A few days later, Liz attended a cousin's wedding, this time without Paul. At dinner, she sat next to her grandfather, Conn, and told him she was about to marry Percy's grandson. "He locked his piercing blue eyes on mine and said, 'You don't love that guy.'"

Stunned, Liz says she talked about what her grandfather had said on the drive back to the Smythe cottage with her older sister Vicki. Without intending to, she'd already confided to her sister the story of discovering Paul's unfaithfulness. At the time, Liz recalls now, her sister had herself settled for a "'right marriage,' with a chap from a good family, a stockbroker and a philanderer." If Liz married Paul, Vicki said, she too "would be choosing to put up with that kind of behaviour. We talked about how men don't change and that the entitled ones feel it is their birthright. I sunk into a state of gloom."

A few days later, an old friend of her brother's who'd just been dumped by his California girlfriend came to visit the Smythe cottage. He and his girlfriend had been planning a fishing trip to an isolated cabin up north on the Montreal River, he told Liz, and he was now reluctant to go alone. Would she like to accompany him?

She rebuffed him at first, she says now, but—still stinging from her discovery of Paul's unfaithfulness, which she hadn't confronted him about—abruptly changed her mind. "A truly mad love affair began."

She broke up with a bewildered Paul. He only knew "we had gotten as far as the meeting with Gail and Helen about arranging the wedding, and he thought that's where we were," she explains. "And then ... *What on earth happened?* He was understandably stunned and tried to dissuade me."

But it was already too late. Liz, only twenty, was ready to make a complete break with her past. She "quit school, was disowned by my family, kicked out and told to change my name. But at that point, I wanted to escape everything and everyone."

Although the affair with her brother's friend ended quickly and disastrously—"it turned out he had a debt of about twenty thousand dollars that was due on some land he owned, so he figured he could kill two birds with one stone if he managed to whisk me away"—she had already decided she wouldn't go back to Paul. "There were indicators of trouble to come. I feel I was brave enough to turn away from a mountain of security and jump off the end of the road into a very uncertain future."

Paul, for his part, wasn't ready to let her go. After Liz's affair ended and she'd moved back to Ontario to live with some college friends, Paul "showed up in the middle of the night, banging on the door, demanding that I come out. I said no. One of my more gallant friends told him to go home. But there were incidents like that."

And yet, Liz says, she couldn't help but wonder if there wasn't some way to patch things up between them, to at least be friends. That winter, she agreed to accompany him on a sailing adventure.

"Why I took such a chance remains a mystery. I was crazy for adventure, for one thing, still longing for escape for another, and wanting to see if we could manage to be in a platonic friendship. But I made it clear that there would be no romance as I was too injured at that point."

Paul acquiesced. He had sailed alone from California to Panama, and she flew to Panama City to join him for the next leg of an adventure around the Caribbean. The boat was "not at all large," she recalls, "and was crammed with computer equipment," which had become a fascination for Paul. "I wrote daily on the first portable computer in the world!" They ended up in a storm on the ocean, "battered and flailing, focused on literally staying afloat." Teamwork saved their lives. "We both remembered that moment forever. In spite of everything," she says now, "our friendship was cemented."

But it would never be the same.

Back in Toronto, Paul invited Liz to a party attended by many of their old friends. Paul was with someone new, Rundi Dick, the woman who would eventually become his wife. "I could see great attraction between them," Liz says now. As she prepared to leave the party that night, she remembers, she approached them to say her goodbyes. "Paul stuck out his foot and tripped me." She fell. Paul's friends "cried out, asking him, 'What on earth?' To me it was a declaration. He made it quite clear. We were through."

Paul's own writerly dreams went nowhere. After a while, remembers Liz, "his father said, 'Okay, it's time to come down to the office with me.'" He didn't actually start in the office, but worked "briefly" as a Cara line cook before eventually joining his father at head office.

The reality was that Paul had long been fascinated by business, though not necessarily his father's business. Fred Farncomb, a fellow student at Upper Canada College who would become PD's stockbroker, would later tell the *Globe and Mail* that a teenaged Paul David would sometimes go to visit the Toronto Stock Exchange gallery, as well as the trading room at Gardiner, Wardrop & Company, his grandfather's brokerage firm.

He became an astute investor, and after personal computers debuted in the mid-'70s, he would use them to work out algorithms to trade in commodities and currencies. By his later "tongue-in-cheek telling," he was the "first individual to use a personal computer."

His office at Cara doubled as the head office of his private investment firm, and initially at least, he spent more time playing the markets than he did learning the intricacies of Cara's food business.

Paul's relationship with his father had become even more complicated now that he was an adult. On the one hand, PJ saw his only son as his rightful heir. He wanted him beside him at Cara. On the other, PJ had no intention of going quietly into his own good night and regarded any sign of his son's interest in advancing his place within the company as a kind of disloyalty.

Their corporate differences often spilled over into their personal relationship. Liz remembers one incident in 1973 when she and Paul were still a couple. They'd arrived half an hour late for one of the Phelans' "great parties. PJ came to the door and said to his son, 'I want you to stay out of my milieu. Stay out for some time.' Then he turned and walked away. I didn't know what the term meant so I asked Paul. 'He wants to kick me out of his life.'"[33]

That said, Paul had finally, if not wholeheartedly, taken his place in the Phelan family business. As his father hoped.

And he would finally have the wedding his mother hoped for—though not with the young woman Helen had expected. On June 4, 1977, Paul David married Rundi Dick, a stunning young woman, the daughter of an Alberta engineering consultant and granddaughter of a Norwegian immigrant who'd initially homesteaded in Saskatchewan. "Hence," noted *Globe and Mail* columnist Zena Cherry in her account of their society wedding, "her Norwegian name."

As was often the case with Cherry's society notes, much space was taken up establishing the couple's parents' bona fides in the business and social firmament. After a brief nod to Rundi's more rural rustic roots, Cherry devoted several effusive paragraphs to the Phelans. "Paul David is the grandson of the late Percy R. Gardiner, industrialist and philanthropist. His great grandfather was TP Phelan who ... founded the firm that is now Cara Operations.

"The bridegroom's father is chairman of Cara and an international yachtsman, who hopes his new yacht *Mia VI* will represent the Royal Canadian Yacht Club in the 1978 challenge for the Canada Cup.[34] The bridegroom's mother, Helen, is volunteer chairman of Toronto Arts Productions, which runs the St. Lawrence Centre."

Some of Paul's friends had been surprised at Paul's choice of partner, not because they disliked Rundi personally—"I liked her a lot," Andrew Hunter says—but because she hadn't gone to an exclusive private school and her first degree was from the Ontario College of Art. "You partner inside the box, and at Upper Canada College, that meant [Bishop Strachan] or someplace similar," Hunter explained. "I mean it's about love, of course, but still..."

The wedding took place in Holy Rosary Church—PJ and Helen had wed in its rectory—with the boys of St. Michael's Choir School singing from the choir loft. John Brooke, Paul David's pal from UCC, was best man. Two other UCC alumni and close friends—Gary Slaight, son of broadcasting executive Allan Slaight, and Jeffrey Heintzman—served as ushers. Paul's sister Rose was a bridesmaid, and his nieces—Gail's daughter Ellen and Sharon's daughter, Holiday—were flower girls. Gail's son Timothy was one of Paul's ushers.

The reception, as Helen had long planned, took place at the Phelans' Old Forest Hill mansion. Cocktails were served on the upper terrace while a trio played Irish, Canadian, and Norwegian music in the background. Dinner was served on the lowest terrace where tables for ten, decorated in yellow with flowers in white stands, had been set up. "After the speeches," Cherry wrote, "there was dancing on the middle garden terrace. At midnight, another band performed in the playroom of the main house."

There were, of course, other moments that didn't make it into the pages of the *Globe and Mail*. When John Brooke began making his "silly little best man speech," for example, describing how "Rundi and Paul David were already set up for marriage with their Volvo, and had been setting up their house together," PJ's eccentric aunt, who was in the front row with the family, "started yelling at me to stop it. She didn't like the fact I even referred to the fact that they'd been living together before being married. PJ had to tell her to shut up."

John adds, "After that, it just turned into a wild party, guys jumping into the swimming pool with their tuxedos on." The only thing about the wedding reception that surprised Andrew Hunter was that it took place "at the groom's house and not the bride's" as was then usual. "But that," he says, "was just sort of an indicator of the balance of power, how things worked. The Phelans ran the wedding."

Zena Cherry's official account of the wedding ended by noting that the couple were now on their honeymoon in Nassau, planned to live in Toronto, and "will also have a winter home at Red Mountain in Aspen, Colorado."

Cherry did not describe Paul by his day job in Cara's head office but by what seems to have been his preferred title, "research analyst."

Rosemary Anne Phelan, the baby of the family, was smart. Like her oldest sister, Gail, she had skipped two grades in elementary school. But in other ways, Rose wasn't like her sister at all.

In part, there was their age gap. A dozen years separated them. "I never remember ever living in the same house with Gail," Rose allows today. Gail had married young and begun her family before Rose was even a teenager. The result was that, growing up, Gail's oldest children were closer in age to Rose than Rose was to Gail.

But the very different times in which they came of age also shaped them. If Gail was the dutiful daughter of the 1950s, Rose self-reports today as the "rebellious teenaged hippie" of the 1960s and '70s.

Rose had good reason to be rebellious. "My parents were very difficult," she explains. "I mean they were glamorous and busy, and they did a lot, and they had a big life. But I think, as parents, they were just absolutely ghastly."

Like Paul and Sharon, Rose was primarily raised by Betty, the family nanny. "Betty was my caregiver." And then there was the cook, and the driver, and a general household helper, and Helen's personal assistant, more present in Rose's life than her own parents.

Rose's daily interactions with her parents mostly took place during dinners in the formal dining room. "There was my father at one end of the table, my mother at the other, and my brother, Paul, and I were in the middle. My dad had this buzzer under the table, and he would buzz, and the meals would be brought to us at the table by 'the help.'"

Parental table tensions were palpable. Rose can't remember what her parents argued about, or if their disputes were even about anything at all. "They just seemed to fight and be in bad moods all the time—my mother, especially." Rose and Paul kept their heads down "and just tried to get through dinner."

Sometimes, her mother's bad moods could escalate, and her wrath was often directed, for no obvious reason, at Rose. "She'd have violent rages, particularly when she'd been drinking, but sometimes she'd have rages just because she was in a bad mood."

Rose remembers one such incident. She was in her mother's bedroom combing her hair in front of the mirror with a silver comb that had once belonged to her grandmother. By accident, Rose knocked an arm off a Dresden doll on the vanity. "My mother just went through the roof. 'You did that on purpose! I know you did that on purpose!' Well, no, I didn't do that on purpose. It was an accident. But she could be very hurtful, purposely hurtful."

Rose was only thirteen—having completed grade 9 at Bishop Strachan School—when she announced she wanted to attend a boarding school in the United States. "My parents were thrilled. My brother was about to go to university, so he wouldn't be at home anymore, and they wouldn't have to think about us."

Rose chose Chatham Hall, an all-girls boarding high school in rural southern Virginia with small classes and a "mission to equip curious thinkers to lead lives of impact." Perhaps most important for Rose was that the school boasted a first-rate equestrian program. Rose had been riding since she was ten. It was a family passion she shared with her older sister Sharon, and which she could also trace back to the famous great-grandfather she'd never met. "My sister rode, so maybe it was some weird sister yearning, but the horses really got under my skin and remained a passion for me."

But Rose also arrived at Chatham Hall at the beginning of the 1970s, a time of cultural, social, and racial ferment in the southern United States. Chatham Hall was located not only to the south of the rarified world she'd known in Toronto but also south of the Mason–Dixon line that had divided warring states during the American Civil War. The school attracted "a mix of southern girls and northern girls" all trying to understand how they fit in this new world order. "It was a fascinating time," Rose recalls. "I was very sensitive to what was happening around me, and I learned a lot." She adds today, "In hindsight, it was great."

In hindsight...

"I think I probably suffered from depression. I wasn't coping academically. I wasn't coping emotionally. I was sorry after that I didn't stay."

Instead, in the summer before what was supposed to be her final year of high school, Rose travelled to visit her sister Sharon at her horse ranch in Mendocino, California. Sharon was married at this point, and she had a baby daughter, Holly. "I just went out there to visit her for a couple of weeks," Rose remembers, "but I was really into horses, and she was living on a horse ranch, and I was, 'Hell, no! I'm staying.'"

She was still only fifteen. "It was ridiculous that my parents would let me do that," she says now, especially given what they knew about Sharon's addiction issues and her lifestyle in California.

Rose's decision to stay with her sister did create a "big family crisis" back in Toronto, remembers Liz Smythe. But instead of going to see what was happening for themselves, "PJ and Helen decided the solution was to send Paul out to either fetch her or decide if she should stay. And so, I went with him, and we went out and saw that scene." What Liz remembers of that scene:

"Sharon ran this horse farm out there with a complete cast of ne'er-do-wells who came and went and basically sponged off her."

That wasn't what Rose saw in the moment, of course. "I was a star-struck teenager who'd landed in this hippie Shangri-La in Mendocino, California—and there were horses!"

The first months of her stay went well enough. She attended a nearby public high school. "But then my sister split up with her husband and everything became too chaotic. But, by that point, I was there. I had a boyfriend, and I started doing serious drugs, which was not great, of course." She shuffled between living at her sister's ranch and a commune nearby where she lived with her boyfriend.

A year and a half after she arrived and after graduating from high school in California, Rose finally returned to Canada. But in the fall of 1973, she left Toronto again for the US East Coast and enrolled at Goddard College, a small progressive private liberal arts college in Vermont. She remembers her four years there fondly. "I was starving [intellectually], and I enjoyed the academic side." She followed that up with two years of graduate school at the University of Vermont where she studied English, completing her courses but not her thesis. By then, she says, "I had started straightening myself out and becoming serious and goal oriented."

Some things, however, didn't change.

At one point after Rose wrapped up a semester of college in Italy, she remembers flying to Bermuda to spend time with her parents whom she hadn't seen in six months. "Dad came in from sailing, and we all went for dinner. My parents had a tremendous argument." Later, she confronted her mother. "Why? What was that all about? You didn't seem to be the slightest bit interested in me. Why was it all about you?"

Her mother didn't answer her directly, "but she actually paused. I sense that it resonated with her in some way because it wasn't a normal reaction." Still, what happened fit with a pattern Rose, then twenty, could trace back to her first memories of childhood. "There didn't seem to be any interest in me whatsoever. No respect, no consideration..."

Liz Smythe also remembers when Rose would return home to Toronto for school holidays after six months in the United States. "The chauffeur would meet her at the airport. Betty would have something nice for her in the kitchen. And her parents weren't even there." The upside of that, Smythe adds, is that Rose "grew to be a strong and independent woman."

After college, Rose finally returned to Toronto full-time, moved into a third-floor apartment in a building her father owned in nearby Forest Hill—close but not too close to her parents—and found work in publishing at Methuen's Canadian office. Her father soon tapped her to serve as the primary researcher for a book he was planning to celebrate Cara's 100th anniversary. "It was a really good project, a good and positive thing."

By this point, she had been a board member of Holdings, the Phelan holding company, since she was seventeen. She wasn't sure why her father had decided to bring her into the company so young—"Did he just want a body to fill the chair. Or did he want to educate me in the systems and the way the business worked?" In the beginning, her duties consisted primarily of attending the Christmas dinner followed by the company's annual general meeting. But even that began to give her a new and more complicated perspective on her complicated father.

"He was a fascinating character," she says today. "I get conflicted about my dad. Of course I do. He had a big personality. He was very outgoing. He was charming and good-looking. He loved sailing. He was really, really into sailing. That was a huge part of his life. My father was ambitious, and he married my mother who came from a wealthy family, a wealthy entrepreneurial family. I think my father was ambitious and entrepreneurial and really had a vision for the family company. I think he was a sensitive person and creative person. He wasn't a traditional businessman. He was Catholic, and maybe he had more of a flair and less of a discipline. He didn't graduate from high school. I think he had a lot of conflict. I think he had conflict within his own family and his own demons."

Some of those demons he'd inherited, some he would pass on to members of the next Phelan generation.

~

Despite the five years separating them and their own very different teen years—Rose as a boarding student in the United States, Paul as a day boy at Upper Canada College—the siblings' relationship evolved for the closer after Rose returned to live in Toronto in her early twenties.

"We crossed paths and began to connect socially," Rose says now. She became friends with Rundi, Paul's new girlfriend and then wife. She dated some of Paul's friends, including—briefly—John Brooke and then, more seriously, Michael Robbins, a graduate of the University of Guelph who worked as a planning consultant for a Toronto-based international engineering consulting firm.

Although Michael had grown up in Don Mills, a self-contained middle-class Toronto neighbourhood, he and his sporting family "spent every weekend since I was born, basically, in Collingwood," where the Phelans had their farm.

He and Paul bonded over their mutual love of windsurfing, which combined sailing with surfing. Invented in California in the late 1960s, windsurfing had quickly become a highly competitive sport.

"We were among the first guys [in Canada] to get into the sport, to compete," Robbins remembers. "Once we did, all we thought about in the summertime was windsurfing. We'd look at the trees, and if there was wind, we'd rush down to Georgian Bay with our boards on our cars." On hot summer days, they'd hang out for hours on the sandy beach at Northwinds Beach Park in the nearby resort town of Blue Mountains, just waiting for the wind to come up.

Although he and Paul were friends, it was clear from the beginning that they hailed from very different worlds. "Paul was different, obviously, because he came from money. Paul didn't work. He played the commodities market, and he had a program that he used to play the market."

Once, Robbins recalls, he and Paul and some friends decided to travel to Virginia Beach, Virginia, for a windsurfing vacation. Robbins and the others drove, "our boards and all of us crammed into a little van. Paul flew down." During the trip, Michael won a "bit of money at the casino," so he decided to fly back with Paul. "We were late for the plane, so Paul just pulled up in the rental car to the departures level. We jumped out, ran for the plane ... just left the car there." He marvels. "I guess Paul called the rental car company afterwards and told them it was sitting there on the curb at the departures."

When Robbins first met Rose—at a friend's birthday party at a restaurant in downtown Toronto—"I didn't even know Paul had a sister, to be honest." But, he adds with a laugh, "I will never forget when I did meet her. She was wearing a leather skirt, which I thought was pretty hot."

When they did talk, Robbins quickly realized Rose was a Phelan, a sister of Paul and a friend of Paul's wife, Rundi, who'd grown up in Don Mills and was one of Robbins's friends too.

For Rose, those connections, especially the one with her brother, were important. "At first, I think our relationship began because he was my brother's friend," she explains. "I wanted to please my brother." But she was also in love, "and I wanted to be a part of something."

In contrast to her own complicated, argumentative upbringing, Michael's "very sporty" suburban family seemed—on the face of it, at least—"lovely, lovely, lovely," and a family into which she could be accepted.

Michael's father, Jake, an engineer who'd played varsity football at the University of Toronto, had spent most of his career as the vice-president of Miller Paving, a Canadian highways contractor. In the 1950s, he and his wife,

Geri, a Finnish-raised ski instructor, were among the thirty founders of the Osler Bluff Ski Club on the Niagara Escarpment in Collingwood. Jake volunteered to cut the first ski runs. The Phelans, of course, whose farm was near the base of the ski hill, became prominent members.

All four of the Robbins children became competitive skiers: Derek, the oldest, was a member of the Canadian team at the Sapporo Olympic Winter Games in 1972, while Lynda, the youngest, would become a member of the Canadian national team and marry Ken Read, legendary member of the Crazy Canucks. Michael, the second son, not only became a champion competitive skier but was also a competitive sailor. That too brought Michael into Paul's orbit.

Although the Robbins family lived comfortably enough—Jake eventually branched out on his own, becoming president of J.A. Robbins Construction Ltd., a Collingwood-based paving and maintenance company—they were never in the Phelans' wealth class. And that was fine with Rose.

"There was always a lot of talk in my family," Rose says today, "lots of talk. I was tired of talk. I wanted a simpler way of life, but also to be part of something where people did things, purposeful things, even little things like go to the grocery store or drive a car."

Michael Robbins, for his part, delighted in being welcomed into the far-from-simple Phelan world. "PJ and Helen were larger-than-life characters, especially PJ," Robbins recalls. "He'd come into a room with his booming voice and his approach. He'd command attention in the room." Robbins quickly became a regular at 8 Old Forest Hill. "They'd have these amazing parties. One time I was up at the oyster bar in the backyard and the king of Norway was standing beside me ... Christmas, Thanksgiving, whatever, they always put on a big event for family and friends. PJ sat with his drink in what he called his 'coming and going chair' in the front hall to receive people." He pauses, considers. "You know, it was fun. It was exciting, a whole different world than I grew up in. But looking back on it, there was definitely a lot of drinking and partying. That was a big part of it. In those days, I never even thought about addiction."

On June 1, 1985, Rosemary Anne Phelan, twenty-eight, and Jeffrey Michael Robbins, thirty, married in the chapel at Bishop Strachan, the exclusive private school Rose had left behind fifteen years before. *Globe and Mail* social columnist Zena Cherry would describe the ceremony performed by Rev. Cheryl Kristolaitis, the school's chaplain, as "the first I have seen conducted by a woman, and it seemed most apt."

Rose's white wedding gown, which came from Creeds, had been designed by Priscilla of Boston, the legendary wedding dress designer who'd become famous in the 1950s for designing Grace Kelly's gown when she married Monaco's Prince Rainier III. Rose's attendants' gowns, made in Paris, featured white lace dotted with pearls over pink. Sharon's daughter, Holly, and Gail's daughter Ellen, served as bridesmaids while Rose's younger nieces, Gail's daughter Honor and Paul's daughter Jennen, served as flower girls. Paul David and Rose's nephew Timothy Regan were ushers.

The reception, of course, was at the Phelan home, where three marquee tents had been erected for the two hundred and fifty wedding guests. For cocktails, they had the choice of two bars, one on the upper level of the garden and a second at the middle level. The formal dinner was served under a large, very high, third tent that covered the tennis court.

PJ, "known for his Irish wit," as Cherry reported, "was at his best as master of ceremonies." Guido Basso's orchestra played until the wee hours of the morning. And Paul David, unsurprisingly, proposed the toast to the bride.

"I thought that by marrying a friend of my brother's, I'll be in, I'll be accepted. My brother will like me."

That didn't work out exactly as she hoped.

But something else did work out—and for the better. After an extended honeymoon, Rose and Michael visited New Zealand. They fell in love with the South Pacific islands' nation. As someone who "liked to travel and see new places, always a bit adventurous," Rose took the lead. *What if…?*

Their New Zealand future, Rose jokes today, "started on a whim in a phone booth on a rainy day on the North Island in New Zealand." While staying at a bed and breakfast, they began chatting with the owner, a local consultant. One conversation led to another, and the consultant suggested there might be an opportunity for someone with Michael's skills at an Auckland-based international company, which was looking for someone to develop its own tourism division. "Michael called up and went in for a couple of interviews and got the job." Rose laughs. "We ended up living there for three years."

Rose, Michael, and their growing family—daughters Raewyn, a popular New Zealand name that Rose liked, born in 1986, and Michaela, born in 1988—settled in Auckland, 14,000 kilometres and more than thirteen hours by plane from Toronto, the Phelan family, and the gathering storm over Cara that would change all their lives forever.

"Any Problems with Alcohol?"

Hiring David Bork had been Gail's idea. But it was her mother who'd inadvertently planted the seed more than a decade earlier. Hoping to take the edge off what she saw as Gail's bluntness, Helen offered to pay for Gail and her husband, Tim, to attend a National Training Laboratories Institute for Applied Behavioral Science summer session in Bethel, a small, isolated resort town in the mountains of Maine.

The NTL had been founded after the Second World War by Kurt Lewin, a German Jew who'd immigrated to the United States soon after Hitler came to power. He later served as the director of the Research Center for Group Dynamics at the Massachusetts Institute of Technology and is considered one of the founders of modern social psychology.

Working with small groups known as training or T-Groups, Lewin had developed a technique of facilitated dialogue he called "sensitivity training," which was designed to encourage individuals to become more aware of their own goals and prejudices, and more sensitive to the needs and dynamics of the larger group. The methodology was experiential, the goals to encourage team building, conflict management, and group effectiveness. Given his focus on "group dynamics" (another term, among many, that Lewin coined) and the ways in which organizations can be made to change and adapt, Lewin's ideas became increasingly popular during the 1960s with modern business leaders.

Including Helen Phelan.

Given her own family's dynamics and what would become the increasingly fraught relations among her own children, she might have spent more time considering what became known as Lewin's Equation. Dismissing the popular arguments over nature versus nurture in explaining human behaviour and individual personality, Lewin had posited his own theory of behaviour as an equation, which he expressed as $B = f(P, E)$. Behaviour (B), he argued, was a function (*f*) of personal characteristics (P) and environmental characteristics (E).

That would go a long way to explain what ultimately happened inside the Phelan family—and Helen Phelan's own role in its outcome.

By the time Helen suggested Gail attend that first NTL workshop, Lewin himself had been dead more than twenty years, but his ideas still shaped the training.

"The first time we went," Gail recalls of her trips to Bethel, "was 1969, the year of the moon landing. That's how I remember when we went." What she also remembers is that "I loved it. I thought this really, really helps to understand people and to get along with people." She became a devotee, attending "pretty well" every year for the next decade. "I cycled through a lot of sessions, including ones with a more specialized focus. I remember one was called the Power Lab. It was an authority program. So, after that session, I went to the facilitator of the conference. 'I think I need help,' I said."

After Gail joined Cara, PJ tasked her with organizing the national celebration of the company's 100th anniversary in 1983. After that? "I realized there wasn't a plan for me past the centennial."

She knew, of course, the traditional pecking order for the children of family business owners. "The brothers went into the family business and the women played tennis."

She didn't want that for herself. She had an MBA. She'd already spent a lot of time thinking about business, about family business, about the Phelan family business. "I wanted to be part of it." But she still wasn't sure what that meant or where it might lead. "I was in no rush," she explains, nor immediately ambitious for a particular position.

That said, she told her family she did want to be named president of Holdings—specifically because you had to be the president of a substantial company before you were forty to be eligible to join the Young Presidents' Organization. YPO was a US-based worldwide group of executives whose goal is to "become better leaders and better people through peer learning and exceptional experiences in an inclusive community of open sharing and trust." Gail's cousin, Michael Gardiner, was already a member "and found it a great way to stay up to date on what was happening in business." Gail, the lifelong learner, thought she could benefit from that too.

Larry Hynes, Cara's long-time lawyer and PJ's confidant, wasn't keen on Gail becoming president of the holding company. "I don't think my brother was thrilled either because then he theoretically would be reporting to me. But my position was, 'This is just so I can represent us, so I can qualify for YPO, but I don't want to boss you guys around.' After that, they said fine."

Gail's goal at this point was still primarily finding her own comfort zone within Cara. "I just wanted to prepare for it. I wanted there to be a plan. Maybe there were courses I should take, or ... also, the rest of the family? How would they be involved." She laughs. "Then, of course, my brother promptly showed up. Because he wanted to be the successor. He just thought he was entitled."

She wasn't sure what her brother really wanted. On the one hand, Paul David was on the board of Cara and had an office across the hall from Gail's at the company's head office. On the other hand, he spent most of his time in the office—when he spent time in the office—running his own separate commodities trading business. He'd only seemed to begin to take an active interest in Cara and its future after Gail arrived on the scene. Jealousy? Rivalry?

Gail knew what her father wanted. Or thought she did. PJ wanted his son to be his successor. Someday. But PJ didn't seem eager, or even ready, to contemplate his own retirement. And yet he seemed, to Gail at least, to have become "fragile." He was in his sixties and disengaged. She couldn't put her finger on specifics, "but his mind seemed to wander. He didn't seem to be as directed or as ambitious as he had been."

Gail decided she needed help figuring out exactly where and how she fit in the Phelan scheme of the future. As importantly, she decided, her father, her brother, and the rest of the family needed help too.

Gail explained the situation to her training group's leader at NTL. "We need to sort ourselves out. Could you do it?" He couldn't. "It's not my specialty," he said. "I don't know anything about family business. The person you want to talk to is David Bork. He's the family business specialist."

David Bork didn't set out to become a family business specialist. He graduated from the University of Minnesota with undergraduate degrees in arts and in applied science, with specialties in the even more specialized fields of medical microbiology and bacteriology. But he inexorably gravitated toward applying that scientific thinking to the corporate world. He eventually trained as an organizational behaviourist and opened his own private practice in Frederick, Maryland, in 1968.

Though Bork wasn't aware of it at the time, the state and fate of family businesses had by then become an increasingly important subset of the practice of business consulting, as well as an increasingly rich focus for serious academic research.

Fifteen years before, in 1953, a University of Indiana School of Business student named Grant Calder completed the first doctoral dissertation on family business studies in North America, "Some Management Problems of the Small Family Controlled Manufacturing Business." That same year, Harvard University published Roland Christensen's book *Management Succession in Small and Growing Enterprises*. By 1962, Leon and Katy Danco had founded the Center for Family Business, the first national organization for small business owners in the United States. In 1975, the first consulting firm specifically dedicated to family business would open in Brazil. In 1978, Baylor University would establish a Chair in Family Business. In 1983—the year Cara celebrated its 100th anniversary—the Canadian Association of Family Enterprise, a non-profit association of family business owners, was founded in Canada.

David Bork was only vaguely aware of all that was happening in the world of *family* business consulting when he hung out his consultant's shingle in Maryland. "I was thirty-one years old and naive."

But Bork's own first clients turned out to be members of a family enterprise consisting of three separate operating companies, collectively owned and run by five by-blood or by-marriage relatives. Their business goal, they said, was to merge the three entities into one. They hired Bork to help them develop long-range goals for their newly unified company.

Bork quickly realized he wasn't simply dealing with *business* issues. "I had no idea what was going on in the relationships between and among the family players. If I had invited those five people to cocktails and dinner, the social dynamics would have been complicated. To have them in business together..."

Realizing he "didn't know what the hell was really going on," Bork reached out to "psychologists, psychiatrists, social workers, experts in the human potential field." Finally, he says now, "I bumped up against Bowen Family Systems Theory."

This theory, developed by Dr. Murray Bowen, a psychiatrist who directed family programs at the Georgetown University Medical Center in Washington, DC, considers the family not, as Freud did, as a series of distinct individuals—as lone trees in a forest—but examines the forest/family as one emotional unit employing "systems thinking to describe the unit's complex interactions."

During Bowen's earlier work treating schizophrenics, he had discovered that when he treated his patients as individuals, they would often make progress, but when they returned to their families, their behaviours would not only revert to what they had been before he began treating them but also often become worse.

What was happening inside those families? Bowen began digging deeper into his patients' family histories and discovered patterns of behaviour that replicated generation after generation. The family is a system, he concluded, and it transmits its rules, messages, behavioural expectations from parent to child, to grandchild, and beyond. If those emotional messages are negative or self-destructive—parent-child conflict, sibling rivalries, alcoholism, addiction, and so on—the family dynamics become self-perpetuating.

The good news, Bowen postulated, is that past is not necessarily prologue. Family members can learn to behave better by responding with their minds instead of their emotions. The key is to learn new and more positive thought-based behaviours and then use those to short-circuit their natural emotional tendencies to revert to what they'd learned inside their families.

What did any of that have to do with business?

Everything, argued Bork.

A family business isn't just another family. And it isn't just another business. The business is the family with all the baggage that implies, but it is also a business in which family members must engage in business, financial, and personal relationships simultaneously. While emotions influence decision-making in all human enterprise, the emotional tensions that arise when you mix family and business can be off the charts. It can be difficult, for example, to unremember a childhood slight.

When Bork began promoting his own business application of the Bowen theory, he says he smacked into plenty of skeptics. "The psychologically oriented folks told me, 'Well, you don't have a PhD, so you shouldn't be doing that.' And the businesspeople said, 'That sounds pretty soft.'"

Bork laughs. "Of course, we know today that it's really the hard part. So, what I did is I introduced the Bowen Family Systems Theory into the whole process of looking at family businesses, and I feel personally responsible for having done that."

Dennis T. Jaffe, another pioneer in the field of American family-business consulting, says that while others were still trying to figure out what they could do to help those in family businesses, "Bork offered not just a few ideas but a new framework to define what they were doing and how to see the field."

By the mid-1970s, Bork's company, which now focused entirely on helping family businesses with their specific issues, had become known as Coda Corporation. According to an explanation on the company letterhead, Bork chose the name because *coda*, a musical term, is "a more or less independent passage at the end of a composition, introduced to bring it to a satisfactory resolution."

That was how he saw himself. Coming into a troubled family business and helping its members find a satisfying way back from the brink and into the future.

By 1980, Bork had become recognized as a go-to expert when it came to family business. "One day, the *Wall Street Journal* gave me about six inches of honourable mention in a story ... *There's this guy in Frederick, Maryland, and he's doing some interesting stuff with family business*. The very next day, *Fortune* called and said, 'Would you be able to help us with an article?' So, I supplied a number of cases for them to look at. And that really put me on the map."

Soon, he was working with families from the YPO, the group Gail had been keen to join. The organization invited him to present at a week-long event at Venice International University. His lectures on family business were so popular he was asked to repeat them on the conference's last day. "And the next thing you know, I had all these clients all over the world."

By the time Gail called, Bork had worked with more than two thousand business families. He had helped them negotiate family decision-making processes, understand the complexities of the entrepreneurial personality, deal with complex compensation issues, resolve conflict inside the family and inside the family business, and, ultimately, navigate the perils of succession.

At the time, Bork was in the difficult early stages of structuring a book about what he'd learned. Its cheeky working title was "Patricide, Matricide, Fratricide, Suicide and Other-cides of Family Business." By the time it was published in 1986 under the more buttoned-down title of *Family Business, Risky Business*, Bork had created a fictionalized composite family he called the Harwoods to help him illustrate the many issues families face.

"That family," Bork jokes today, "had more shit inside their family than any family should have."

Although he insists the Harwoods were based on a variety of his clients, it is hard not to extrapolate the real-life Phelans from the fictional Harwoods: an alcoholic patriarch unwilling, unable to let go; a smart eldest daughter more than capable of assuming the mantle but stymied at every turn by her father and brother, an alcoholic; troubled son who, though he was the father's favourite, was clearly neither up to the task nor driven to ready himself for his designated role as successor to his father.

In the pages of Bork's book, there is a happy ending. With the help of an outside consultant, the Harwoods come up with a family succession plan to be phased in over a three-year period "with benchmarks to measure each stage." Louis Sr.—the book's PJ Phelan—agrees to step away for a well-deserved rest and reconsideration of his future life. The favoured but troubled son, Charles—PD—sticks around long enough to help with the transition of generational power to his sister, but then checks himself into a substance abuse program to deal with his own "complex medical condition." Though he continues to struggle with severe depression, including a suicide attempt and hospitalization, Charles/PD eventually finds happiness too in a new, unrelated business and can reconnect with the family business in a less-pressured role as a board member and consultant. Elaine/Gail, the eldest daughter, takes her rightful place as the next-generation leader of the Harwood family enterprise. As Louis/PJ continues to recognize Elaine's/Gail's entrepreneurial qualities, "he also understood that she would become the business peer in whose hands he could safely entrust his life's efforts. She totally appreciated the skill and determination he had expended to make the company successful."

And everyone lived happily ever after.

Would that real life worked out as well.

Paul David Phelan was unhappy. And frustrated. "Dear Mother, Gail, Sharon and Rosemary," his August 29, 1983, letter began. "It has been over a year since you turned down my request for funds from my own inheritance, which I wanted in order to hold my house in the city. Since then, several thoughts have been pressing in on me about this matter and associated concerns. I must relate them to you."

PD wanted to sell off some of his Cara Operations shares—"a small percentage" of what would eventually be his $7-million inheritance—but he couldn't do that without the okay of the others. Given that selling off those shares would dilute the family's control of Cara Operations, the others had said no.

"You think you acted nobly and shrewdly in order to protect your own inheritances," he wrote bitterly, "whereas it seems to me that you have prevented me from realizing what is rightfully mine, and you have prevented me from properly providing for my dependents and heirs. This troubles me very much and we must come to terms about the matter."

PD contrasted his own pressing personal needs—"I have four dependents, my wife and three children, who are also my heirs, and it takes a tremendous amount to provide their total support package"—with what he airily dismissed as the relatively stress-free life of his mother and sisters. "None of you, except Sharon, have dependents. Mom's children are grown ... Rosemary has no dependents." He glossed over the reality of Gail's own four children: "They are Tim Regan's dependents, and Tim supports them as well as Gail."

By contrast, he pointed out that when he'd initially asked for the funds, his wife, Rundi, was pregnant with their third child. "I had a desperate and very real need for good accommodation in the city." And then, just before the baby was born, their second child, Paula, was admitted to the hospital with leukemia. Without the funds from his inheritance, his "house [in the city] was gone. I could not afford to carry the cost of the house, some $380,000, at the interest rates of 16 to 18 percent which were current at the time, and without your co-operation, I had to sell the place."

Paul David's anger and frustration were palpable. "I remain bewildered as to exactly why you prevented me from realizing a part of my own inheritance in order to provide properly for my wife and children."

He may have been "bewildered," but he clearly had his suspicions about the reasons they'd refused him. "I have often heard from all of you, especially recently for some reason, that something went wrong with me when I was 18, and I left 8 Old Forest Hill Road," referencing, it appears, his departure for university and his later failed relationship with Liz Smythe. "It seems that you refuse to believe that I have grown, and that now you think I am still some sort of juvenile reprobate incapable of handling responsibility. I am a grown man of 32 with a wife and children to protect." His tone became almost threatening. "I ask that you be most careful to remember this."

Yes, he acknowledged, he had had his financial reversals. "It was common, and probably still is, for you to say, 'Oh, Paul David, he has lost a fortune.' In fact, over the past 10 years, I have amassed a good amount of business experience and have made money. What outside business experience have you gained?"

Boom. That brought the issues back to where they almost inevitably ended up: the future of their family business and who was to run it. "PJ has been insisting that he is becoming increasingly feeble and that he wants to quit," Paul David wrote. "Who is to manage Cara? Sharon? Mom? Rosemary? Gail has less than one year's business experience—are we to leave it all to her?"

Paul had no intention of doing that. "I intend to make sure my father's business is properly looked after," he declared, "and I need a base in the city. I can no longer tolerate sacrificing the security of my wife, children and business by allowing you to prevent me from realizing what I have inherited. We must come to terms about the matter."[35]

It was not lost on anyone that Paul David's shot across the bow to his sisters and mother landed just a few weeks before the family's first scheduled meetings with David Bork.

~

The day's meeting began with David Bork drawing familial circles on a whiteboard at the front of the room. *Great-grandparents, grandparents, parents, siblings...*

It was September 13, 1983, and those present included Phelan family members Paul James, Paul David, Gail, and Rose.

Sharon was not present for the meeting; she remained in California and completely uninvolved in the day-to-day of the family business. The others understood—and agreed—that Sharon and her daughter Holiday's interests would need to be protected in whatever succession decisions they ultimately made.

Helen did not attend the gathering either; she had not been invited. Bork had made the argument she was a member of the family, and therefore the family business, so she should be included in any discussion of its future. Gail resisted. Her mother, Gail pointed out, "was on the board of a competitor [the Gardiner family–owned Scott's Hospitality] and these discussions were about our darker secrets."[36]

That hadn't prevented Bork from meeting with Helen privately already. In fact, in the days leading up to this first gathering, Bork had met with each family member individually.

"As part of my process, I always have an extended interview and probe the relationships," Bork says. "What typically I do is I establish rapport with everybody, so they tell me their stories and they tell me what's going on. I find it really useful to wonder, 'Well, how does that impact on the relationships?' 'Any problems with alcohol?' Then you start digging, 'Who has a problem?' 'Well...' And then you hear stories. To be a family business consultant," he adds, "you need to be a damn good detective. I think my best skill is that I listen to people. If you ask a question and then shut up, they're going to tell you everything."

Paul David hadn't needed to be invited to tell Bork what was on his mind. In early March 1983, he'd shared a draft of what he described as a "job description for Gail as a starting point for working toward a satisfactory final job description." She would become vice-president of Holdings, with Paul David continuing as president. Her functions would include "assisting" PJ, who would remain as chairman of the board.

"I have not included a section which delineates 'Job is Well Done When...,'" he wrote, "but I think it is an important section and should be included in the final job description."

Four months later, he wrote to Bork again, this time in advance of their planned group session to outline to Bork the results of a recent meeting he'd had with Gail to discuss their individual goals.[37]

"Gail's stated objective is to become chairman of the board and/or chief executive officer of Cara Operations, and my objective is to be a responsible owner."

While that wasn't how Gail would have described her own objective at the time, no matter. To fulfill his own role as a responsible owner, PD suggested, it would be his duty to be "very aware of corporate affairs and function in the company, be involved in the corporate planning process, communicate directly with various personnel within the company"—and last on his list but far from the least of his presumed duties —"be prepared to be chairman of the board if necessary."

As for Gail? "I have a certain amount of concern about Gail's objective," PD continued. "As a responsible owner, I would not want anyone with very little business experience to be chairman of the board of Cara Operations. Thus, if PJ 'died tomorrow,' I would not want Gail to become COB or CEO." If PJ continued to be "reasonably healthy" over the next five years, he added, "I would want him to remain as COB and not be superseded by Gail." PD's bottom line: "I suggest Gail form alternative plans for the possibility that PJ might not step down within five to 10 years."

Ironically, Paul David's own "very limited" business experiences—unmentioned in his letter—didn't speak well for his preparation to ever assume the role of chairman. He'd recently taken charge of a Swiss Chalet franchise owned by Holdings in Richmond Hill, a Toronto suburb. It was not going well. Costs for labour and food were both too high. Joe Leilich, the national general manager for Swiss Chalet, had had to step in, personally advising PD's store manager and then reducing the outlet's rents and royalties just to keep the Richmond Hill operation afloat.

By the end of March 1984, PD would write to his father and sister: "I am totally embarrassed," he declared, adding that "we have dismally failed so far" and losses would almost certainly continue to mount. Unless they could find a way to better control costs, he wrote, "we should either divest ourselves of the franchise or get a new manager."[38] It would not be the first—or last—time he would blame someone else when things went wrong.

Two months later, he was ready to move on. He had plans for a combined Swiss Chalet and Harvey's in Collingwood.[39] Despite the losses in Richmond Hill, he said, "I have learned a great deal about our company. I feel the learning experience has not been too expensive because Bernie [Syron] and Mike [Maguire, Cara's chief financial officer] are willing to buy the franchise back at a price that would recover most of our loss."

That, of course, was still in the future.

As they gathered in Toronto for their first group meeting with David Bork, it was clear PJ continued to be ambivalent about the entire process. Although he had agreed to Gail's proposal to hire Bork as their family business consultant, he did so, Rose says today, mostly because Gail had asked him to. But while PJ admired Gail as "the academic, research-oriented, best-practice-oriented person who had deep family knowledge and was seeking new and better ways of doing things," he remained unwilling—perhaps unable—to take the process seriously. And he certainly showed no intention of stepping down or even back from his twin-towering roles as head of the family and head of the family business.

When he met with Bork for their one-to-one, for example, PJ insisted it happen over lunch at his Toronto Club where he would clearly be in control. "He set up a private room and the bottles of wine just kept coming," Bork marvels today.

"They both had hangovers," Gail remembers with a laugh.

Although Bork was careful to maintain his role as the detached, helpful-to-all business consultant, it didn't take him long to reach his own private conclusions about PJ. "This is my opinion," he explained years later. "PJ was impaired from when I began working with the family. He was not functional. He was not a contributing person."

Bork had learned much about the ways in which the Phelan family did—and didn't—work during those individual conversations with family members, including, especially, the central role alcohol played in too many of their lives.

For example, Bork says, he discovered that Helen would usually spend time around the beginning of December at spas he referred to as "'spin dries' where you dry out and get your face worked on, and then you're ready for the holidays when you can drink every day."

Bork was less surprised than he might have been. In his fifteen years of working with family businesses, several themes had emerged, including two that seemed to encapsulate what had careened off the rails in the Phelan family. The first, of course, was the insistence on following the practice of primogeniture, even when the family's first-born son seemed unready for the job. The second was the prevalence of substance abuse among family members and the cascading issues that that created within the family and within the family business. That, in fact, would soon become a primary focus of Bork's ongoing meetings with the Phelans.

That was not what Gail had expected. She'd hoped Bork would "get the family to outline a training program for me. I wasn't necessarily going to be Dad's successor, but I wanted to be a success. I wanted to become for Cara what Mom was for Scott's—be on the board, understand the strategic choices. I wanted to be trained for that. But nobody gave me a whit of attention, nobody seemed to care."

Substance abuse had not even been mentioned when Bork first laid out the structure for the first session in a table-setting but generic memo to family members the week before. The session would begin, he wrote, "by sharing information about a process the Phelan Family members named above have engaged in since early 1983. That sharing will include generic information about families in business as well as selected data about the Phelan family."[40] This part of the meeting, he added hopefully, "will take approximately two and a half hours, depending on the extent of the discussion.

"The second purpose and primary focus of the meeting is to begin a process of grooming successors to Paul J. Phelan (Chairman, President, Honorary Commodore at Sea, *et al*)," Bork continued in a jaunty tone. "While any public announcement is premature, it is anticipated that PJ will remain in his current capacity through 1988. It has been agreed among family members that his children will succeed him. There are skills, knowledge, special understandings and insights they must have in order to provide the quality of leadership required.

"No one is expected to come to this meeting with completely formulated ideas," Bork was quick to add in the memo. "We do ask, however, that some advance thought be given to the task and to the successor group. Among the successors are people at different stages chronologically, personally and professionally. Through our discussion we will refine the task and make specific plans. It is anticipated that some decisions about grooming can be finalized while other issues will require further data collection and analysis before decisions can be made."

The group never did get to that second agenda item, or to decisions about grooming the next leader.

Instead, they quickly got sidetracked—or focused, depending on your perspective—on the family drinking problem.

Bork's "generic information about families in business" had highlighted his finding that alcohol and substance abuse were "rampant" in family-business families. His "selected data about the Phelan family" made clear those issues had long been rampant in this family too.

Rose couldn't help but be impressed—and distressed. She was twenty-six years old, back in Toronto after years on her own, working for the family business as a researcher on its celebratory anniversary book project, "and trying to figure out what I was doing, where I was going."

As the sibling at the meeting who was least directly involved in the day-to-day workings of Cara, the one who had the least vested interest in who should succeed their father, Rose seemed the most clear-eyed about the strengths and weaknesses of her brother and sister. "Gail was an academic. That's really her world and her forte, not necessarily the business world. She didn't really have the business experience nor was she terribly practical." Paul David? Despite his assumptions of entitlement, Rose wasn't sure he really wanted the job or, if he did, what he would do with it.

She watched that day as Bork filled in the details in the familial circles on his flip chart. He would "draw these little heads. Grandfather, grandmother … Then he'd put little *X*s on people's heads to indicate the alcoholics." There were a lot of *X*s, she would recall.

A lot of baggage to be dealt with.

Bork did his best. In a follow-up letter to PJ and Helen in March 1984, he again suggested that the "issue of alcohol" treatment would be a suitable topic for the next family meeting. "I think you both know that I see this as a family systems issue. We don't have to shake the family trees very hard to have the issue appear. Further, I see your children 'at risk' in a variety of ways. There can be little doubt that the issue has impacted on your lives. My objective is to assist you in getting 'on top' of the matter and minimizing the deleterious effects the substance had on your health and family life. I do not believe it is too late for positive results in all areas."

But it was.

The meetings with Bork would go on for much of the 1980s. In the beginning, Gail says, "David was better than Christmas. He would come and we would meet with him and share our inner thoughts and feelings and visions for the company." The sessions would usually take place three times a year, though never during the summers. Why not during the summer? "Because everyone was away and partying," Gail says simply.

What about after their group sessions with Bork? Would the family ever meet to discuss what had happened, what they should do next? "No," Gail answers. "We all just went home. The meetings were very intense, and everyone was just exhausted by them."

Eventually, adds Rose, "they petered out. I think there was resistance from my father and my brother." Paul David eventually stopped attending. PJ stopped paying attention. The more Bork tried to focus the conversations on alcohol and substance abuse, "how prevalent it was and how it was passed on ... I don't think my father was comfortable with that."

PJ insisted he wasn't an alcoholic.

"Well, Dad," Rose shot back at one point. "I agree with you. You have problems that go beyond alcoholism."

To which PJ responded: "Well, I guess I'm just an alcoholic." At one point, he agreed to check himself into the Betty Ford Center, the residential treatment centre for persons with alcohol and substance dependence in Rancho Mirage, California, but he only lasted a week. Nothing changed as a result.

As an exercise early on in his work with the family, Bork asked Paul David—still the putative heir to the Phelan family business—to write a letter to himself from the perspective of the state of his world "five years down the road."

"Dear P.D.," begins the typewritten one-page letter dated "Feb. 10, 1988." It offers an extraordinary glimpse into Paul David's thinking—or at least what he wants the reader to think he is thinking.

"Your 30-year plan is unfolding in a very interesting way," PD reports to himself, adopting an almost *ex cathedra* voice as he catalogues the "current" status of Phelan family members. "PJ has remained strong over this time and has allowed his immense experience and sensitivity to guide our operations successfully. Gail has made very good progress towards grooming herself for the chairmanship, and if she continues the way she is going, she will indeed be able to assume those responsibilities in another five years.

"Rosemary has proved invaluable to holding us together with her sensible conclusions and advice and, although she will be busy with her new young family, I am sure she will continue to perform her essential and valuable role in this firm.

"I am very glad to see that Sean and Tim Regan have shown an interest in the company," he continues, referencing Gail's two sons, "but I am concerned that they might not get enough entrepreneurial training by working outside the company either with their own company or another firm."

Turning to himself, he notes, "I congratulate yourself for the success you have had with your fund management and also the valuable advice you have offered to our group of companies."

Although he notes that his letter is already crystal-ball gazing five years down the road, he also makes the point that "we still need to look to the future now more than ever because our affairs have now become bigger than ever. If something should happen to PJ, and we do commit him to Happy Acres Rest Home as he requests, then I suggest we ask Boyd Matchett to be chairman of the board of Cara Operations."

Matchett, of course, was the president and CEO he and Gail convinced PJ to shunt aside in 1983. "Despite trouble in past and recent years," the letter says, "Boyd has a wealth of experience and I believe he could continue to work well with our family. We need a diplomat in this position, a diplomat with at least 10 years of business experience."

His work here done, PD signed off his letter to self: "Well, despite all the work that has been done and the need for constant attention and planning, a North Wester is coming through this weekend, and I will see you on the beach and out by five-mile shoal this weekend."

~

On February 25, 1985, Gail wrote a chatty, mostly upbeat letter to David Bork to let him know "how things are with the Phelans, the

Regans and the Robbins to be"—Rosemary's busy ski season with her fiancée, Michael Robbins; Sharon's latest stay in Toronto; Holly's life at boarding school; family plans to gather during the winter in the Bahamas...

The first item, however, contained anything but good news: "Paula Dawn Phelan died at 5:30 a.m., February 12, 1985. Rundi and Paul were with her, holding her hand. Mum did a fabulous job of negotiating who was to decide what re: the funeral, and the decisions were well made. It is very sad to lose a child, especially a child who fought for life so tenaciously."

Paula Dawn—Paul and Rundi's second daughter—had turned five only a few months earlier. By the time she was two years old, she'd been in and out of doctors' waiting rooms and emergency rooms with fevers, trouble breathing, and what had initially seemed like an especially nasty, persistent flu. "She's just very prone to flu," one doctor suggested.

"But what about these funny little blue spots on her legs?" Rundi asked.

The doctor looked more closely. "Oh, dear," he said. Paula was rushed to Toronto's Hospital for Sick Children that same day. There followed three years of treatment and trauma, and a series of "breakthrough" procedures that inevitably failed to break through. Despite the best efforts that modern medicine and Phelan money could buy, Paula's condition steadily worsened.

Gail believes Paula's illness may have been a "trigger" that helped transform Paul from an excessive but mostly outgoing social drinker into a dangerous-to-himself-and-others alcoholic. "I think it might have been a trigger for Dad too," she adds. "He had developed a sense that he could do anything, that he was a golden man. And yet, he couldn't stop his grandchild from dying. It was just a slap in the face."

In the beginning, Gail remembers, "I had such hope for Paula's recovery, but I could see that she was coming out of each procedure weaker." Gail wanted to say something to Paul that would "be honest and open" but also helpful, "to give Paul a safe place to come to if Paula failed."

Instead, she says now, "my stupid autism" got in the way. One afternoon, she asked Paul to drive her home from the office. In the car, she broached what she wanted to say.

"Paul," she said, "I'm not sure she's going to make it."

She didn't get a chance to say more. "He was very reactive to my saying that," she says now. "What he wanted at that point"—and what Gail hadn't recognized because of her autism—"was for everybody to buy the party line and be really hopeful about her recovery." Paul didn't say anything directly in response, she says, but "I could feel the tension from him."

Today, nearly forty years later, Gail still wonders if that moment permanently changed the dynamics of their relationship, exacerbated the gulf between them, made reconciliation impossible.

At the time, however, as she noted in her letter to Bork, she was still hopeful. She and Paul had met twice since their last session with him, as well as once with PJ. "We were all upset about Paula in these meetings," she noted, "yet, despite this, they went quite well. I am hoping things will get even better."

She was equally hopeful—and equally unrealistic—about her father's drinking. "Around Christmas time," she wrote, "Dad had chest pains, indicating to his doctor that he had had a heart attack, or was about to have one. Mum got him into Women's College Hospital, who motivated him to stop drinking and quieted his hiatus hernia, which was causing the pain, with antacids. His heart is fine and so is his liver. Dad drinks wine now, in modest amounts. He seems to have given up his enthusiasm for drinking."

~

By the time the next Christmas rolled around, Gail was far less hopeful about her father's drinking, the family business, even the family itself.

"I have always preferred a close family, one that gathers often for celebration and for the free exchange of ideas and feelings," she wrote in a "Dear

Dad" letter on December 16, 1985. "This is the type of togetherness which I like, and I feel the others like too."

Cara, the family's business, she added, "is another thread which weaves our lives together. Rosemary edited a book on it. You have dedicated your life to it, as have Paul David and myself. It is important that our business life together proceed smoothly and happily. Business tensions spilling over into family occasions make the family tense and unhappy."

The family, she suggested, was indeed tense and unhappy. Paul David had recently resigned as an officer of Holdings and was not even participating in the Phelans' usual family Christmas functions. Sharon was pondering moving Holly back to California; Rosemary was considering living overseas. "The unresolved tensions are making my family restive."

At the same time, Gail did her best to placate her father. She didn't mention PJ's drinking, and she tried to empathize with what had been "a time of physical and emotional stress in your life. Paula's death, the constant pain of bladder irritation, the isolation of the office, the retirement of old hands like Tom Plewes [a director and senior vice-president of finance and administration at Cara Operations], the loss of Malton [airport concession] ... have interfered with your cheerful disposition.

"Normally," she pointed out, "this should be a time when the family would pour out love and support for you. Family affection would compensate for these setbacks until they are overcome. Instead, I see a family drawing away from itself."

Near the end of her one-page letter, Gail offered what she hoped would be at least a partial solution from a business and family perspective. "I recommend that we combine share repurchase for you with an enlargement of the role of the trusts." Gail wanted to be sure that, even though PJ and Helen's grandchildren would be the ultimate beneficiaries of the trusts, Gail and her siblings could still control the trusts and their children in the short term. In turn, she and the others would appoint PJ chair of Holdings. That, she suggested, "will give you the chance to see that the family wants you to have this position because you deserve it. By enfranchising your children, you reduce their fear of your power, and return to them the feeling of command over their individual family's destiny."

David Bork's focus on substance abuse wasn't just about family history or even how it was affecting the generations running the business now but on trying to prevent the damage from destroying yet another generation.

By the time Gail's first-born son, Sean, was in his late teens, he was acting out, failing at school, travelling down a too-well-worn path for first-born Phelan sons. In 1986 when Sean was twenty-two, his father, Tim, suggested Sean call Bork. Sean did, confided he was struggling.

"Give me a sec," Bork said, and arranged for Sean to fly down to Washington. "I've got a place for you to go." When Bork had suggested an addiction treatment centre in Virginia, Sean initially imagined it would be the kind of Arizona spa his grandmother checked into once a year for a few weeks to dry out before the Christmas holidays. At the time, he allows today, "that was my idea of getting better. No one goes into rehab thinking they're never going to drink and do drugs again. They go in thinking, 'How do I learn to control this?'"

But the Virginia centre wasn't his grandmother's spa. While there, Sean learned to create his own family genogram, a graphic representation of a family tree that allows the user to see relationships among individual family members, including hereditary patterns and the psychological factors that help explain those connections. Sean's genogram showed that three-quarters of his family struggled with addiction issues of one sort or another. During his stay, Bork visited him every week just to talk and listen. When Sean was ready to leave, counsellors advised him, "Never go home again."

He didn't. Not at first. He moved to Montreal, found a "great psychiatrist and started the journey of growing up." Sean would occasionally visit his grandparents—"I loved my grandparents"—but PJ invariably, incredibly, continued to offer him alcohol. So, Sean made sure to arrive early in the morning before his grandparents had begun drinking heavily.

In the end, Sean not only maintained his own sobriety but also would eventually become the last Phelan standing at Cara, the one direct member of the Phelan fifth generation who would find a permanent place in the family operating business.

~

At 2 p.m. on October 8, 1986, Gail, Paul David, and PJ met in PJ's office "to discuss Cara Operations, Cara Holdings and the succession to the chairmanship of both companies." After the meeting, Gail prepared a "Dear Dad" memo about what they'd agreed to, "amplified by my thoughts where appropriate."

Gail, ever the MBA and academic, began by citing a recommendation from the Canadian Association of Family Enterprise that companies have strong boards "made up of fellow risk takers" and reported that "it was agreed that all members of the Cara board who are not family or management would receive a term of office. At the end of the term, some could be asked to continue. Others would be replaced by entrepreneurs, perhaps of the second generation."

At the same time, she reported that PJ himself had expressed a wish "to be bought out [to] ensure the transmission of the firm to the next generation." They had agreed, she noted, that the buyout price would be no higher than market price, with $10 million to be paid out immediately. That initial $10 million was to be financed by repayment of the loans PJ had already taken out of Holdings to support the America's Cup Challenge. "PJ will then gift $10 million of his Cara Holdings stock to the Challenge and Holdings will purchase it."

The remainder of the payment of the eventual purchase price was to be financed from Holdings cash flow and spread over the next decade "without dividends or interest." To ensure that there was sufficient cash, Holdings would pay off all its debts and then issue preference shares to Langar, the holding company controlled by Helen and her daughters, at interest rates "lower than what it is now paying the Bank of Nova Scotia." Under the terms of the deal that Gail said she, Paul David, and PJ had agreed on during the meeting, Holdings wouldn't be allowed to incur more debt or dispose of any more Cara Operations stock without Langar's okay. "Langar," she wrote, "may use its own lawyers to draft the terms."

At this point, Gail noted that she personally "was no longer willing to deal with Fraser & Beatty," Cara's law firm, whose key player was PJ's friend Larry Hynes. PJ, she wrote, had suggested that "she use her own lawyers." But they had eventually agreed PD would use Fraser & Beatty to handle the legal sales arrangements.

Perhaps most importantly, Gail wrote, "PD is to be actively supported toward becoming the chairman of Cara Operations." Gail, Sharon, and Rosemary "are to show their agreement with this plan by voting PD in as vice chairman of Holdings."

Before he would be handed the Cara Operations brass ring, however, PD would need to demonstrate not only that he was "competent in business" but also that he was "healthy and known in the community as a good family man." Gail explained that she and Rosemary were worried about PD's—and PJ's—chemical dependencies. If PD is "ill," as Gail decorously described it, Gail, Sharon, and Rosemary would withdraw their support for their brother, and PJ had allowed that he would accept that decision as "reasonable."

Perhaps *amplifying* with her own thoughts at this point rather than simply representing the consensus of the meeting, Gail "questioned whether control of Holdings and Ops through the ... voting preferred shares has been good for PJ personally and for the family."

Those 1,000 voting preference shares, you will recall, were the shares PJ owned and could use to prevail in any disagreement with his children over decisions not only about Holdings but also, indirectly, for Cara Operations.

Gail's preference, she explained, was for a shareholders' agreement or, failing that, a deal under which the preference shares were held collectively, and their power wielded by "one leader chosen for a term, say five years, on the basis of competence and talent. There would be no wrangling with the leader, who would be free to make decisions and to make mistakes." One of the designated leader's responsibilities would be to "train a leader from the next generation and to make room for him or her when the candidate is ready."

If the members of the family trusts concluded any leader had become "personally incompetent, he could be removed after proper discussion at any time." Grounds for removal included "extreme physical illness, active chemical or alcohol dependence, inability to recover from dependence or nervous breakdown."

Given that the focus of the meeting had seemed to be on supporting Paul David to become chair of Cara Operations if he proved himself worthy and the ways to remove him if he didn't, where did that leave Gail? "Gail," she wrote of herself in the third person, "is to be the 'den mother' of the group with particular responsibility for educating the next generation to commitment to Cara Operations. Gail is to continue to be president of Cara Holdings. She will emphasize managing liquidity for the buyout and may use budgetary discretion to do so. She will continue as chairman of the Ops executive committee."

Gail ended her memo by circling back to the Canadian Association of Family Enterprise and instructed that all Holdings board members "are to read C.A.F.E material on succession."

After PJ sent Paul David a copy of Gail's memo for "your advice,"[41] Paul David fired back with his own memo disagreeing with virtually every point his sister had made—except, of course, the suggestion he be supported to become chair of Cara Operations.

"First of all, our meeting was not planned or formal. I was under the impression that we were really just having a discussion of various concerns, yet Gail implies and actually states that a number of matters were agreed upon. Not only did we not agree on most of the matters her notes indicated we did, but such a casual meeting is no place to make such sweeping decisions, especially without input from other family members or the experts and professionals."

While acknowledging his father's point to him that the memo "just comprises Gail's ideas," Paul David worried that it will "cause problems if we accept a memo which sets out these ideas as agreements, when no agreements were made."

~

In 1986, almost everyone outside the Phelan family but inside the Cara tent—bankers, lawyers, accountants, management, all of whom had a vested interest in the answer to the multi-million-dollar question of which of PJ Phelan's fractious children, his first daughter or his only son, should become the heir to the Cara throne—was invited to weigh in on the issue.

Although David Bork continued to meet with the family, Paul David had mostly stopped attending his sessions. PJ continued to play the genial paterfamilias in the group conversations, but ignored Bork's encouragement to change his personal behaviour and dismissed the argument that he needed to finally make decisions about succession. Without full buy-in from PJ and PD, Bork became increasingly marginalized, seen within and outside the family more as Gail's adviser than as Cara's succession guide.

Even though PJ refused to make definitive decisions about succession, the issue was never far from his thoughts. In August 1986, for example, he invited Coopers & Lybrand, Cara's accountants, to come up with three options for succession arrangements for him to consider.[42]

Their starting point was PJ's 1977 will. It provided that, in the case of his death, his executors, subject to the agreement of Helen or a representative of the law firm Fraser & Beatty—meaning Larry Hynes—would make "decisions dealing with the control of Holdings," the family company that controlled Cara Operations.

But that arrangement, as Richard Cole and John McClelland, the authors of the Coopers & Lybrand report, suggested, "could be onerous on your wife as she will be put in a position where she might have to make a decision which you yourself find to be a very difficult one." The upside, however, their report added, was that if Helen survived PJ long enough, "she would have the opportunity of seeing your children achieve further maturity and skills and might be in a somewhat better position to make the ultimate decision."

One alternative to the provisions of the existing will, they suggested, would be for PJ himself to name his successor in a new will but keep that decision to himself until after he'd died. "The provisions of your will could remain confidential between you and your lawyer, giving you the opportunity to change your decision should your views change over time."

There was a third possibility, they noted, which would not only allow PJ to avoid making a definitive decision but also "take some of the pressure off your wife." That would be to create a voting trust so the estate could oversee the family's holdings in Cara Operations. It would be "composed of your wife, the chief executive officer of Operations and your four children." The report then carefully laid out how the trust might work. "The voting trust would elect the directors of Operations and make such decisions for Operations as would normally require shareholder approval. Decisions of the voting trust would require four out of six possible votes, including the vote of your wife if she is alive. Your wife by her will could appoint a successor to herself on the voting trust." The voting trust could also decide to add new members or replace existing members "as long as there was unanimity." A faint hope.

The trust itself should have a limited shelf life, the report added. At the end of ten to fifteen years, there would be an orderly sale of the investment in Cara

Operations "unless there is unanimity as to the appropriate course of action between your four children represented on the voting trust." Again unlikely.

"While this is more a matter for personal judgment than a professional view," the authors of the report added delicately, "we might comment that many would consider it better for your family to ultimately sell the shares rather than to create an irreparable family rift if your children cannot reach agreement between themselves as to how Operations should be managed and controlled."

By then, it was clear—if it had not been before—that PD and Gail could not agree on much, even on the facts of what had transpired during a meeting that year that both had attended.

After the Coopers & Lybrand report landed on Larry Hynes's desk in October 1986, he quickly prepared his own seven-page "Dear Paul" response.[43] Perhaps not surprising for someone who owed much of his own legal success to his personal connections to PJ, Hynes's tone was deferential, almost obsequious.

"As lawyers," he began, "our expertise does not lie in the area of financial counselling," deferring to Coopers & Lybrand's suggestions about how PJ should maximize his Holdings assets, then added: "It seems to me that it would be a brave man who would purport to tell you, of all people, how to invest! There is no one else I know who has taken an investment of $300,000 in 1961 to $180 million in 1986! ... In my opinion this is a matter on which the personal judgment of PJP is worth more than that of anyone else! Amen.

"I feel somewhat more confident in offering suggestions about the 'succession' matter," Hynes continued, "about which we have already had so many chats. First of all, there is no pressing need for you to do anything about this matter in the immediate future. You have as good a chance of achieving 'four score' as anyone, and if you should disappear suddenly, your present will at least provides a mechanism for the ongoing control of Holdings and Operations even if it does not determine the result."

Like the Coopers & Lybrand authors, Hynes worried that following the provisions of the existing will "may simply push off onto Helen the thorny issue of deciding ultimately between Gail and PD—a decision which is still a difficult one for you to make. Helen may not find it any easier than you do, but circumstances could arise in which it would be critically important for her to make a choice between them. I know that it is your wish that the family operate as a harmonious and cohesive unit for the mutual benefit of all, but I think there is already some fairly cogent evidence that Gail and PD will find it difficult to do this when you are no longer on the scene."

That said, Hynes did not support Coopers & Lybrand's suggestion of a voting trust, which he described as "cumbersome to operate and present[s] significant technical legal problems." Arguing that a voting trust isn't "really appropriate for a majority shareholder," he added, "I would like to make a somewhat related proposal."

He suggested the creation of what he called a "'proxy committee,' which would have nothing whatever to do with the administration of your estate," but would determine how the shares of Operations "were to be voted at any meeting of shareholders of Operations."

Hynes suggested the initial proxy committee consist of Gail, Paul David, and Bernie Syron, "all of whom are, of course, directors of Operations." Hynes made a strong case for Bernie's participation. "I suggest Bernie as a member of the committee because he now has your confidence and, so long as he continues in his present position (and he is a young man) it must be presumed that he will act in the best interest of Operations—and therefore of the family—in all matters pertaining to Operations."

While acknowledging that PJ might be concerned this would give Syron "more of a voice in your family's affairs than you would wish any outsider to have," he argued that key decisions about the future of Operations after PJ's death would inevitably need to be made "with the active participation" of Cara's CEO.

"You will appreciate that the key decisions, which would be made by the proxy committee, are those which you alone can now make—such as the number and composition of the board of directors, the appointment of auditors, any form of corporate reorganization involving shareholders' approval, and, as a practical matter, any decision to acquire a new business or sell off any significant part of the present business."

Although Bernie could be outvoted on the committee by Gail and Paul David acting in concert, he noted, "in the event of any disagreement between them," Syron would have the deciding vote.

"I do not think this should disturb you," Hynes added. The market would need the certainties of "a clear decision-making mechanism for the exercise of the share control." Uncertainty might not only undermine the morale of the company's officers, employees, and franchisees, he pointed out, but it "might also be disturbing to your bankers."

If the idea of a proxy committee "has any appeal to you, we would have to consider it in more detail," Hynes noted.

It's not exactly clear what happened after that. But by the following year, the idea of the proxy committee had made it into a new draft of PJ's will—with one key difference. Instead of a committee made up of Gail, Paul David, and Bernie Syron, the new proposed proxy committee comprised Paul David, Bernie ... and Larry Hynes! Gail was out. PD would be the sole family representative on the committee, and even he could be outvoted by the committee's two non-family members.

For very different reasons, Paul David and Gail would both object to the proposed changes to PJ's will.

~

Perhaps inevitably, there are random documents and half-remembered but weakly documented incidents that seem to be important in understanding what was really happening inside Cara and the Phelan family during this period but that are difficult to connect directly to the unfolding narrative.

Consider, for example, the strange encounter Gail had with two close friends of PJ: lawyer Larry Hynes and John Gordon Weir, a heroic Second World War RCAF pilot[44] who'd gone on to a hugely successful career as a bond salesman with Wood Gundy.[45]

Gail recalls the meeting in some detail but can't be sure exactly when it happened. She eventually found a notation in her calendar for Friday, November 13, 1987. "Talked Larry re trusts," it says. She now believes this might have been the meeting "with Weir dropping in and not noted," but she isn't certain. What she is certain of now is that "I did not notice the import at the time."

She does remember that the meeting took place in her office at Cara headquarters in a renovated building at the end of a cul-de-sac tucked behind the side-by-side landmark Harvey's and Swiss Chalet locations on Bloor Street. That would suggest the meeting occurred sometime after Cara moved there from 55 York Street as part of the 1983 reorganization when Bernie Syron had replaced Boyd Matchett.

"We moved in after the renovation," Gail adds, "probably in 1984 or 1985." Gail's office—which was opposite Paul David's at one end of a long corridor that led to PJ's "huge, very elegant" office—had been designed to look like a library. There were a lot of books, mostly about family business, on the shelves, "and I'd bought very attractive china that sat in front of the books. The windows had flowered curtains to express femininity." Her office looked out on a small courtyard, and she remembers the morning light made the office "sparkle." Her recollection is that the meeting with Hynes and Weir took place on a sunny day.

Hynes had made an appointment to see her that day, she believes, but without explaining the purpose in advance. That purpose, Gail eventually came to believe, was at least in part to sideline David Bork from his role in succession discussions. While she doesn't believe Hynes and Weir were acting on explicit instructions from her father, "they were both very good friends of Dad. I think they homed in on Bork because they believed he had too much influence, and so it was their role to orchestrate the succession on Dad's behalf." That was the second part of their mission that day—to encourage Gail's own exit from Cara, paving the way for Paul David to succeed his father. Eliminating any role for Bork.

The two men began by setting the table, outlining their concerns about what would happen to the company if her father were to become legally incompetent or die.

Gail herself had become increasingly concerned about those issues. Her father's arms "looked thin, and he'd become pot-bellied. From having had an athlete's figure," she says now, "he began to look like an old man." And then there was his drinking to excess and his inattention at meetings...

If something did happen to PJ, Hynes and Weir continued, they were concerned there would inevitably be "quarrels" among the siblings that would sow doubts among employees, customers, and investors about the future of the family business. Specifically, of course, they noted the "rift" between Gail and Paul David. "Paul David feels alienated from you."

Gail must have surprised them when she downplayed that as an issue. The two had perhaps become more "distant," she explained, but that was likely because Paul David was "managing his own stuff and doing the commodities [trading business]. We were both busy." She reminded them of how she and Paul David had worked together "beautifully" just a few years earlier to convince their father to ease Boyd Matchett out and Bernie Syron in. That transition had been "so successful. We did brilliantly." Although she acknowledged there had been tensions in the aftermath of Paul David's daughter's death—something for which she took responsibility—she suggested they "were getting along just fine now."

If that surprised Weir and Hynes, her follow-up must have shocked them. The real breach, she suggested, was not between her and Paul David, but between Paul David and Rose. "The relationship between Rose and Paul is intractable," she said flatly. "I don't know that it can be healed."

At this point, Gail herself wasn't certain of all the reasons for the split between her youngest siblings, but she had no doubt of its seriousness or the unlikelihood that it could be patched over easily. "It was personal."

She remembers the men were surprised to hear that. "Well," they responded, "they don't show it."

The meeting soon sputtered to an end with no real conclusion.

It was only later and slowly, Gail says, that the incident came into focus. Her father's joking reference to the new will "you won't like." Random disclosures about plans for a proxy committee that would effectively "disinherit" and disempower the Phelan women.

She believes the meeting with Weir and Hynes, whenever it actually took place, was part of a process intended to put her in her place.

"I subliminally sensed the reduction of my power," she reflects now. "I had depression, but I didn't know that I was disinherited for a couple of months. Once I found that out, the depression instantly lifted." The unfairness rankled. "I had been groomed for this, hauled out of an academic career I was enjoying. I had had another baby, I did an MBA with an infant, and that wasn't fair to the infant, wasn't fair to me ... Now, I was angry."

The real war for the future of Cara and the Phelan family was about to be joined.

~

"FOR DISCUSSION." The two letters, written by PJ to his oldest daughter and his only son, each dated December 12, 1987, began the usual way.

One was addressed to "Dear Paul David," the other to "Dear Gail," but PJ had crossed out the secretary-typed Gail in the salutation to the second letter and replaced it with the fatherly nickname "Gaily," handwritten in pen with his ubiquitous aquamarine ink.

The opening paragraphs were almost identical. "This is further to our conversation between you, Paul David and me on December 1st, 1987," he began his letter to Gail. "It seems to me that there is needless rivalry between you and Paul David. I feel indeed that all my children are not sympathetic enough with each other. Coming from a family of 10 children, one knew it was reasonable for parents to have difficulties and sympathize with them, and then to know that one's brothers and sisters, for mutual preservation, should be loving and kind to one another, 'gentle love' as expressed by St. Francis."

PJ employed the same words in his letter to Paul David, but then continued: "In view of all this, and realizing that you are a practical thinking man, I recommend that you and Gail separate yourselves from each other."

His letter to Gail came to the same conclusion, but the route was more circuitous and clearly part of an ongoing conversation. "Considering your request, and the discussions we have had, and in my best judgement [*sic*], I think that you and Paul David should make sure that you continue your sister and brother love, but I think you are incompatible and should be separated."

He wanted, he'd written to Paul David, for him to become "the family operating officer within Cara Operations Limited. Gail's main thrust should be with Holdings, where she should do her best to see that the company thrives with my assistance. In this way, I think we could find a happy stress-free working relationship."

In his letter to Gail, PJ suggested she continue in her existing role as chair of the executive committee at Cara Operations. "Remember," he added, "you are also a director of that company and have a right to put forth whatever ideas you wish to advance to management through the board of directors." More importantly, however, he suggested she take a "more active" role in Holdings. "You were supposed to alternate with Paul David, but I suggest you settle in as president of Holdings as part of your 'den mother' role."

He tried to put the best face on it. "We could build [Holdings] into quite a successful investment instrument. What should we do with our land at Russell Hill and St. Clair? If we cashed in our holdings there, we would be in instant possession of a very useful investment portfolio base. In essence, think of how we together, all of us, sharing in Holdings, could build a portfolio together." But he also made it clear that, when it came to Operations, she was to leave that to her brother. "You and I are really just owners. We must leave 'operating' to others and I think it is only fair that we support Paul David in his operating role as the vice chairman of Cara Operations Ltd."

It was already too late for that.

~

Too many years of cozy sounding but purposely wounding correspondence between and among PJ and his son and daughter...

Endlessly upbeat but equally endlessly inconclusive individual and family conclaves with David Bork about how to guide their family and their family business through to its next glorious generation ...

Various on-the-one-hand-this, on-the-other-hand-that consultants' reports PJ had commissioned on succession options, followed by the inevitable counter responses to them, followed by nothing of substance...

"Disinheriting" provision in PJ's new, you-won't-like-this will that had been teased out elliptically instead of simply explained...

Coming together of Gail and her sisters and their reluctant decision to give up trying to fix their family and demand a corporate divorce instead, unless...

Unless...

All of that had served as the backdrop for what everyone now anticipated/feared would be one final family showdown meeting in the living room of the Phelan family mansion at 8 Old Forest Hill Road on the morning of May 12, 1988. This is the meeting with which we began this account of the Phelan succession showdown.

There were, of course, still so many subtexts nibbling at the edges of the conversation this morning that, if you didn't already know what was at stake, you wouldn't have had a clue what was really being said—or meant—simply by reading Dorothy Pyfrom's carefully constructed minutes.

PJ began the meeting by asking for a dictionary. He said he wanted to look up the phrase *noblesse oblige*. It was not that he didn't know the literal meaning of the words or what the concept implied, of course. He simply wanted to make a point.

Noblesse oblige is a French phrase meaning that privilege entails responsibility, an inferred responsibility that privileged people should act with "honour, generosity and nobility" toward those less privileged. PJ Phelan measured his own noblesse oblige not only by his behaviour toward his company's employees—"Thirty-six thousand lives touch mine every payday," as he'd noted in the book celebrating the company's 1983 centenary—but also in his leadership of his family.

According to the minutes, PJ recounted for the assemblage "how he had looked after his grandfather's and father's estates, how he took care of his brothers and sisters and every month saved his $100 allowance to buy shares of Canada Railway News Company as there was very scattered family interest in the company at that time. When he had bought up enough shares for control, he reorganized the company, which then became Cara. Pensions were established for old Cara management and long-time employees. He provided humanity for all."

His continuing control of Holdings' preference shares, he added pointedly, made him "the captain of the ship so all can be protected—family, business and employees in the thousands ... If the 1,000 preference shares were now divided equally among [his children]," he asked, "how could he keep control of the operating company?"

"With your own natural authority," Gail replied.

But the real question, as David Bork, the family-business consultant, pointed out, was "What happens after PJP? ... Would not the holder of the 1,000 preference shares really make the final determination of what can happen."

Gail reiterated the sisters' position that the relationship they'd had with their father could not be "instantly duplicated" or automatically transferred to Paul David.

"I will not lose my son," countered PJ, insisting almost plaintively that he "needs his son and wants his children to be a close loving family." Any doubts PJ may now have been harbouring about his only son's fitness to lead the next generation he kept to himself. But it also appeared that if PJ had to choose, he would choose his son over his daughters, or that close loving family.

If Gail really wanted to "butterfly," he told the meeting, "they" would buy her out. According to the minutes, there would be other consequences. "Paul David would be chairman of the board [of Cara Operations] as he has great qualities of leadership ... Gail should relinquish her position as chairman of [Cara Operations'] executive committee."

Larry Hynes then tried to bring down the temperature in the room by reminding everyone that "the desired objective was to find a means by which PJ's issue could harmoniously control this great business."

"As opposed to who controls their assets," retorted Bork.

"Nobody wants to do that," Hynes fired back.

Finally, Paul James Phelan cut off the back-and-forth. He wanted to follow his father's and grandfather's "solid philosophy ... to share and share alike," he said. Unexpectedly, he declared he would try to do this by preparing a new will to return control of the preference shares equally to the four children.

The sisters had won!

Or had they?

Even if PJ changed his will, that wouldn't resolve the larger—and largely unspoken—issue. Who among the next generation would succeed their father?

While Bork allowed that he "fully understood and agreed with" PJ's hope to see his son succeed him, he added that "it was important to keep open an avenue to continue dialogue to find a solution that would treat all with dignity." As he often did, Bork, the polished, experienced, consummate family-business consultant, laid out a pathway forward, which the minutes vaguely described as a "profile of best solution."

The goal, Bork said, should be to share and share alike—income streams, assets, and opportunities—among PJ's four children and their families. This could only be achieved by the families working together in ways that would allow the most talented in each generation to reach leadership positions. Each generation should then choose its own leader. They would collectively need to agree that there would be no dismembering of Cara, and that they would "prudently discharge their responsibilities to Cara shareholders and employees." If any family member wanted to, they would be free to leave "with provisions that don't undermine Cara."

"Suppose," Bork finally suggested, Gail's lawyer, Glen Macarthur, and PJ's lawyer, Larry Hynes, "meet and jointly develop a plan for next steps."

Noted the secretary's cryptic but hopeful minutes: "Want best possible leadership in every generation ... Want to have talent rise to the top ... Together invent a solution."

Easy to say. Would it ever be possible to accomplish?

"I understand some of you are worried about your estates," PJ acknowledged in a three-page letter to "Dear children *all*," written a few weeks after that contentious family meeting in Toronto.[46] By then, he was in the calming Gulf Coast waters off Venice, Florida, aboard his yacht, *Pleiades*.

He seemed to sense that his rationale for what he'd initially proposed in his will was still not fully understood by his children, and he wanted to try again—for them, and perhaps for himself too.

"You are now largely vested in Langar very successfully, thanks to your mother and Uncle George," he began, referring to his children's personal stakes in the enormous wealth generated from the Gardiner side of the family. He praised Helen and George Gardiner for their roles in helping Scott's achieve "its present great success."

And then he turned to his own goals. "My objective was to save my grandfather's and father's business and to free it to grow to its full strength, which is now being achieved."

Because PJ's four children were already "vested" in Langar, he had decided—for tax reasons—"to bypass your generation" and make the children of the fifth generation the ultimate beneficiaries of the trusts in Cara Holdings Ltd. "when they come to maturity. In the interim," PJ was now quick to point out, "you individually will be responsible for your children's affairs as long as you think it prudent and wise to continue in that role."

PJ was clearly responding to veiled accusations in the minutes of the family meeting. "Gail's great fear," the minutes stated, involved "children being subject to the authority of family members other than their parents ... Gail believes that the parent should control not only dividends held in a trust fund, but the assets that generate these dividends," the minutes explained. "In this way the individual family takes the risks, and children are subject to the authority of their parents."

And now, PJ appeared to be saying, the children would be.

With that clarified—he hoped—PJ proceeded to lay out his longer-term plans. "PJP will arrange to slowly and gracefully retire and become honorary chairman of Cara Operations Ltd., but he will remain chairman of Cara Holdings Ltd." He and Helen would set up the Helen and Paul Phelan charitable foundation "so that I can make sure in my lifetime that it gets off to a good start." But they would do it "in a fair and equitable way, using the resources of the Holding company and the assets of my estate. Half of my estate will remain intact, which in the end could be used for your own interests, tax purposes, etc."

With PJ's continuing role in Operations and Holdings clarified, Gail, for her part, "could" continue as president of Holdings "if she so wishes." Paul David, meanwhile, would be elected chairman of the operating business and "be responsible for its ongoing success ... Paul David is shrewd and wise," he told his other children. "I am confident that he will succeed. All of our staff will support him, as shall we."

As for PJ's will, "Mr. Hynes has been instructed to prepare a will which gives the controlling shares of Cara to my children and a referee. This follows the principle of 'share and share alike,' and I trust you will use this principle to enhance clear strong leadership of our company ... You are all very gifted people," he admonished them. "Live up to your heritage received through your parents and grandparents, through the generations. Your interests are being carefully looked after by all of us ... Have no fear. Love you all."

Settled? No. In fact, no new will was ever prepared.

~

It was supposed to be a pleasant evening. Dinner, a few drinks, some light, meaningless conversation.

It was January 1989. Rose, Michael, and their young daughters, Raewyn and Michaela, had carved out a new life for themselves in Auckland, New Zealand, far from Cara, far from family meetings. They lived in a small house that couldn't compare to Old Forest Hill Road, "but it was cute with a really nice garden and a beautiful view. I loved New Zealand," Rose says today. "I loved that experience." She juggled her family responsibilities with a job at Bateman Books, a small independent family-owned publisher in Auckland where she did "a little bit of editing. I learned a lot."

They'd made friends in the community, but they also welcomed a steady stream of visitors from Canada, including PJ, who flew in several times. He'd stay for a week to ten days each time at a nearby bed and breakfast and enjoy "adventures" with Rose's family. "PJ loved New Zealand," Rose's husband, Michael, remembers. "It's a sailing country, and sailing was his sport."

Helen never accompanied him. "First of all," explains Rose, "she would not have wanted to travel with my dad, and second, she just was not a traveller." (Ironically, Betty, the nanny who'd raised Rose, did fly out to visit twice.)

On this night, the dinner guests included PJ and a couple from Toronto, former work colleagues of Michael's. "My dad just took a 'scunner,' as he would say, to the woman," Rose remembers. "He just didn't like her, took an immediate distaste to her."

It probably didn't help that the Auckland bed and breakfast where PJ was staying doubled as a pub, "and the owner would invite all his friends over. Dad loved it." Perhaps too much. He began insulting the woman. "He just lost it completely," Rose recalls, "not enraged but just saying the most inappropriate things." She can't remember now exactly how the evening ended. "I remember being horrified and embarrassed. And I probably apologized."

The next day, she and Michael confronted PJ about his behaviour. "'That was completely inappropriate, Dad. I mean, let's just reverse the situation. If I was at your house and around the dinner table with your friends, and I started saying words like that, how would you feel?' And I think that sort of shamed him."

But she refused to let it go. "What's your problem, Dad?" she pushed. "What's your problem?"

"He thought, and he thought, and he just said, 'I have a monkey on my back.'"

Perhaps surprisingly, perhaps not, PJ seemed most at home in his later years in the original Bloor Street Swiss Chalet restaurant at 234 Bloor Steet West. By then, his boozy lunches at the York Club were mostly in his rear-view mirror.

That particular Swiss Chalet had established its place among Canadian cultural icons,[47] attracting not just university students in search of cheap meals but also local professionals and politicians like former NDP premier Bob Rae and Progressive Conservative prime minister Joe Clark, not to forget various levels of Hollywood stars from Mr. T to Brian Dennehy to even Jennifer Lopez, who'd ordered takeout.

Northrop Frye, the famous literary critic, had been one of its first documented customers. On January 7, 1955, Frye—as he wrote in his diary—bought "an Imperial standard typewriter for $180" at a nearby office supply store, after which he and his wife attended a lecture on Chinese silk at the nearby Royal Ontario Museum and then "we went to dinner at the new chicken place on Bloor St.—chicken & finger bowls."

Margaret Atwood, who lived nearby, was obviously a regular customer too. Elaine Risley, one of the characters in her 1988 novel, *Cat's Eye,* specifically references the restaurant: "I've taken a job at the Swiss Chalet on Bloor Street," the Risley character notes, adding, "This is a place that serves nothing but chicken, 'broasted,' as it says on the sign. Chicken and dipping sauce, and coleslaw and white buns, and one flavor of ice cream: Burgundy Cherry, which is a striking shade of purple."

When the outlet finally closed in 2006—the building was about to be demolished in favour of a new condominium development[48] — the *Globe and Mail*'s Anthony Reinhart interviewed some of its long-time servers about their memories of the place and its customers.

One server, whose nickname on her name tag was "Sunshine," would fondly remember PJ. He was known among the servers as "Mr. Slippers," she said, "for his choice of footwear. [He] would descend from his office in an old house immediately behind the restaurant and come in for lunch."

"He owned the joint, and he paid," she marvelled. "He'd buy everybody's lunch who was sitting around him."

Down on the Farm

Rose had had enough. Yet another of Paul David's friends had just zipped along the driveway in front of the old farmhouse on the Phelan property in Collingwood. They were on their way to PD's house further up the road, "whipping past" Rose's playing children and romping dogs as if the driver were cruising along a major highway.

If the driver wasn't one of PD's friends, of course, Rose knew it could as easily have been PD himself. "For some reason, he would just speed up when he went by the farmhouse." At one point, Rose's father even had signs erected beside the driveway in front of the farmhouse urging drivers to slow down. But they didn't.

On this day, an angry Rose picked up the phone and called her brother. "PD," she demanded, "could you please tell your friends to stop driving so fast? And could you stop going so fast yourself?" PD was not apologetic. He was "enraged."

It was the summer of 1989. Rose, Michael, and the girls had recently moved home from New Zealand. It had been a delightful two-and-a-half-year adventure, a needed tonic to Phelan family life in Toronto. But "it was just time," Rose says now. "I was feeling isolated and lonely." For all her ambivalence about her own upbringing, she wanted her children to have the opportunity to bond with their cousins, to spend time with their grandparents, their aunts, and, perhaps, even their uncle, to be part of a larger family.

That said, and despite her desire to keep her family's many ongoing feuds at arm's length, she'd found herself increasingly drawn back into the fray as a somewhat reluctant ally of her sister Gail and a less and less reluctant opponent of her brother in the battle over the future of the Phelan family and its business interests.

Back in Canada, Rose and her family spent their weeks in Toronto—Michael had arranged to return to his previous job there—and then they'd decamp for the weekends to Collingwood. Conveniently, Collingwood was both Michael's family's home turf and the site of the Phelans' rambling country homestead. By the late 1980s, what had begun as a 100-acre hobby farm twenty-five years earlier had become a 350-acre Phelan family compound known as Braeburn Farm.

After Paul David married Rundi in 1977, he had legally "severed off 10 acres" and built his own "gorgeous" house on a hill above the original farmhouse.

Perhaps to even things up within the family, Helen told Rose before she and Michael left for New Zealand that she intended to bequeath 10 acres, including the farmhouse that had been built in the 1870s, to Rose—and would gift Rose and her family the use of it during Helen's lifetime.

Paul David objected. His real if unspoken reason may have been as simple as the fact that he'd had the farm property mostly to himself since well before Rose left for New Zealand. While the property at the base of the Osler Ski Club had served as a winter playland for the Phelan kids growing up, PJ and Helen now rarely spent extended periods there. "My mother never really went there," Rose says. Gail and her family preferred summers at Gail's cottage at Pointe au Baril where the breezes from Georgian Bay cooled the hot summer sun. "I think PD just resented our presence," Rose says today.

But there was probably more to it than that. The growing tensions between the two once friendly siblings had ratcheted up following Rose's return from New Zealand.

Fuelled by alcohol and who knew what drugs, Paul David had become increasingly angry and aggressive. Rose had come to believe he was capable of physical violence. Did her parents not see that? Did they not understand why she could not support PD as her generation's leader? "I believe my parents were aware," Rose says now, "but they wouldn't—couldn't—face it."

No one stepped up to confront Paul David until that summer when Rose herself finally called her brother out during an emotional phone call. "I have no idea of the context of the conversation or why we were even talking," she explains today. "But I do remember I was at Number 8 Old Forest Hill in the library talking to him on an old-fashioned phone. And I just lost my temper. I said, 'I can't support you as a leader because of your alcohol and drug use, because of your controlling behaviours and your rages, and because of your own mental health issues.'"

Her brother was "furious," she remembers today. He denied everything.

Later, Paul David himself suggested they try counselling to see if they could rebuild their relationship. They did sit down with Kathleen Metcalfe, a Toronto-based family therapist with McWhinney, Metcalfe & Associates, "and got absolutely nowhere." Whenever Rose attempted to confront Paul David about what she saw as his personal issues, "my brother would call me a liar, say I was making it up, and that was the end of that."

Rose's newfound willingness to call out Paul David for his personal transgressions as well as her mere presence on his turf no doubt played significant roles in his hostility to Rose. However, his formal objections were couched in far less personal, far more legal terms.

The problem, which he correctly pointed out, was that Helen didn't legally own the farmhouse and surrounding land she attempted to gift to Rose. When PJ and Helen bought the original property in 1963, half the funds had come from Helen's personal accounts, but the other half had been paid out of Cara Holdings. That meant Holdings' board would need to sign off on any transfer of the farmhouse and its acreage to Rose. That meant...

"The farm issue was a side issue," Rosemary begins as she tries to explain how the 1990s battle over ownership of Braeburn Farm fit into the larger Phelan family disputes over succession, but then she stops, reconsiders. "It wasn't really. It was an example of my father's mismanagement." PJ blithely mixed his personal pleasures—from buying and running the farm, for which Holdings picked up the tab, to funding his personal contributions to various America's Cup challenges through Holdings—with the corporate responsibilities of the family holding company. It was supposed to be mainly focused on safeguarding and enhancing the family's wealth for future generations while exercising ongoing oversight over Cara Operations and its management. PJ's belief that Holdings was also his personal piggybank frustrated Holdings' board as well as his family, most of whom, of course, were one and the same. As for her mother's gifting of the farm and surrounding acreage, Rose says, "I was leveraged into a position that I didn't ask for, and nothing was clear."

Since she'd been told PJ and Helen would find a way to sever the house and its 10 acres so she could have free title to it "until the rest of the issues were cleared up," Rose settled into the farmhouse and began to make it her own. She fixed up the garden, which her mother had long since abandoned. She moved one of her horses from a stable near Toronto to the barn at the Collingwood farm. She agreed to pay the farmer's wife to look after the horse and arranged for some renovation work on the old barn to accommodate the horse. She said she would have been happy to pay for that out of her own pocket, but "that sent my brother into a tizzy."

Again, Paul David's concerns, at least in theory, were well founded. Holdings' accountant eventually informed Rose she couldn't pay for the renovations herself—"You cannot"—because they represented a "capital improvement" to a property she didn't own. Since the renovations would increase the value of both Cara's and her mother's share of the property, they would need to pay the costs. That infuriated Paul David and complicated matters that would not finally be uncomplicated until the lawyers—or someone—sorted out the ownership questions.

Over the next few years, while the lawyers dreamed up ever more complicated scenarios to sever the farm's connection to Holdings while dividing up the land among warring family factions, Paul David's responses to his and Rose's differences became increasingly personal—and petty.

Although Lake Helena—a "beautiful pond" PJ had built and named after his wife in the 1980s—was technically on Paul David's side of the property line, it had always been considered a shared space.

"The properties were just directly adjacent," remembers Rose's husband, Michael Robbins, "so our kids used to play down at the pond where there was a little sand beach. We used to hold mock Olympics there in the summer, swimming events and different things." At one point, Michael built a raft for Brodie, their third child and first son who'd been born after they returned from New Zealand, because he wanted to "float around on a raft."

But then Paul David erected a fence between the properties. "One of the saddest points was the day that Paul carried that raft from the pond and just tossed it over the fence and forbid us to ever go back down to the pond again." Michael pauses. "How do you explain that to a little guy? His uncle has just taken his raft and broken it over the fence. And now he's saying we can't go down to the pond where we've always gone down ... It became a sore point."

It was one of many, and not just with Rose and her family. Paul David demanded a full forensic audit of Holdings and its wholly owned subsidiary, Braeburn Realty Ltd., to try to untangle the complicated interconnections between PJ and Holdings. In 1994, he even filed a lawsuit on behalf of 1003749 Ontario Ltd., his numbered company, against Braeburn Realty Limited et al. The et al. included his sisters, his father, and his mother.

But that would come later. Soon after Rose's angry phone call, PD himself showed up at the farmhouse. "You've got to go," he told his sister. "You have to leave. If you don't leave on your own, I'm going to physically throw you out of here."

Paul David didn't, not then, not there, but Rose was already convinced her brother was capable of violence against someone he claimed to love.

Sharon Gertrude Phelan died on November 8, 1994, in Mendocino, California. She was predeceased by her former husband, Stanley Grossman, with whom she'd had a daughter, Holiday, now twenty-four. Sharon Phelan herself was just forty-seven years old.

Everyone, including Sharon, had known her death was only a matter of time. While still a young woman, she'd contracted hepatitis C, a liver infection caused by the hepatitis C virus. No one in the family knew—or perhaps wanted to know—exactly how Sharon had contracted the virus, but they assumed it was probably the result of her "lifestyle" in her late teens and twenties.

Not that the cause mattered, so much as the effect. By the time Sharon's Hep C had been finally diagnosed, hers was no longer a short-term, easily treatable illness. It was a chronic long-term infection with no good outcome. Although she was told she could be assessed for a liver transplant, Sharon had also been warned by her doctors that even that likely wouldn't cure her Hep C. The infection could return, requiring antiviral medication simply to prevent damage to her transplanted liver. She was also told that she would need to be alcohol-free for at least six months before the operation in order to be a suitable candidate for a transplant. Although Sharon had long since given up using drugs, she still drank alcohol. For whatever reasons, Sharon did not pursue the possibility of a liver transplant. "Too many needles" was her simple explanation to Gail.

There were celebrations of Sharon's life in California and in Toronto where she was laid to rest on November 16, 1994. The funeral service took place just a fifteen-minute drive from 8 Old Forest Hill Road.

Rosar-Morrison Funeral Home & Chapel at the corner of Sherbourne and Wellesley was another historic family business that, like the Phelans' Cara, could trace its roots in the same location back to 1861. Gail thought it appropriate for another reason. The chapel where the service took place had once been a stable for the horses that pulled the coffins. "I remember we remarked on this," Gail says today, "how suitable it was for her funeral because Sharon had loved horses."

The small chapel was filled to capacity with immediate family members—their many feuds shelved for the day—and various Phelan aunts; Sharon's daughter, Holiday; friends of Sharon like her business adviser Steven Stutz; and many of PJ's business associates.

PJ had had a special relationship with Sharon. Sharon reminded him of his own sisters in both looks and manner, explains Gail. Unlike Helen, who was "harsh with Sharon, trying to get her in line, trying to discipline her," her father also seemed to understand and empathize with whatever "monkeys" she carried on her back. In his eulogy that day, he said, "Sharon has run down the wind before us."

Gail and Rosemary offered their own tributes too.

Gail, always more direct than some might have preferred, remembered her sister's careening childhood moods—"this sweet child, this angel, raging, bellowing"—but also how she'd found peace in California, "a place where it is easy to believe that God is busy with the smallest things." Sharon, she added, had "accepted her early death." She had once reminded Gail that "life is not a race. It is not necessary that we all live the exact number of years, that we finish at the same time. There is God's pace for each person and a special choice had been made for her."

In her eulogy, Rose, who'd travelled to California to visit with Sharon earlier that fall, recalled the time when she'd lived with Sharon there as a teenager. "I had forgotten just how beautiful the Mendocino coast and the redwood forests were," she said, adding: "Sharon sometimes had a restless spirit and a troubled soul, and I could see why she found freedom and security in Mendocino."

During the last months of Sharon's illness, Rose explained, she had kept in touch with her sister by phone or "by being with her. Never did we fail to have a laugh over the latest family foible or her current predicament, even when it came time for us to say goodbye. In one of her more optimistic moments, she said to me, 'At least when I recover from this illness, I will have missed menopause.' I think those that knew her well appreciated her humour, her finely tuned sense of what was absurd, and her love of 'characters.' She could have us laugh at ourselves.

"The time I spent with Sharon a few weeks ago was not an unhappy time," Rose was quick to tell the mourners. "Sad, yes, but her home was not an unhappy home. She was at home, surrounded by people who cared for her and loved her. We even managed a Halloween party because Sharon loved Halloween.

"In the last few months," Rose added, "I really do think Sharon was at peace; she was accepting of where she was going and had found forgiveness for herself and others. She had really let go of so much. She knew she was loved and in turn she was free to give love. I know I loved her, and I know how much I will miss her. God bless you, Sharon."

Sharon had found her peace. There would be no such peace for the rest of the Phelan family.

~

"I am very sorry about Sharon and offer our family's condolences," Paul David's hand-delivered "Dear PJ" letter on November 21, 1994, began appropriately enough. "Her ceremony was a beautiful one and your reading was inspirational. I know how hard a loss like this can be, and you know the importance of faith. You have our thoughts and prayers."[49]

But then Paul David quickly pivoted to other matters on his mind. "Losing Sharon is bad enough, but it will probably also cause some pressure in the business because I think some taxes will have to be paid. Will you please call a shareholders' meeting?"

His concern was not simply about the taxes Sharon's death might trigger. There hadn't been a Holdings shareholders' meeting in a year and a half, he pointed out, and it was more than a year since the directors had met as a group.

During that October 1993 directors' meeting, the board had tabled two letters from Brian Levett, Paul David's lawyer, and a third "personal letter" from PD himself. All focused on Paul David's latest proposals to resolve the still-unresolved issues about how to carve up the Braeburn Farm property and untangle who really owned what.

According to the minutes, "Mrs. Regan proposed that these matters should be dealt with in discussions among the solicitors for three shareholders of the corporation, viz: Paul J. Phelan, Paul D. Phelan and the holding company owned by Gail Regan, Sharon G. Phelan and Rosemary Robbins, and that counsel for Cara Operations should be entitled to participate in such discussions. On motion duly made and seconded and unanimously carried, the proposal was agreed to."

In a letter to Paul David later, Gail explained the motion as a way "to address everyone's concerns out of court. Personally," she added to her brother, "I'm in favour of your purchase of the Greenwood property"—one of the land parcels Paul David wanted to purchase, according to his proposal—"but I believe there must be an open process."[50]

In his own letter to PJ, however, Paul David characterized Cara's board's motion as "Regan's directive" and complained, "Regan refused to let us discuss the issues and insisted that the lawyers take over ... It has been very expensive ... to let the lawyers find a solution."

Paul David certainly wasn't wrong on that score. Their collective billings would end up in the millions of dollars.

Everyone, it seemed, needed a lawyer to protect their own interests. Given the number of high-priced partners and their associates from Toronto's most prominent law firms all exchanging memos and drafts, you could probably have staged a full-scale, high-level contracts course. Start with Brian Levett of Aird & Berlis, Paul David's representative at the discussion table. Add in David Hague of Robertson Perrett, who represented PJ, and John C. Murray of Genest Murray DesBrisay Lamek, whose client was 373027 Ontario Limited, the numbered company whose owners included Gail, Rose, and their late sister, Sharon. Plus, of course, there was Larry Hynes of Fraser & Beatty acting on behalf of Cara Operations and John Evans of Osler, Hoskin & Harcourt who carried the brief for Cara Holdings Ltd. itself. And that was just the case of Braeburn Farm.

As the conflicts evolved and escalated—negotiating a shareholders' agreement, dealing with the still-unresolved issue of PJ's preference shares, navigating the fraught state of PJ's mental competence, brokering a deal to remake the ownership structure of Cara Holdings—so did the numbers and specialties of the lawyers.

The unlikely constant among them all was Stephen Christie, who'd grown up in Collingwood and now practised law there. He knew and liked all the players. He'd been "sort of part of" Collingwood's windsurfing community with Paul David. He was a close friend of Rosemary's husband, Michael Robbins. Christie's wife was friends with Gail's sons, Sean and Tim. "So," Christie says today, "everybody kind of knew one another. I was the 'friend of the family.'"

He actually first became involved years before the latest conflict, helping PD legally transfer a building he owned in Collingwood to the National Ski Academy. "I helped Paul with that project and a bunch of other real estate–related projects where he was acquiring pieces of land," Christie remembers. "And then because of that connection, [Paul David] asked me to help the family try to sort through a severance of the farm."

Christie didn't represent any of the players directly. "Everybody had legal counsel and I wasn't counsel to anybody. But I could call Rosemary and say whatever, and I could call Paul and say whatever, and so on. Whereas, of course, Rosemary's lawyer couldn't call Paul; he could only communicate through Paul's lawyer." Christie became a trusted go-between for the Phelans. "I know that it was irritating for some of the lawyers that I was talking directly to their clients."

Given the ever-higher level of hostilities among the members of the family, it seems clear the Phelans—and their various lawyers—needed all the help they could muster to navigate Braeburn's ever more well-seeded minefields.

Paul David himself had proposed a dizzying number of alternatives for how to divide up the pieces of the Collingwood pie, aided by a sketch of the property, to which his lawyer had conveniently if confusingly added various number labels. "I have renumbered the 88.73 acres west of the township road as '5' and the two parcels east of that road as '6' and '7,'" wrote Brian Levett. "I have also added numbers and letters to certain of the buildings on parcels 3 and 4 of the property."

One "simple" solution, which Paul David suggested through his lawyer on April 7, 1994, was that he would pay $2.5 million to acquire "all the real property at Collingwood" for himself. Failing that, he said, he'd be prepared to pay $126,000 ($6,000 per acre) for the 21 acres referred to as Greenwood, located to the north and west of his existing 10 acres. All Phelan family members, including himself, he added, could then share ownership of parcels 1 and 2, while PJ, Rose, and Gail could buy parcels 3 and 4 for the same

$6,000 an acre "plus the un-depreciated cost of the buildings on the property plus the costs of improvements."

Finally, the remaining parcels could be sold to the highest bidder "within the family or leased to PJ at $10 per acre net to carry on the cattle operation with PJ to pay all real property taxes. If PJ bought Braeburn's farming equipment for its net book value," Paul David's proposal added, PJ "could charge back to the owners of the other Collingwood properties a fee for the cost of snow plowing and maintaining such properties."

Phew! It seemed complicated, and it was.

"We went through a million potential iterations," recalls Stephen Christie, adding that the solutions became even more complicated after the lawyers' drawings and napkin notes ended up in the hands of "the Township Planning Department and this, that and the other thing became involved."

Hanging over the negotiations were Paul David's demand for a forensic audit of Holdings to determine the extent of PJ's mixing of business and personal expenses, and his threat to take everyone to court.

Even as the lawyers were digesting Paul David's April 7 proposal, PJ signed a separate agreement with his daughters Gail and Rose. It was a direct response to Paul David's threatened lawsuit, which they argued "has been seriously disruptive of family relations and had inflicted needless pain and suffering."

This father-daughters deal called for the daughters to buy all the Braeburn real estate at its appraised value as well as the farm business and assets at their net book value.

So long as he was "mentally competent," they would allow PJ to not only be the ultimate decision-maker regarding the farm operations but also have the right to "direct the manner in which the daughters shall vote their common shares and Class A shares in Cara Operations Limited in respect of all matters."

In return, PJ agreed to vote in favour of a "butterfly reorganization of Cara Holdings Limited" under which all its assets would be distributed among its shareholders—no matter the ultimate outcome of the daughters' offer to buy Braeburn.

Paul David's lawyer flatly rejected the idea of the butterfly, which he claimed would result in PD and his family ceasing "to be participants in the control block through Cara Holdings ... A butterfly to 'punish' PD for the issues he has raised (and in fact have been conceded) is not appropriate. The butterfly has not been requested by PD, will not satisfy his claims and has been and continue to be objected to by him."

If it went ahead, Paul David, the lawyer added, threatened to resist through discussions with Revenue Canada or "in the courts if necessary."[51]

There was nothing new about Paul David's threat to take legal action. As far back as February 1994, John Murray had written to Paul David's lawyer, Brian Levett, on behalf of the Phelan sisters complaining "it is apparent your client intends to commence legal proceedings in the spring of this year." If that happened, he warned, it could have an "unnecessarily prejudicial impact on the operating company" as well as create unwanted "public speculation regarding the controlling shareholders."

Murray suggested instead that the parties—PJ, PD, and the sisters' numbered company, referred to by the shorthand "373"—agree to a private dispute resolution process, beginning with mediation and then, if that failed, binding arbitration. "In this way," Murray offered hopefully, "outstanding matters could be adjudicated privately before an arbitrator in whom we all have confidence."

That never happened. "Unfortunately," Paul David wrote in his letter to his father after Sharon's death, "nothing has been accomplished" despite thirteen months of lawyerly back-and-forth. "I have been forced to start a court action." To add insult to injury, Paul David said, he had been informed that "you, Robbins and Regan had signed an agreement to forever cut my beautiful family out of the control block of Cara Operations."

But his lawsuit, he was at pains to tell his father, was "not an attack" against him but a "defence against Regan and Robbins using corporate assets improperly for their own benefit."

Although the court had set a date for late January 1995 to consider his lawsuit, Paul David told his father he still "very much want[ed] to settle before then. Please, PJ, let's all meet and resolve our differences."

Despite all of Paul David's continuing bluster and braggadocio, the fact is he already knew an out-of-court solution to the farm problem had progressed beyond the proposing stage. Two months before Paul David's letter to his father, John Evans, who represented both Holdings and its subsidiary, Braeburn, had noted in a letter to Paul David's lawyer that he was aware of "discussions" between Paul David and Rosemary facilitated by someone he described as an "intermediary."[52]

"As a consequence of those discussions," Evans wrote, "I understand that PD has indicated that he would be agreeable to an arrangement substantially as set forth below." That eight-point "arrangement," it's worth nothing, did not include one or the other party buying the entire property and shutting out the rest of the family, or the nuclear option of putting it all up to the highest bidder and everyone walking away with their share. The terms instead were:

- Braeburn would sell to Rosemary Robbins the pond, house number 2 and land over to the town line (being approximately 170 acres) for $1.2 million.
- Braeburn would sell to PD the Greenwood acreage (20 acres) plus a further 10 acres near the pond for $5,000 an acre or $150,000 in aggregate.

- Braeburn would retain the 150 acres it currently owns on the east side of the town line (the "residual farm").
- The residual farm would be rented out to a tenant on a net-net lease basis for say three years at $1.00 per year rent.
- The cattle operation would not be continued.
- The net proceeds from the sale of the 170 acres and the 30 acres would be applied to repay the inter-company debt to Holdings.
- In connection with the foregoing, PD would substitute his easement rights to the road past Helen's house for an easement over the other access road on the farm property.
- The costs currently incurred by Braeburn would be reduced.

Evans said he'd already discussed this proposal with PJ's "advisors," as well as with John Murray, the lawyer for the sisters' numbered company, "and they are generally supportive" with only a few caveats. They wanted the price for the acreage Rosemary was buying lowered to $900,000, including the farm machinery, cattle, and equipment on the farm, and for the matter of the amount owed to Braeburn negotiated and settled as part of the arrangement. Everyone would sign mutual releases, he added, and there would be, of course, "a termination of the existing litigation."

"My suggestion," Evans concluded, "would be that PD make a proposal along the lines set forth above, in which case I am reasonably confident that all parties would agree to it."

Paul David's lawyer later suggested adding a provision that two independent directors be added to the board of Cara Holdings. This, he said, was "a very important part of the settlement to PD. Independent directors would have a duty to ensure that only reasonable expenses be incurred by Holdings, that Holdings not incur personal expenses and that the assets of Holdings not be available for personal use."

Theoretically, PJ's misuse of Cara's assets as his own was at the heart of Paul David's differences with his family over Braeburn, and the reason he had demanded a forensic audit of the company.

Rose did not disagree. In retrospect, she says, "PJ's intermingled structure of corporate and personal assets was offside when it came to acceptable corporate structure. What PJ was doing, really, was tax evasion."

That said, she and everyone else were surprised when the audit revealed that Paul David had been among the beneficiaries of his father's free hand with Holdings' cash. His father had lent Paul David $2 million from Holdings to buy stock in Cara Operations. "That," says his sister Gail, "was completely against the interest of the women. If that two million dollars was going to be spent on Cara stock, Cara Holdings should have bought the stock."

In the end, Paul David was required to pay the money back—one of the few concrete actions resulting from the audit. "I didn't want the money back," Gail says today, "because it looked bad on him. It showed his self-dealing nature. He would come across as concerned for his father but ... This was a struggle for control of a public company. He had been caught with his fingers in the till. And I liked it that way."

On November 28, 1994, PJ and Helen paved the way for a final settlement of the farm issue by paying Braeburn $300,000 "to settle the outstanding litigation" over unauthorized spending and agreeing to personally "cover all expenses and costs of operating the farm" going forward.

One week later, Paul David's lawyer wrote to the lawyers for Cara Holdings and Cara Operations to inform them that, "in light of the agreement which he has reached with his father, our client has instructed us to advise you that he will not proceed with the [court] application in this matter."

On February 5, 1995, the Ontario Court's General Division (Commercial List) dismissed the case of 1003749 Ontario Limited et al. v. Braeburn Realty Limited et al. (Court file B181/94) without costs.

It was over.

Rose's reaction? She laughs. "I think I probably said, 'Why wasn't that done years ago? Why was it so complicated?' We spent so many years discussing how we were going to divide it along these lines or divide it along those lines, when, in fact, it's just 'divide it,' and be done."

On January 6, 1995, two days after meetings of the Holdings board and shareholders, Paul David even wrote an upbeat letter to Gail: "I am sincerely very glad we made some progress the other day, and I hope we can continue to," he wrote. "I have a number of comments or ideas I would appreciate if you could find time to consider."

One of the issues Paul David wanted to put back on the table was how to deal with PJ's infamous 1,000 voting preference shares, the shares that left their father in continuing ultimate control of Holdings and, by extension, Cara Operations. Any discussion of a shareholders' agreement—the next big item on the family's conflict resolution to-do list—"will be hamstrung by the existence of the preference shares and the provisions of PJ's will regarding them," he wrote. "Perhaps we could agree to redeem these ... if we become trustees of PJ's estate and thus remove this uncertainty."

In a handwritten PS, he mused: "Or why don't we just redeem the pref shares now?" Then he answered his own question. "No, an agreement would be easier."

~

Paul David's affability was short-lived. Within the month, in fact, Paul David had written to Holdings vice-president Peter Gaunt to complain—among other things—about how long it had taken him to distribute draft minutes from the early January meetings he'd written so positively to Gail about. "Given their relative simplicity, we should have had them within a few days of our meetings rather than a few weeks."

In his January 25, 1995, letter, Paul David also proceeded to micro-edit the draft minutes—arguing there was no need to "overly detail" the provisions of the Braeburn Farm agreement, for example, and noting the shareholders' meeting, which the minutes listed as beginning at 10:30 a.m., did not start until "at least 11:15 or later."

He also pointed out that the shareholders had "agreed not to just have another meeting but to proceed and work on the shareholders' agreement. I believe the process was for Regan and myself to come up with something, which we would then show to PJ."

And then there was this, which may have been the point of Paul David's pointed letter. "Under election of officers, I would prefer wording something like this: it was noted that Paul David stated that he thought the corporation would benefit from his greater involvement in the company and suggested that he be elected chairman."

He wasn't.

Disagreeing to Agree

Even as the endless family dramas played out in and around Holdings Ltd., Cara Operations continued to operate. Bernie Syron had been its CEO for more than a decade. He'd made his Cara business bones back in the late 1970s and early 1980s, helping PJ engineer the acquisition of Swiss Chalet and Harvey's, and then consolidated them into what became the Cara restaurant and food services empire.

Thanks in no small part to his early triumphs, Syron won the unanimous backing of PJ Phelan, PD Phelan, and Gail Regan—the three key members of the Phelan family, who rarely agreed about much—and became the CEO of Cara Operations in late 1983. In 1990, when PJ decided to transition from being Cara Operations' "active chairman" to its honorary chairman for life, Bernie Syron had added chairman of the board to his CEO title. Gunter Otto, the veteran Cara executive who'd run Cara's airline services division, became president and chief operating officer.

But that was then. This was now. By the spring of 1995, the question became what have you done for us lately?

For public companies like Cara, acquisitions are one of the keys to show sustained growth and credibility in the marketplace.

Bernie Syron's record was, at best, mixed. Whose fault was that? It depended on who you asked. And which acquisitions you were talking about.

In late 1986, for example, Cara tried to buy iconic Canadian Tire Corporation Ltd., offering to pay holders of the company's common stock $100 a share in a deal the *New York Times* estimated to be worth $1.58 billion."[53] But within a few days of going public with the offer, Alfred, David, and Martha Billes, the siblings who controlled 60.9 per cent of Canadian Tire's stock, revealed they had already thrown their lot in with a rival bidder, a group of independent Canadian Tire dealers. That was an obstacle Cara should have known it would face.

But Cara's offer probably wouldn't have succeeded anyway, in part because of PJ's own marching orders to Syron. In a memo entitled "Cara Holdings Limited and PJP's terms of reference for Mr. Syron re Cara Operations Limited – Canadian Tire merger," PJ laid out his terms: "Holdings to remain in command with 54–60 percent of a merged consortium. Holdings to spin out at the top and is not to be at risk ... The family will HOLD."

There likely was never a deal to be made there.

In 1989, Cara's target became Dunkin' Donuts, the world's largest coffee and doughnut chain with more than two thousand locations worldwide. This bid began with a chance encounter between PJ and his neighbour, George Mann, at a Toronto cocktail party in the spring of 1989. At the time, Mann, the larger-than-life chair of the investment firm Unicorp Canada Corporation was considering a bid for Dunkin' Donuts. Mann, who revelled in the media's description of him as "Canada's original corporate raider" and its fascination with his "penchant for grandiose schemes," considered Dunkin' undervalued and therefore a prime target, but he was looking for a knowledgeable partner to share the risk.

"I remember Cara made fabulous doughnuts when they ran the concessions at Toronto's airports," Mann later told the *Globe and Mail*'s *Report on Business Magazine*,[54] so he approached PJ at the party. According to Bernie Syron, PJ told Mann to "talk to my number one man. I don't do deals, he does them." Mann and Syron then put together an offer of $308 million. "That was a good deal, a really good deal," Syron says today. "Everything was fine, except somebody outbid us." No deal there either.

Syron had better luck in 1990, acquiring Grand & Toy Ltd., a family-owned corporate office supply company that had opened its doors in 1882, one year before the Canada Railway News Company. The price tag: $137 million, including assumed debt. Syron called it a "meaningful acquisition" and told analysts he had plans to expand the mostly Ontario-based company nationally, doubling its size and possibly franchising future outlets. None of that happened.

Gail Regan acknowledges she voted for the acquisition at the time. "We got it for six times cash, which was a good price. I thought it was not a fancy business but something that people need. Everybody needs paper."

But did an office supply company really fit with the rest of Cara's restaurant and food services portfolio? And how did such an acquisition line up with the expectations of the market, or with the hopes of Cara's shareholders, or with the goals of management?

Gail Regan, the MBA with a penchant for the theoretical, sees their objectives as different, but not necessarily incompatible. "What the market wants is single concept companies. It doesn't want empires where nobody knows how to run a particular concept. But what the shareholders want is to diversify, to hedge their risks." Management, meanwhile, "tends to be paid as a function of sales, so the bigger you are, the higher your salary."

Gail initially hoped Grand & Toy could satisfy all those competing interests. Grand & Toy was a "logistical company" that matched inventory to delivery, "and so is airline catering. We should have grouped them together after the acquisition. I didn't see how Grand & Toy was a fit unless we worked on its integration, but Bernie just wanted the diversification. So, he bought Grand & Toy but didn't do anything with it. We just left it autonomous." She thinks now that may also have been, in part, because "Bernie had health problems at the time. For him, it was enough that we had bought it, and it should be left alone."

Six years later, Cara would sell Grand & Toy to US-based Boise Cascade Office Products Corp. for $140 million, barely breaking even on the original purchase.

Something similar happened after Cara's 1990 friendly takeover of Arvak Ltd., a London, Ontario–based holding company that provided catering services to more than one thousand dining facilities in schools, colleges, universities, remote camps, and business and industry locations through its Beaver Foods and Summit Foods divisions. That seemed like a good fit, but a decade later it too would be sold off, this time to Compass Group.

The reality was that those 1990 acquisitions—whatever their individual merits—added to Cara's debt just as the economy cratered, forcing the company to focus on paying off old debt rather than looking for new acquisitions or improving on what it had.

Still, the ever-ambitious Bernie Syron had recently pitched yet another deal, this one an unquestionable fast-food game changer, merging Cara with Tim Hortons. The legendary Canadian coffee chain boasted more than one thousand outlets across the country and was growing at the rate of two hundred new Tims a year. Syron had initially broached the idea to Tims' co-founder Ron Joyce at a US food service conference at the PGA National Resort in 1994.

"I knew Ron Joyce very well," Syron recalls. "So, I went to him, and I said, 'Ron, why don't we do something? You're mucking around with a doughnut business and I'm mucking around with a hamburger business, and you and I have been in this business since we started.' And he said, 'Sure, Bernie, we can look at something.'"

That something initially was the idea that Tims—legally TDL—would go public and become the largest shareholder in a new merged entity with Cara, already a publicly traded company. Though Joyce "initially approached the idea with a degree of hesitancy," as he later wrote in his autobiography, *Always Fresh*, "I grew enthusiastic about its chances of succeeding." Still, he knew, "the deal would have to be sold to the Phelan family and it was not clear they would have supported the idea."[55]

They didn't. PJ, as always, was keen on maintaining control. Syron lobbied PJ hard, reminding him that he'd accepted a similar arrangement when he bought Foodcorp in 1970, "and then he bought us [Foodcorp] out. So, we thought he'd do the same this time ... The brokers were all involved and everything. It was a good deal." He pauses. "But then the family got together and turned it down."

It was complicated. Michael Robbins, who was then representing the family's interest on the board of Cara Operations, reported to the board of Holdings that the issue had not simply been about control.[56] While the Operations board "had been informed that there was serious concern within the Phelan family at the price and control problem," the real issue for the Operations board was that "the price was not enough to justify loss of control. The deal might have been satisfactory," Robbins added, "but not at the price offered." The board of Operations, Gail noted, had commissioned its own consultant's report and come to a similar conclusion.

Soon after negotiations on the merger collapsed, Paul David—now the Phelan family's contrarian-in-residence—told a Holdings board meeting the deal "would have been an excellent transaction for the company and felt that a mistake had been made in turning down the deal just because the family would have lost control of Cara Operations Limited."

In reply, Robbins was careful to point out that Paul David had, in fact, supported Cara's initial decision to say no to Tims' merger offer.

In the end, Ron Joyce, Tim Hortons's sole owner, opted for a $425-million deal with Wendy's International. Under its terms, Tim Hortons was absorbed into Ohio-based Wendy's, and in the process, Joyce himself became the largest shareholder in the third-largest hamburger chain in the United States, with a 13.5 per cent ownership of the newly configured company.

No matter who was responsible for Cara's track record with acquisitions, the CEO—like the coach of a hockey team—was the one most likely to lose his job over it.

The bottom line, according to a report Holdings commissioned by Monitor consultants "on the value to Holdings of the portfolio of businesses in Cara Operations" was that "Cara's acquisition strategy has reduced shareholder wealth and diverted capital from Harvey's-Swiss and the shareholders."

The reference to Harvey's and Swiss Chalet was significant. "Cara," Gail noted in a May 1995 letter to Syron, "is a company that, if it gets two things right—Harvey's and Swiss—will be prosperous. Grand & Toy is a distant third, followed by Beaver-Summit and Airline Services." To compound Cara's problems, the Monitor report's assessment was that "the competitive position of each division except Beaver is weakening."

Focusing too much attention—and money—on its other businesses undermined the spending needed to grow Cara's key fast-food division. Sales in many Harvey's restaurants, for example, had stalled during the early 1990s recessions, thanks to a combination of slumping markets and "ferocious" competition from McDonald's, Burger King, and Wendy's. Monitor described the situation as a "dog fight" in a cost-driven competitive environment.

All of which had created years of what the *National Post* would refer to as "lacklustre returns ... stagnant and, lately, declining annual results."[57] Between 1991 and 1995, Cara's annual profit had steadily declined from $35.6 million in 1991 to $26.8 million in 1995.

All of that put Cara's future as a Phelan family business in jeopardy. Short-term shareholders, Gail noted, were "an important, volatile constituency, totally fickle and capable of selling us out to the highest bidder. If the Phelan family held more of the stock, management could do what it liked and the Phelans could defend the company with a share buyout." But the family didn't have the resources necessary, she acknowledged, so "management must take responsibility, not only for the operation of the company, its development and business reputation, but it must take account of the expectations of shareholders."

After considering all of that—the Monitor study, the profit decline, the need for a different style of management—Gail explained in her letter to Syron, "family members ... concluded that more strategic leadership is needed at the divisional level."

That had been the purpose of the special meeting of the Holdings board. PJ, Gail, and Rosemary—three of Holdings' five directors—were present and constituted a quorum. Gail noted for the record that all five directors "had been given notice of the meeting and those not in attendance had signed waivers giving their consent." Although Paul David wasn't present, his lawyer, Brian Levett, was. So were lawyers John Evans, representing Cara Holdings, and David Hague, PJ's lawyer, as well as family members Helen Phelan, Tim Regan, and Michael Robbins, now director of Cara Operations.

Based on the minutes, there was very little discussion about whether shuffling Bernie Syron out of his CEO's position was a good idea. The discussions about whether to push Bernie out had already taken place offstage. Helen said she would "fully support the family in this decision" and viewed it "as a vote to support the transition to the new generation of family ownership and control of Cara Operations." PJ said that "in the interests of harmony," he would support Gail's motion.

The real questions now were legal and logistical. Although PJ had suggested he "would like to be the one to talk to Bernie and present their family's direction, Helen argued it would be better if PJ and Gail visit Bernie together." John Evans recommended that "the approach to Bernie should be expressed in such a way that it is clear that the will of the controlling shareholder is that Bernie retire as CEO, and either stay on as chairman or leave totally."

Bernie's "golden parachute package" was already in place, and Gail was instructed to contact an executive search firm to begin the process of finding his replacement.

"There being no further business, the meeting was then duly terminated."

That had been how it was supposed to happen. On Thursday, April 20, the day after the board meeting, PJ and Gail did meet with Syron. They met again the next day. It did not go well. On May 3, Gail wrote to Syron that "a misunderstanding has evolved. My family has asked me to write this letter in order to clarify and to apologize for the miscommunication. I am not certain of the cause, or whether I said something or did not say something Friday to upset you, or whether other parties intervened to pursue goals of their own."

That idea that someone—never identified—might be pursuing goals of their own had gained credence on April 28 when Gail "received a shocking and inaccurate letter, purportedly written by my father ... The first paragraph of the letter says that PJ and I asked you to step down as chairman of Cara Operations. We did no such thing." What they wanted, of course, was for Syron to vacate the role of CEO; they were happy for him to stay on as chairman if he wanted the position. Gail would suggest to Syron that PJ, whose cognitive issues were becoming more apparent, "may have had problems following this discussion and has reconstructed it as something else. I can only speculate."

In her apology letter, Gail went out of her way to praise Syron and his role in the company. "We see you as our leader, loved by the Cara family and trusted by franchisees. You are the glue that keeps the organization together." The reason that the company wanted Syron to step aside as CEO was not because of his performance but because of the demands of his CEO job. "We do not see how in light of the competitive environment and the diversification of Cara that you can attend to these responsibilities *and* the strategic development of each division."

Syron, she said, had "concurred" with that assessment during their earlier meetings. "Although there is an emotional attachment to the present reporting structure, we agreed that a quick transition to a new CEO was the best course for the company."

The big questions for the family had been whether Syron would be willing to continue as chairman once the CEO role had been transferred and whether the organizational change was "of sufficient importance [to the company] to risk losing you. Our answer was that we were willing to take that risk," Gail wrote. But she quickly added, "We believed that you have the personal maturity and avocational interests to handle the transition, and that you do not need a disadvantageous reporting structure to artificially protect you."

Though it didn't go nearly as smoothly as hoped or planned, Bernie Syron did finally agree to stay on as chair. The man who replaced him as CEO was Gabe Tsampalieros, an energetic forty-eight-year-old, who was no stranger to Cara. He was the founder and CEO of his own company that already owned and operated fifty-seven Harvey's and Swiss Chalet locations, making it Cara's largest corporate franchisee.

"Internal expansion is our new thrust," Tsampalieros told the *Globe and Mail* in December 1995, just two months after taking over as president and COO. Theoretically, he replaced Gunter Otto in those positions—Otto had retired—but everyone knew the plan was for him to quickly add the CEO title to his responsibilities.

Tsampalieros's initial approach was to take "an aggressive run" at expanding the company's core businesses. He announced plans to add thirty new

Harvey's outlets within the year, most in the Maritimes and Western Canada where franchises were scarce on the ground. After years of simply holding the line because of the recession, he also announced plans for twelve new full-service Swiss Chalet locations in the next year.

Within that year, Tsampalieros also sold off both Grand & Toy and Beaver-Summit and acquired a 39 per cent interest in Second Cup, the Toronto-based coffee company. While Second Cup dominated the café trade with sales of $125 million a year, most coffee was still purchased for home consumption. Tsampalieros's goal for Second Cup, he told reporters, was to get its branded coffee onto supermarket shelves in prominent aisle-end displays, which would not only generate sales of coffee but also create awareness for its cafés.

Paul David, Gail, and their mutual friend and adviser Stephen Christie had agreed to meet in Paul David's current office on Prince Arthur Avenue, a five-minute walk from Cara's headquarters. The purpose of this preliminary meeting in the summer of 1995 was, as Christie explains, "to discuss what might go into a shareholders' agreement and how [Gail and Paul David] might work things out going forward."

During the conversation, Christie recalls, one of the siblings asked what would happen to their agreement if somebody died. "PD said to Gail, 'Well, you're older than I am so you'll probably die first.' And Gail said to PD, 'Well, you have a high-risk lifestyle so you're likely to die first.'" Christie chuckles. "I was thinking, okay, well, these are both fair comments ... But really, what they're saying is, 'I hope you die first.'"

It was the beginning of what was about to become yet another series of bitter, protracted family and business negotiations involving yet another overlapping, rotating cast of some of Canada's highest-profile corporate legal minds, this time focusing on the creation of a shareholders' agreement.

To crib from Investopedia, a popular plain-language business website, a shareholders' agreement is simply "an arrangement among shareholders that describes how a company should be operated and outlines shareholders' rights and obligations. The agreement also includes information on the management of the company and privileges and protection of shareholders."[58] And usually, of course, provisions on how the agreement can be ended.

It is simple to define, but this particular shareholders' agreement would swallow another six years of time and money before the shareholders could agree to agree on the agreement.

An early draft of a deal had circulated back in October 1992 just as the disputes over the Braeburn Farm properties began to boil. That draft included provisions that no shareholder would be permitted to sell their shares "unless all of the shareholders have consented thereto in writing" as well as a modified shotgun provision that allowed any shareholder to offer to buy all the shares of another shareholder for cash. The agreement was set to end after seven years, but during those seven years, it would remain "in force so long as the preferred shares"—back to *those* shares—"are outstanding." The draft was resurrected and recirculated in August 1995 after the family had reached its out-of-court settlement to divvy up the farm properties.

On August 5, 1995, however, Paul David made a pre-emptive move, offering to buy out his sisters and his niece for $5 a share of Cara Operations stock. When that didn't elicit the response he claimed to hope for, Paul David came back a month later with a new proposal, this time asking for a directors' meeting "to discuss and possibly approve" a new scheme for Paul David and his family to butterfly out of Holdings. Oh, and once that was settled, he wrote, he would also like to be bought out of Braeburn Realty "at a fair price."

In an October 6 response to Paul David, Gail attempted to catalogue his vacillating views. "At the last directors meeting, you said that you had changed your mind [about the butterfly] because of the tax considerations involved.

When it was pointed out to you that those tax matters could be resolved in your favour, you then said that the—presumably real—reason for not wanting to butterfly was the existence of the preference shares in Holdings. You thought that these shares were of great value, and you did not want to preclude yourself or your family from participating in that value."

According to the minutes of that September 19, 1995, Cara Holdings Ltd. board meeting, Paul David also suggested his father "would be prepared to give up [his] preference shares on a suitable basis provided the other shareholders could enter into a shareholders' agreement." While Paul David made it clear he wasn't interested in any agreement that had been proposed so far, he suggested that "it would be desirable that his father, Mr. Paul J. Phelan, name a proxy for these [preference] shares and advised the meeting that he was prepared to hold this proxy, and that his father might agree to that."

That—no surprise—was a non-starter for the others for all the obvious reasons, plus the fact that, as the minutes noted, "quite apart from any proxies, Mrs. Helen Phelan held Mr. Paul J. Phelan's general power of attorney."

By this point, PJ's dementia had reached a point where he was no longer able to make decisions on his own, meaning Helen was now the one to speak and act on his behalf. That, of course, became part of yet another interconnected, interrelated family side drama.

On August 26, 1995, Paul David wrote a letter to his sister Rose, accusing Gail of "abusing PJ ... mentally, verbally and emotionally ... [Gail] has also threatened him with physical violence."

That bizarre reference was to an incident involving PJ that had begun the month before at Gail's family cottage in Pointe au Baril. "My dad was out of control," Rose remembers. "His drinking was out of control. He was really misbehaving. He was falling down a lot. His face was bruised, and my mother was really having a hard time managing him. Everybody was. So, my mother demanded that my dad go back to Toronto. And I totally agreed."

To convince him to leave, Gail says, she "faked a temper tantrum and made this tai chi gesture" in her father's direction. Somehow, her foot brushed against his pants cuff. "Sorry, Dad," she said. "That was supposed to miss." He wasn't hurt then, but later that day, after he'd been driven home to Old Forest Hill, he fell while putting a log in the fireplace and broke his shoulder.

Although he couldn't have seen the incident clearly, Jim, the family cook, told Paul David about the incident, which PD connected to Gail's earlier tai chi move, and then combined the two unconnected incidents to claim Gail was responsible for his father's shoulder injury—and a perpetrator of elder abuse.

The ostensible purpose of Paul David's letter to Rose—which she had refused physical delivery of, insisting he mail it instead—was to convince Rose to represent what he saw as PJ's personal and business interests. Gail, he said, was "too much of a loose cannon," while Helen "is having trouble coping with her existing problems ... And that leaves you! I DO think you would be a good person to represent PJ, and we need someone in that position because there are many matters to be attended to."

First, of course, was his "takeover bid," to which there had been no reply from Holdings. And then, he pointed out, "just a week or so ago, on his own initiative, PJ wanted to give me his proxy, as he always has, but Helen would not—and will not—allow this.

"Could you please try and persuade Helen to allow PJ to give this responsibility to someone who can do the job. But the person has to know the situation and can't just be off the street. Since I am not allowed to do it, I see you as the next best option."

Five days later in a response—pointedly addressed not to Paul David himself but to PJ's lawyer, David Hague; Cara vice-president Peter Gaunt; and her niece Holiday—Rose wrote she was "shocked and disturbed" by her brother's allegations, which she insisted were groundless.

By this point, PJ had 24-hour nursing care at 8 Old Forest Hill Road and, "never, except when he is asleep, is he alone for much more than a minute. Every moment can be accounted for. Never does he lack for concerned, active and involved care. But, as we all know," she added, "he is a handful." She herself had been in daily contact with Betty, the family housekeeper, "monitoring Dad's condition and offering at least moral support."

As for the "business issues arising from PD's letter ... I think we all agree the 'proxy' issue and PJ's position as controlling shareholder is problematic. I believe that Helen and PJ are committed to the notion that they will not favour one child over another. And I believe, deep down, PJ is committed to equal representation in voting his shares."

Clearly, Paul David did not agree. He had reached the point where he now saw his mother among those conspiring to rob him of his birthright. "Perhaps," he had written, "Helen is counting on getting PJ declared incompetent," giving her the ultimate power over the family's future.

In the winter of 1996, Dr. Barry Goldlist—chief of geriatric medicine at Toronto's Queen Elizabeth Hospital, co-winner of the 1984 Munk Geriatric Award, and an editor of the *Canadian Journal of Geriatrics*, among other specialized medical distinctions—conducted a professional assessment of Paul James Phelan to determine his mental competence.

Such tests generally involve evaluating a patient's cognitive functions, including orientation—who they are, where they are, what day it is—their attention and concentration, short- and long-term memory, verbal and mathematical abilities, judgment, and reasoning.

Goldlist determined what everyone already suspected: Paul James Phelan was no longer mentally competent to handle his own affairs or those of Holdings Ltd.

Thanks to the provisions of her husband's will and his power of attorney, Helen Phelan was now PJ's voice and his vote.

Although Helen herself was not a director of Cara Holdings Ltd., she "received all information in advance of board meetings," and PJ's lawyer, David Hague, and Helen's own lawyer, Christina Medland, both attended board meetings on her behalf. As Medland explained in a letter to Paul David's lawyer: "By receiving information in advance, Mrs. Phelan is in a position to deal appropriately with the board of Cara Holdings Ltd., even to change the composition of the board, if necessary, to protect the interests of Paul J. Phelan. This control is no less active because it is indirect."[59]

Paul David wasn't convinced. "Mr. Phelan's concern has to do with his father's present state of health and his mother's ability to fully represent her husband under the power of attorney," Lindsay Histrop, another of Paul David's lawyers, explained. Even with all the information the board provided Helen Phelan, she argued, "her inability to take an active role on behalf of her husband under the terms of the power of attorney potentially puts his assets and his interests at risk."

Not to mention Paul David's assets and interests.

At his lawyer's suggestion, Paul David had already met with a vice-president at Canada Trust, Murray Nicholson, to determine if he'd be willing to act in "a supportive role as an independent third party, assuming a position as a director of Cara Holdings, thereby representing Mr. PJ Phelan's interests without burdening Mrs. Phelan with the stress of doing so."

Given Dr. Goldlist's assessment of PJ's competence, Paul David's lawyer added more ominously, "it is clear that Mrs. Phelan cannot ignore her responsibilities under the power of attorney to take a proactive interest in representing her husband's assets."[60]

"Mrs. Phelan is very aware of her responsibilities as Paul J. Phelan's attorney and of his condition," Christina Medland fired back. Any suggestion that Helen Phelan might be ignoring her responsibilities, she added, "would be unfounded."

That same day, Medland wrote another letter to all the Phelan children on Helen's behalf. "As it would not appear that the issue respecting the voting preference shares will be dealt with on Mr. Phelan's death, Mrs. Phelan strongly urges you to attempt to resolve this issue now."

It had long since become clear that Paul David was less interested in finding a solution than in provoking a fight, particularly with his sisters, but also now his mother.

Facts no longer mattered. Remembers Rose: "You'd have a conversation with him, and you'd say, 'No, no, no, no, no, Paul. A goes to B, goes to C, goes to D, goes to E, and here are the facts.' You could present him with the facts, and he just wouldn't believe them. It was conspiracy theories, paranoia, *his* mental health issues."

Much of it may have been exacerbated by Paul David's increasing substance abuse. "I had a rule of thumb," Stephen Christie remembers. "Don't talk to Paul after eleven in the morning. I can remember driving back from Toronto in the afternoon after some of our meetings, and he would get me on the phone. It would never be pleasant."

On November 20, 1996, Paul wrote a letter to his mother, addressing her as "Dear Helen." He and his mother had met on October 29 at Paul David's request because he said he "wanted to discuss PJ's improved health, legal advice for PJ, the shareholders' agreement and your attitude towards PJ."

During that meeting, he wrote, "You were adamant that PJ was completely mentally incompetent, he couldn't do a thing, and he could not remember anything. And that it was useless to get him any kind of advice because he couldn't use it. You also said that if PJ could sign over a power of attorney to someone else, you wish he would because you did not want to have anything to do with it."

Two weeks later, Paul David claimed, PJ had invited him for lunch at the York Club. Russell, the family chauffeur, had driven them "and accompanied us for our meal. Over a period of three hours PJ spoke eloquently and reasonably without once making a silly comment or an out of place remark or losing track of the conversation. His recall of past events was exceptional, and he related events from the past equally well whether the event was 30 years or three weeks ago. Numerous distinguished gentlemen offered their greetings, and PJ responded in a cordial, meaningful and sensible way ... [They] all treated PJ kindly and with respect.

"I have great difficulty," he continued, "reconciling the differences between your description of PJ and the way PJ conducted himself at our recent luncheon and indeed on the numerous occasions I have been with him this fall."

He ended his typed letter with: "Given your attitude towards PJ and your reluctance to fulfil your role as his power of attorney, I think it is time we found some other parties who can assist PJ with his affairs."

Paul David then added a perfunctory but threatening handwritten PS: "PJ is perfectly capable of signing [a new power of attorney]. If he is not, I will apply to the court to appoint [someone else]—so keep him healthy!"

Helen Phelan didn't respond directly to her son. Instead, she asked her lawyer, Christina Medland, to reply on her behalf.[61] Medland wrote that Helen would continue to fulfil her obligations as attorney in accordance with legal advice and in PJ Phelan's best interests. "This would be less arduous," she added pointedly, "if she was not subjected to accusations such as those you made at the October 29, 1996, meeting. I do not propose to comment on your views about PJ Phelan's capacity except to say that Mrs. Phelan spends a great deal more time than do you with PJ Phelan and has a very different view of his capacity."

As for Paul David's threat to apply to the courts, Medland retorted, "It is, in my view, counterproductive to suggest court action with respect to PJ Phelan's power of attorney rather than to focus your attention on completing the shareholders' agreement."

The shareholders' agreement? Oh, right. That.

In the spring of 1996, the family, in desperation, turned to a Toronto-based chartered accountant and professional facilitator named Michael Shulman to try to find a path to that elusive shareholders' agreement.

"My role," Shulman explained in a May 1, 1996, letter to Gail, "will be to facilitate you, your siblings and your niece Holiday through a process to determine the issues surrounding your co-share holdings and assist you to arrive at resolutions for those issues. As you are aware," Shulman continued, "my approach is very personal and highly collaborative with most of the work being done on a face-to-face basis."

The first session with Shulman was supposed to be with just Gail and Paul David, who, Gail says, "could not bear to sit in the same room with me." For her part, Gail found time spent with her brother emotionally draining. She'd warned Shulman she wouldn't tolerate abuse in the session and urged him to have a second person from his firm attend to make sure the session didn't get out of hand. Shulman allowed that he had done that in other cases, "but you guys are getting along well enough. You don't need a second person."

Early in their first meeting, Gail recalls, "Paul said to me, 'If you do this or that, you won't be so financially desperate.'" Gail wasn't desperate, she insists now, but she was "financially distressed" because her second son, Tim, had been making poor investment decisions.

Her issue with Paul's comment, however, was more complicated than that. By then, Gail had carved out a respected place for herself in Toronto's business and good works community. She was vice-chair of Cara. She was the chair of the Women's College Hospital board and had helped save the hospital from an unwelcome amalgamation. "So, they worship me at the hospital, and then I'd go to Cara and Dad and Paul would insult me."

At first, she let Paul David's jibe pass her by. "But then I felt the sting of it, and I said to Shulman, 'In retrospect, I find that remark about my financial distress abusive.' Michael said, 'If it was abusive, I would have stopped it, but I don't see how it was abusive.' At that point, my brother said, 'I can't take this anymore, I'm not putting up with this.' And he stormed out."

That was the end of the negotiations until an unlikely source stepped in to save the day.

Holiday Rose Phelan, the late Sharon Phelan's only daughter, was just twenty-six years old. She'd grown up shuttling among her mother's California horse ranch, her grandparents' Toronto mansion, and a series of private boarding schools. None of that would have seemed to prepare her for a crucial role at the family bargaining table. But she was a Phelan and probably the only family member who could claim to be on good terms with all the others. From Paul David's perspective, her most important qualification was that she was not Gail or Rose. That seemed to be more than enough.

They got down to business, and on December 30, 1996, Paul David sent a letter to Cara's directors and shareholders. "Holly and myself have come to a consensus," he wrote.

The final draft shareholders' agreement included provisions covering what seemed like almost every eventuality.

The new Holdings Ltd. board would consist of the five family members—PJ, PD, Gail, Rose, and Holly—or their representatives.

There would also be two independent directors in case there were conflicts among the siblings. Each shareholder would be entitled to submit the name of one candidate and their CV. Shareholders would then cast their ballots—three votes for their top choice, two for their second, and one for their third—with the two candidates with the most votes becoming directors. If PJ's shares were eventually distributed among the other shareholders, the draft agreement provided that the number of family directors would be reduced to four and the number of independent directors increased to three.

If anyone wanted to sell their shares, that would require the agreement of six of the seven directors, with other shareholders having a 30-day right of first refusal.

In this version of the agreement, there was no sunset clause. Termination could only happen with the written agreement of all the shareholders, dissolution of the company, bankruptcy, or in the event that one shareholder became the beneficial owner of all the company's voting shares.

Thinking ahead, given that Holly then had no children and had indicated that her will provided for her Holdings shares to be distributed among the other families, the draft agreement even suggested that "Cara Holdings shareholders, other than Holiday, should consider the acquisition of insurance on Holiday's life to pay the income taxes on death." Those taxes, it was suggested, should "perhaps" be paid by Cara Holdings.

Given all the legal, financial, and tax complications, the agreement allowed the board to hire a "sophisticated corporate tax lawyer to whom it can refer questions."

During the summer of 1996, Michael Shulman, the facilitator, had met with Paul David and Holly regularly to create the broad strokes of a deal. Then Shulman met separately with Stephen Christie, still playing the Phelan family go-between, who not only did the legal drafting but also kept all the family members and their lawyers in the picture, answering questions, fine-tuning the wording. "It was a protracted negotiation," he remembers.

Finally, in early December, he was ready to share the final draft with the five different lawyers representing the families and the family business, with copies to Shulman and the individual family members themselves.

By then, Christie had already had numerous detailed conversations with Gail and Rosemary. "I think this is about as good as we're going to get," he explained. "My guidance would be that you should agree to this." They had.

John Evans, the Osler, Hoskin lawyer who represented Gail and Rosemary and had been copied on Christie's message to them, was not amused. "John was a gruff kind of guy," Christie says today with a laugh. "He probably walked into his office that morning with his raincoat on and his briefcase, saw my message and hit the speed dial."

"Who the hell do you think you are telling my clients what is appropriate for them to sign?" he shouted into the phone. "Okay, full stop. Call me as soon as you get this message."

Before he spoke to his clients, Evans fired off a six-page, close-reading, single-spaced memo to Christie, raising questions about virtually every clause in the agreement. "As you will see from the foregoing," he concluded, "it is somewhat difficult to provide exhaustive or meaningful comments on all portions of the shareholders' agreement."

"I didn't call him back right away," Christie says today. "Then I had another message from him two hours later, I guess after he'd finally gotten through to Rosemary and Gail." Evans's message this time was similarly simple and succinct, but without any of the bluster. "I'm instructed to ask you to prepare execution copies of the agreement and send them to my clients," he told Christie. They had an agreement.

But, of course, their consensus did not encompass PJ's contentious preference shares, which meant that real control of Holdings was still in the hands of a man who was no longer capable of wielding the power those shares gave him.

On this point, Paul David cast himself as his father's protector. "Any agreement that reduces the power of the prefs would reduce their value," he wrote, "which would not be in PJ's best interest and thus would be in breach of trust ... I still think we should have a shareholders' agreement," he added, "but I believe we need to respect the pref shares, which should control Holdings and Operations through the boards of Holdings and Operations."

Perhaps ironically, Paul David signed off his end-of-1996 letter: "Best wishes for the new year."

It wasn't to be.

Paul David, still not satisfied with the outcome of PJ's initial competency test, demanded a second one. PJ failed that one too. The testing process itself was apparently so "upsetting," Gail says now, that PJ had a seizure and had to be admitted to the hospital later that day. That was the end of the competency testing, "because they were too risky for Dad's health."

Instead, Paul David applied to the courts again, this time to appoint a co-trustee with his mother, who would "have veto power over the decisions of Cara Holdings and its own board appointments."

If possible, things then became even messier.

Gail, Rosemary, and Holly countersued. Paul David countered their counter by calling for the three women to resign from the Holdings board. They didn't. Lawyers' letters flew. In one, Helen's lawyer wrote to Paul David: "Mrs. Phelan asked me to convey to you her strong wish that you not raise with her or Mr. Phelan issues respecting the preference shares while the litigation is ongoing."[62]

There were personal affidavits. In one, Rose complained about Paul's personal behaviour. In another, Paul David accused Gail of poor fashion sense. According to Gail, that was a result of an earlier incident at Pointe au Baril. She had been returning to their host's house after a sailing race wearing what she describes as "a half-wetsuit, kind of torn and ripped, wet weather gear, a hat that was drenched and running shoes." Spotting Paul David talking to someone, "I just stopped to say hello before continuing up to the house to get properly dressed. But I embarrassed my brother." In his deposition, Paul David used the incident to claim not only that his sister had "difficulty dressing properly" but also that, "if you get to know her, you can tell that she's mentally ill."

Perhaps luckily for all concerned, the wiser head of Madam Justice Susan Greer of the Ontario Court of Justice prevailed. She granted a request to seal the embarrassing court file—PJ, after all, had been war a hero, a leader of Canadian business, a recipient of the Order of Canada—but she warned the parties she would reopen the file if they didn't reach a settlement on their own.

They settled. And then Paul walked away.

There were all sorts of obvious reasons why Paul David Phelan would want to walk away—from Cara Holdings, from his Phelan family.

It was increasingly difficult for anyone except Paul David to remember that PJ had once praised him as his prince and promised he would one day be king of all the Phelans.

But PJ had never placed the crown on his head. Why not? Was PJ's reticence a reflection of the reality that he couldn't imagine Cara without himself at its head? Or were there other calculations? How much had PJ understood of Paul's increasing mental health issues, his addictions, his weaknesses? Was that why he had lured PD's oldest sister, Gail, into the family business, making her an unacknowledged but understood rival?

Whatever the case, events had spiralled from there. Rose had sided with Gail in the fight over their father's will. And then it all got personal. The farm, the business, the family ... PD had seemingly fanned the flames of discord at every turn, consuming all their personal relationships in the process.

Even Paul David's mother, who'd "gently" excused his absence from the infamous 1988 family meeting to discuss his father's will—"she felt he might be hurt by the demands of his sisters"—now rarely communicated with him except through her lawyers.

There were, indeed, all sorts for good reasons for Paul David to want to walk away.

But his decision in the end had had nothing to do with any of them.

Gail Regan had to read the words of the letter again. And then again. And then parse the unwritten words between the written words. Could this really mean what she thought it meant? It was late August 1998, and Gail had just returned from a vacation at her family cottage in Pointe au Baril. The letter had been sitting on her desk when she arrived back at her Cara office. The letter was from Paul David. He wanted, he explained without explanation, to invoke the exit clause in their freshly minted shareholders' agreement.

That shareholders' agreement, which Holly and Paul David had negotiated in 1996, and which the lawyers had then lawyered, and which all the participants, including PJ's trustees, had finally signed off on just two weeks earlier, had been carefully crafted to guide and guardrail relationships among the contending, contentious Phelan family members for the foreseeable future.

PJ himself was no longer in the picture. Dementia had swallowed the man he'd been. His contentious preference shares, the ones that had caused so much family strife for so many years, were no longer a factor either. As part of the new agreement, Helen, PJ's trustees, and his lawyers reached an agreement with his children to simply eliminate them. As Larry Hynes, PJ's long-time adviser, explained in a blandly unemotional affidavit prepared to put an end to the never-ending litigation: "On July 31, 1998, the articles of Holdings were amended as contemplated by section 5 of the Letter Agreement and the Preference Shares were redeemed for $570." The shares were gone, bought back for almost nothing and then dissolved, disappeared.

Gail and Rose agreed to buy their father's remaining shares using money from Langar Investments, the Phelan-Gardiner holding company that had recently sold its marquee investment in Scott's Hospitality for more than $800 million.

The letter...? Gail read the letter again. Paul David wanted out. As per their shareholders' agreement's exit provision, he wrote that he was requiring Cara Holdings or 373027 Ontario Ltd.—the numbered company owned by Gail, Rosemary, and Holly—to purchase his 34 per cent stake in Holdings.

Why? And why now? On one level, it didn't matter. "Thank god," Rosemary remembers of her immediate response to Paul David's letter. "Just relief."

She and Gail quickly scrambled to raise more cash—again tapping into the Gardiner side of their family's wealth as a guarantee for a loan from the Bank of Montreal—to buy out both their father and now their brother.

Their mother had been disappointed at just how much of the Gardiner wealth they seemed to be giving up in finalizing the deal. "No, we're keeping a big chunk of it," Gail told her mother. "But, Mom, this has to be done. We have to have succession on the Cara side."

After the sale was officially announced in a Canada Newswire press release on August 28, 1998, Paul David offered what would be his bland official explanation for his surprise decision to sell his stake in the historic Phelan family business. He preferred to be in cash, he said. "I think we're in the first stages of a bear market," he told the *Globe and Mail*, "and, with the year 2000 coming up, I think it's going to be more serious than people have experienced or can understand, and therefore I just want to be in cash."[63]

In 2003, during another battle, this one over his sisters' desire to privatize Cara, Paul David would offer a different explanation: "I was politely getting out of my sisters' way," he said. "'Okay, girls, if you want to be the big pooh-bahs, I'll get out of the way.' They wanted to control the company and I just wanted to ride along.'"

The real reason for Paul's decision was neither Year 2000 skittishness nor a decision to defer to his sisters.

On August 13, 1998—just after everyone had signed off on the shareholders' agreement and just before Paul David sent his letter—the Russian stock, bond, and currency markets had collapsed. Within days, the government dramatically devalued the ruble and announced it would default on private and public debt. That created huge losses for investors, including Paul David, who was then heavily invested in Russian currency and commodities. He probably had no choice but to sell his stake in Holdings.

It was a decision he would come to regret.

PJ was gone. Paul David was gone. Rose's initial overwhelming feeling was "relief." She and her sister had survived the worst. "We stayed healthy. We didn't succumb to the ravages of mental health and alcohol," despite all the pressures they faced. "All that litigation, all the uncertainty with my brother and my father ... I'm sure it took a huge toll on my marriage. I had small children, and I had this thing that was just buzzing and buzzing and buzzing and buzzing around me."

But in the end, "we persevered, we succeeded, we saved the company," she says proudly. "If the company had remained in my brother's hands, we would have been in a litigious negative relationship with my brother forever every day, which in turn would have had negative consequences for the company." By saving the family business from their brother, they had created a "cleaner, better, healthier working environment" for those who ran the operating company, and—most important—allowed the rest of the family members to rebuild their lives as family rather than feuding warlords.

Ironically, while Rose believed she and Gail had had no choice but to fight to save the family business "from...," she says she personally had never set out to save it "for..."

At the time, her own children were eight, ten, and twelve years old. They weren't interested in Cara, and Rose had no interest in trying to influence them to become interested. Given her own experiences growing up in the middle of her own family business storm, her personal goal was to allow her children room to grow up, find and pursue their own passions. And after the decades of intra-family warfare, Rose herself was more than happy to step back and focus on her family, her horses, and other more personal pursuits.

Gail, on the other hand, became more active in the company's business. She was already the vice-chair of Cara Operations, but now she was emerging from the shadow of her father and brother. That didn't mean her presence was necessarily welcomed at the board table. She remembers one incident in which the company's bankers were attempting to talk the directors into buying a derivative—"sort of like an insurance policy, balancing out what you pay in interest on loans. I didn't like it. I thought there were unidentified risks to it. So, in the meeting I spoke up twice against because we were going to go all in on this derivative, and not one person supported me. The bankers thought I didn't know what I was talking about." During the 2008 financial crisis, she notes drily, that decision cost the company $10 million.

That said, Gail had an excellent working relationship with Cara Operations CEO Gabe Tsampalieros. She was also able to bring family-business consultant David Bork back as an adviser to herself, Rose, and Holly. "What I said was, 'We've been fighting, fighting, fighting for years, and now we have to work on our own solidarity. David will help us with it.' And he did. He worked then on forming Holly and Rose and myself as a team."

"When I came back," Bork recalls, "there was more of an inclination to talk about the business issues. There was fundamental respect among the three women, and that was a key theme because they hadn't been respected when [PJ and PD] were around. In fact, there were efforts to marginalize the women, so when they came back, it was, 'We are in charge.'"

"It was more than that," Rose says. "We had the opportunity to work together co-operatively in an environment of mutual respect. All the noise had gone away—for a bit."

"Those were the good years," Gail says now. Rose agrees.

And everyone lived happily ever after...

The Never-Ending Never End

~

In a perfect world, that would have been where our story ended. But this was never—and was never going to be—a perfect world.

On June 28, 1999, not quite a year after the shareholders' agreement and Paul David's unexpected decision to sell his position in Holdings to his sisters and niece, eighty-year-old matriarch Helen Doris (Gardiner) Phelan—the "adored wife and loving life partner of Paul J. [and] devoted mother" to their four children—died "at home with her family." That, at least, is how her obituary framed the life she'd lived.

Helen Phelan was a far more complicated woman with a far more complicated legacy. President of the Junior League, chair of the board of Women's College Hospital, she was, as the Toronto social commentator Rosemary Sexton put it at the time of her death, a wealthy woman very much of her time and place, but also a woman "whose time is passing. She devoted herself to her husband and her community. She was married to a powerful man, and she was a sister to a very powerful, wealthy man, so her identity was based on the identity of her husband and her brother."[64]

That wasn't entirely fair, or certainly complete. Helen had self-described as a "feminist" from an early age and served as a role model for many young women, including Paul David's former girlfriend Liz Smythe. She'd served on business boards, including Confederation Life as well as Scott's Hospitality, "seeking always to be a good example of women's participation in public life." That was how the citation for an Alumni of Influence award from University College had rightly described her. She became a prominent philanthropist too, with a focus on women's health and the arts. She created two chairs in women's health, as well as a drama professorship and the Helen Gardiner Phelan Playhouse at University College, among her many philanthropic works, for which she had been awarded the Order of Canada.

Her own daughters admired this public, social, socially involved, society Helen—they would later credit her as the exemplar who'd given them the courage to challenge their brother and father—but they had somehow missed out on the "devoted" mother of the obituary, a woman they'd rarely encountered growing up but whose passing they now genuinely mourned.

Three years later, on September 2, 2002, Paul James Phelan, the Phelan paterfamilias, died too. He was eighty-five. He was celebrated in his obituary as well, as an "adoring husband" to his wife, but simply as a "father"—no adjectives—to his children.

That was ironic, and sad. In his correspondence, in his conversations within and outside the family, probably in his Irish heart of hearts, PJ obsessed about the importance of family, of family loyalty, harmony, and continuance. As he'd expressed it in his 1977 will: "I recommend to my children that they should always work together with warmth and understanding so that any tendency to pull apart will be submerged—in unity is strength!"

And yet, he couldn't seem to help himself. At every turn, he undermined his own desires. He tantalized "Prince" Paul David from childhood with the promise he would one day be king, but he was never willing—or able—to give up the throne himself. He "toyed" with Paul David, as PJ's son-in-law Michael Robbins described it. PJ also enticed his oldest daughter, Gail, away from a fledgling but fulfilling academic career and encouraged her to train for a future in the family business he never actually allowed her to realize—and probably never intended to. Intended or not, PJ's various machinations managed to sow deep discord between his only son and his oldest daughter, igniting a family feud that ultimately consumed the family he claimed to want so badly to be united and supportive of one another.

PJ's and Helen's final years had been difficult. For most of their married life, they had been locked in an intensely competitive but mutually devoted partnership. By the late 1990s, however, they co-existed in separate sections of their sprawling mansion, not seeing one another for days at a time. "Oh, he used to be in my hair all day long," Helen lamented to her daughter Gail at one point, adding sadly: "Now, I hardly ever see him."

Helen had remained mentally sharp but had been physically weakened by years of attempts—with varying degrees of success—to contain and control her various cancers. She'd eventually decided to abandon the fight. "Eighty is old enough," she'd told Gail. She'd already handed over responsibility for protecting PJ's personal and property interests to three non-family "guardians": two close friends of PJ—Cedric Gyles, a one-time professional football player, and Gordon Norton, an engineer who, like PJ, had grown up and learned to sail on the Toronto Islands, both of them fellow former commodores of the Royal Canadian Yacht Club—and the by-now-ubiquitous family friend and adviser, Stephen Christie.

PJ, who had 24-hour nursing care, was in constant pain from various ailments, including osteoporosis and neutropenia, a blood disorder that made him especially susceptible to bacterial infections. His dementia had reached the point where he rarely recognized his wife or his children.

When Helen died, Gail says, PJ's guardians gave a lot of thought to figuring out how to help him understand she was gone. "They took Dad to sit with her body. I don't know whether they encouraged him to touch her, but they wanted to make sure that he experienced her as dead. It worked for a time, but then he would forget. We'd go over for dinner with him, and he'd say, 'Oh, is Helen not coming down?' He would think she was mad at him and not coming for dinner."

Even Gail's visits created their own complications. "Tim and I came down from the cottage. It was a gorgeous night, and we just had a lovely little chat with Dad. But then he had an epileptic fit, and they had to take him to hospital. I said to the doctor, 'I'm so sorry. I know he can't tolerate conflict, but I was so careful. We had no conflict whatsoever.' But the doctor said, 'It's not that. It's just too much stimulation, he can't take any stimulation.'" Even, it seemed, a "lovely" visit from his daughter.

The night before he died, PJ endured emergency surgery at Mount Sinai Hospital to try to repair an enlarged hernia. "When I got there the next morning," Gail remembers, "Dad literally could not lie in the bed. He was leaping off the bed in pain." She knew it was time for everyone to let him go. At first, his guardians, who'd met with his doctor but had not seen PJ himself, balked. "'We've talked to the doctor, and he's all right,' they told me. Well, I insisted they go see him for themselves, so they marched off and then they came back, grey, the colour just washed out of their faces. 'We see what you mean,' they said."

Paul David was the last obstacle. He had been an advocate for doing everything humanly, medically possible to keep his father alive, but now he too returned from his bedside. "We've had a very aggressive approach so far," he confided to Gail, "but I think we've reached the end."

In its Lives Lived obituary the next month, the *Globe and Mail* charted Paul James Phelan's ascendancy from eighth of ten children to corporate CEO and family patriarch as well as his various roles as "visionary thinker," "dashing yachtsman," and nationalist benefactor.

"In 1992," the article noted succinctly if antiseptically, "Mr. Phelan's health started to decline, and the question of succession arose. By 1995, he was no longer able to continue at Cara. In 1998, two of his daughters and a niece took control, acquiring shares in a family holding company from his son Paul. The sisters are now estranged from their brother. Despite the family pain, Mr. Phelan's children remember him as a true leader who remained a champion of the family business all his life."

The funeral offered its own brief respite as PJ's business associates and family members gathered at the now all-too-familiar—after Paula, Sharon, and Helen—Rosar-Morrison Funeral Home to pay their respects. "Around Dad's funeral," recalls Rosemary, "it was all pretty good. I remember talking to my brother and having an exchange."

The real questions then, of course, became: What now? What next? The answer wouldn't be long in coming.

Helen's will had included a clause allowing PJ to reside at 8 Old Forest Hill Road until his death, "at which time the property would be offered for sale, on certain terms, to each of the children in order of seniority, failing which the property would be sold on the open market." The terms were straightforward enough: the price was to be cash equal to 90 per cent of the "appraised fair market value."[65]

In September 2002, Paul Mills, the estate agent, arranged for three professional appraisals of the mansion and grounds. Those pegged the average value at $6.166 million, meaning one of the children could acquire it for $5.55 million, minus their existing one-third interest in the proceeds of any sale—meaning the actual purchase price would have been $3.7 million.

On October 29, Paul David pre-emptively emailed Mills and his sisters, declaring he wasn't interested in buying the property and suggesting "cleaning it up for sale and perhaps renting it to the film industry as either a residence or site until it is sold." Within the week, both Gail and Rosemary also separately "waived any rights to purchase the property."

At which point, Paul David—as he so often did—changed his mind. Now, he wanted to buy the property for "investment purposes" and, on November 22, requested that Mills's firm draw up an agreement of purchase and sale with a closing set for early January 2003.

But then, in December, inspectors "discovered that there may be a serious environmental issue with respect to the property wherein fuel oil had leaked from an underground tank resulting in the contamination of the soil on the property."

Although Mills initially informed Paul David that the estate would be responsible for the cleanup and that he believed it was "possible that a complete cleanup could be achieved," the environmental issues proved more complicated than expected. Paul David told the estate agent he now "wanted to wait to see what the full picture was before committing to buy the property."

Paul himself then took oversight of the cleanup project, spending $1.25 million of his own money, "on the basis that it will be repaid when the property is sold, or sooner at Mr. Phelan's request." Rose advanced another $500,000 and agreed to pay additional expenses as required.

But then it began to get complicated.

For starters, Paul David, who had split with his wife, Rundi, moved into 8 Old Forest Hill Road. He didn't pay rent. At the time, he claimed through his lawyer that his presence there was, "in part, to save the estate the cost of making other security arrangements, as well as to facilitate his ability to efficiently supervise the [environmental cleanup] work on behalf of the executors." Later, at Rosemary's insistence, he came up with what his lawyers referred to as a "generous" rent of $5,000 a month. "If you now wish to have a professional suggest what the fair market rent for this property in its current contaminated state with remediation work going on, and then discuss compensation to Mr. Phelan for his work on the property, he has no objection."[66]

On February 11, 2004, Paul David offered to buy his sisters' interest in 8 Old Forest Hill for $1 million each and assume all future costs for the cleanup. Rose and Gail countered, agreeing to sell for $1.65 million each with a proviso they wouldn't be responsible for any future costs.

Paul didn't bother to reply until four months later, after the estate agent had pressed him for a response to his sisters' offer, at which point "he reiterated his desire to purchase the property at 90 percent of the 2002 appraised value." You may recall that, after his father's death, Paul David's starting point had, in fact, been that he wasn't interested in buying the property at all.

Now, as had so often happened in the past, the disagreements escalated exponentially. Rose suggested the appraisals be updated to reflect the property's current situation for tax purposes. Paul David rejected that. The siblings exchanged a series of lawyers' letters—Rosemary withdrew her waiver of interest in the property and raised concerns about some of the expenses Paul David had claimed; Paul David reluctantly agreed to an updated appraisal for tax purposes while "questioning its usefulness given the contamination"; and Gail's lawyer asked for a report on the state of the sale—or not.

In January 2005, the updated appraisal estimated the current value of the property at $7 million "on the assumption that the environmental issues have been resolved." That meant the new price for Paul David to buy the property would be roughly $4.2 million, $500,000 more than the price in 2002.

"It would be unconscionable for you to purport to increase the selling price," Paul David's lawyer fired back, "even if you did have a valid appraisal, which of course you do not."

In November 2006, Paul Mills, the estate agent who'd tried to wrangle a deal to sell 8 Old Forest Hill to someone inside the Phelan family, finally applied to the Ontario Superior Court of Justice to determine whether Paul David was entitled to buy the property and, if so, at what price and under what conditions.

Eventually, Paul David himself decided not to buy the property. When it was finally put on the open market in 2008, 8 Old Forest Hill Road sold for

$11.1 million, $2 million over its asking price. The buyer? Ironically, it was Melinda Rogers-Hixon, who in 2021 would find herself on the losing side in a different bitter family boardroom battle, this one with her brother Edward Rogers over the fate of Rogers Communications Ltd.

Considered from one perspective, Cara Operations had done very well for itself, for its thirty-eight thousand employees, and for its major shareholder, Cara Holdings Ltd., in the five years since Gail, Rosemary, and Holly assumed control.

On August 30, 2003, the *Financial Post* reported that—with sales of $1.8 billion a year, up from $1.5 billion the year before, and earnings of $47 million, also up from $35.7 million in 2002—Cara continued to control 5.6 per cent of the Canadian restaurant market, still ranking it third in terms of market share behind only two US-based behemoths, second-ranked Tim Hortons/Wendy's and top-ranked McDonald's.

Over the years, Cara had quietly built on the solid, stolid historic foundation of its behind-the-scenes food service providers like Airport Services ($221 million in sales in 2003), Air Terminal Restaurants ($75 million), and Summit Distributors ($387 million), along with its various marquee food brands, Swiss Chalet ($413 million) and Harvey's ($269 million). A growing stable of smaller but also successful links had also been added to the corporate chain. Second Cup generated $174 million annually in system sales at its 372 cafés; Kelseys Original Roadhouse's 111 restaurants contributed $207 million to the bottom line; Montana's Cookhouse accounted for another $124 million from its 53 restaurants; Outback Steakhouse, $42 million from 16 restaurants; and Milestones Grill & Bar, $69 million more from its 22 locations.

And yet, there were already flashing orange lights signalling potential dangers, many of which would be totally beyond Cara's ability to control.

In February 2003, for example, an elderly woman who'd been attending a wedding in Hong Kong returned to her home in Toronto.[67] She became ill and died at home before doctors understood what had caused her condition. Two days later, her forty-four-year-old son showed up at a major Toronto hospital with a high fever, severe cough, and breathing difficulties. He spent the next eighteen hours in an open area of the busy emergency department, exposing many other patients and staff to what ailed him until officials finally found a space in which to isolate him. He died a week later.

By then, Canadian public health officials belatedly understood that a mysterious disease outbreak in far-off Asia—which became known as severe acute respiratory syndrome (SARS)—had winged its way into Canada's most populous metropolitan area while no one was looking.

Toronto, of course, was also ground zero for Cara's airline services and restaurant operations.

By the end of March, the Ontario government declared a provincial state of emergency, suspending non-essential services in hospitals, cancelling surgical procedures and outpatient appointments, banning visitors, creating isolation units for the expected influx of SARS patients, and preventively quarantining thousands of individuals. In the end, there would only be 438 probable cases of SARS in Canada resulting in 44 deaths, but the World Health Organization briefly issued an advisory that spring, warning against all non-essential travel to Toronto. That created its own pandemic panic.

The American Association for Cancer Research became the first of many organizations to cancel planned annual meetings or conventions in Toronto. The cancer association alone had been expected to bring twenty-eight thousand delegates to the city—most of whom would have arrived by plane, many after eating food prepared by Cara's Airport Services. During their time in Toronto, many more would have eaten at least one meal in a Cara-operated restaurant or fast-food outlet.

To make the situation worse, Air Canada—Cara's Airport Services division's largest customer, not to forget one of its largest creditors—filed for bankruptcy protection, citing the economic slowdown, terrorism threats, increased fuel costs, labour disputes, the beginning of the Iraq war, and, of course, the SARS outbreak. By November, a restructuring Air Canada would announce it had repudiated its deal with Cara and wanted to renegotiate its $155-million-a-year catering contract with Cara.

And then came the news in May 2003 that a single cow in Alberta had tested positive for BSE, or mad cow disease, thought to be the cause of a fatal brain disorder, further undermining confidence in Canada's food supply.

According to later research, SARS and the fears of mad cow ultimately cost Canada's accommodation and food services sector—of which Cara, of course, was a key player—more than $5 billion in 2003–2004.[68]

By August 2003, Cara's profits for its most recent quarter had plunged to just $5.7 million, down from $28.5 million in the same quarter the previous year. Its stock price had been depressed to $5.50 a share.

On August 30, 2003, Cara stunned the market by announcing plans to privatize the company, offering $7.50 a share or $324 million for the stock it didn't already own. (At the time, Holdings owned 79 per cent of the voting shares and 29.6 per cent of the more widely held Class A stock.)

Gail Regan's official explanation was simple. "My great-grandfather founded the company in 1883," she told reporters. "It went public in the late sixties, and the stock is not performing ... At a time when a number of divisions of Cara are experiencing challenging operating conditions, this will provide liquidity to Cara's minority shareholders for all their investment at a substantial premium."

The backstory was more complicated. The issue at the heart of the privatization plan was perception, a perplexing lack of market excitement for Cara's stock that dated all the way back to PJ's decision to take it public in the late 1960s.

In 1997, in fact, a *Financial Post Magazine* Special Report included Cara among "our gallery of firms (fine specimens all) that just don't hit it off with investors."[69] Added *Canadian Business* in a 2004 feature: "Despite remarkable growth and the prevalence of its brands, [Cara] was never able to inspire investors [as a public company] and was a perpetual underperformer: in the period between late summer of 1993 and the day before Cara announced its intention to go private last August, the value of its shares appreciated by a measly 26 percent."[70]

Ironically, one of the most dramatic spikes in stock market activity in Cara in the early 2000s was probably the result of an accident. "Someone shorted Cara stock," Gail told the *National Post* at the time, "but we think they didn't notice that there were voting and non-voting shares." Someone who believed Cara's stock was overvalued borrowed tens of thousands of Cara shares, hoping to then buy them back at a lower price, making a nice profit for themselves. They'd intended to buy the liquid non-voting stock but inadvertently purchased the usually thinly traded voting stocks by mistake, touching off speculation about a bid for the company and driving up the price of the voting stock by $2.50 to $3 a share. "I feel sorry for the person who did this," Gail told the *Post*.[71]

She herself had concerns about how being a publicly traded company affected how Cara went about its business. She remembered a lecture on privatization from her business school days and thought, "Well, here's the answer." In her MBA-influenced assessment, public companies, including Cara, fostered a culture of growth at all costs for no better reason than to keep fickle investors happy with what appeared to be continual growth.

"Management is wedded to these perverse incentives," she says today. "So, they would just keep building restaurants, whether they made money or not." In her view, Cara needed a different mindset. "We had all these brands. We needed to see ourselves as a logistics company, worrying more about distribution of food than brands." The problem was that if a Cara shareholder believed "he bought a set of brands and then finds out it's a company where people are focused on distribution, he'll say it's not the same company he invested in. So, it seemed to me that we'd be lying not to go private first."

First...

We'll come back to that.

Though it wasn't part of any MBA curriculum, Gail also believed prejudice would continue to hobble Cara's short-term stock market prospects. "[CEO] Gabe [Tsampalieros] was Greek, and I'm a woman. We'd gotten control of the company and it did well, but the stock didn't particularly respond. It lingered, so why not go private?"

Privatizing, she believed, offered many advantages. "It would take the stress off growth at a time when the company was consolidating its leadership. People needed to get used to us, the women, and to Gabe because he was still new too."

Since privatization would add a lot of debt, she adds, there was an added bonus. "You don't have the money to do stupid things." (Conversely, of course, that debt would also limit the company's ability to meet new challenges. But that realization came later.)

Perhaps most important, consolidating the leadership would allow the new team to "focus on modernizing our systems, becoming better operators. Once the company was tidied up and tightened up," she adds, "then the goal was always to go public again."

Gail, Rose, and Holly had begun talking about the prospects for privatization soon after they took control, Rose says, "but it seemed like it was too early, too big an undertaking, and there would be too much money involved. But then things progressed, and by 2003, the time was right."

For the company, but not necessarily for the market.

Some analysts, like Scotia Capital, which was acting as a financial adviser to Holdings, saw the logic in the proposal. "The shares are very illiquid, and it has always been a company that, I think, makes more sense to be a private company than a public company," Scotia Capital's James Vaux suggested.

But others not only questioned Cara's end game—was the real plan to split up Cara's assets and spin them off as income trusts, "thereby giving all the gains from such a conversion [to the private owners] and denying shareholders the booty?"[72]—but also the valuation of its stock.

Count Paul David Phelan among them.

Paul David had never really disappeared from the Cara world. He was still a Harvey's franchisee, for example, and he continued to hole up in the mansion at 8 Old Forest Hill even as the legal bickering over its fate continued unabated through the early 2000s. After the tech bubble burst in the spring of 2000, he'd also quietly returned as an investor in Cara Operations. He had begun buying its shares for "investment purposes," as he'd publicly noted after adding another 288,100 Class A non-voting shares in May 2002.

By the time Cara announced its privatization plans a little over a year later, Paul David had amassed about 15 per cent of its non-voting shares. Although there'd been discussions about privatization around the Cara boardroom table for years, he told reporters he was "actually shocked" that it was happening, then added in what could have seemed a compliment: "I didn't think they would be capable of that."[73] But it probably wasn't.

During the 2003 fight over privatization, one *Globe and Mail* journalist would describe Paul David as "a shy but prickly personality [who] says he was once told by a colleague that he had 'a talent for invective.'" Indeed.

In the week after the announcement, Paul David acquired another 1.5 million shares, paying—as he noted—above the offer price for them. That gave him 18.4 per cent of the Class A non-voting shares and 9 per cent of the common shares and made him a player in any deal.

He had become convinced, as he would later tell *Canadian Business*, that his sisters really orchestrated the deal to take Cara private simply to push him out of the business. At the time of the shareholders' agreement, he explained, "I thought my father was catering to his daughters. But I see now that they were controlling bullies...

"You don't realize how much that works on your psyche," he added, "and then one day you wake up and you're not you anymore, and you're not the person you've always been."[74]

Paul David told the *Globe and Mail* his issue was about more than just dollars and cents, and he intended to fight. "I'm still a franchisee, I have a great interest in the company, it's my heritage. But it's not just my situation; it's my children and they want to stay in ... I'm going to try to block the transaction so I can continue to own the shares," he insisted.

He didn't own enough shares "to squelch his siblings and his niece, but enough to be a player when combined with other shareholders."[75]

And the fact is Paul David wasn't the only one arguing that Cara had been "opportunistic," lowballing its offer using short-term issues like SARS and Air Canada's bankruptcy to undervalue the company.

While BMO Nesbitt Burns, who'd been hired by Cara Operations' independent directors to evaluate the offer, pegged its value in the $7 to $8.25 range[76]—in the ballpark of Cara Holdings' offer—others claimed it was worth significantly more. Crosbie and Company, analysts hired by Paul David, suggested the price range should be closer to $8.25 to $9 a share, while an official at BLC-Edmond De Rothschild Asset Management also predicted the final price could top $9.

While most shareholders seemed willing to accept the company's initial offer, there were two very public holdouts—the investment manager Jarislowsky Fraser, which owned 16.3 per cent of the common shares, and, of course, Paul David. Given that the proposal had to be approved by a majority of Cara's minority common and Class A shareholders—and that neither the Phelan women nor senior company officials like CEO Gabe Tsampalieros were allowed to vote—market watchers eagerly anticipated what some referred to as a boardroom "bun fight" between the Phelans and the Phelan, another round in what the *Globe and Mail* described as one of the most prominent examples of family-business dysfunction in Canada.

The anticipated confrontation got put on pause, however, after Air Canada pulled the plug on its critical catering contract with Cara in November, seeking to pressure the company to negotiate a more favourable deal. By December, after those two sides had reached an agreement, the privatization bid was back in play. By this time, Cara Holdings had—slightly—sweetened its offer, agreeing to pay $7.625 a share, exactly in the middle of the BMO evaluation.

When it appeared they still might lose the vote at a special shareholders' meeting, the sisters asked for an adjournment to "further assess and act on all our available options." They noted that although their proposal had "the overwhelming support of Cara's minority shareholders," there was the "regrettable ... exception of Jarislowsky Fraser Ltd. and Paul Phelan."

The sisters soon agreed to up the ante, offering $8 a share. The total price tag—more than $350 million to be financed by the Bank of Nova Scotia and Scotia Capital—was enough to win over Jarislowsky, isolating Paul David. On February 10, 2004, he formally threw in the towel. His sisters had won. Again.[77]

Joining the Phelan family business had never been part of Sean Regan's original life plan. And it certainly wasn't part of his mother Gail's.

After starting his "journey of growing up" in Montreal in the late 1980s, he'd moved to British Columbia where he became a commercial helicopter pilot.[78] But then, in 1997, he and his new wife moved back to Ontario to start a family—and so Sean could pursue his MBA at the University of Western Ontario.

In part, he says, he went back to school because he was concerned about the future of the Phelan family business, then in the worst depths of its succession wars. Without telling his mother, he applied for a job at Cara as a project manager. "I got two interviews. They didn't know who I was."

Once he received a job offer, he says, he went to see Cara president Gabe Tsampalieros. "He couldn't have been more gracious," Sean recalls. "He burst out laughing, and he said, 'Sean, your family doesn't actually want you here, but you got here on your own.' So, I went to work for Gabe."

At first, his mother wasn't happy. "My mom's view was that the company should be professionally managed, and the family should govern. I think that's true. But I also think you lose something in the family when you have talented family members and they're actually not encouraged to be in the business."

Sean rose through the Cara Operations ranks, eventually running its IT group, and leading the company's transformation to a cloud computing environment before being named senior vice-president of corporate development in 2013. That same year, he replaced his mother as president of the family's Cara Holdings Ltd.

"It felt good," Gail says today. "Sean is good at this. He has a mind for structure, promoting this company here and borrowing there and US tax law. He's devoted, and he really enjoys it."

One of his first tasks as president was to negotiate a shareholders' agreement between Cara Holdings and its unlikely, about-to-be new partner, Fairfax Financial Holdings Limited, an insurance holding company that had recently diversified its investment portfolio to include retail and restaurants. It was yet another shareholders' agreement that would change everything about everything for Cara—and the Phelan family.

Before we go there, however, we need to circle back for a moment and understand why a deal with Fairfax had become essential—and perhaps inevitable—for Cara's survival.

The decade since Cara went private had not been kind to the company. Saddled with debt from its $350-million privatization, it struggled to come up with new capital to invest in technology and in new restaurants. The company was still struggling when it was battered by the 2008 financial crisis. To make bad even worse, those financial woes unfolded against the backdrop of increasing competition from new players and new concepts in the restaurant industry.

Until the late twentieth century, the broader Canadian restaurant landscape had been dominated mainly by independent local operators who didn't venture far from their geographical home bases. That had offered the industry's few national multi-brand restaurant consolidators—like Cara—a relatively fertile field in which to grow and expand.

By the early 2000s, however, those advantages were rapidly disappearing as the industry evolved in a multitude of directions all at once.

Start with the emergence of niche chains featuring more contemporary, often internationally themed cuisine. Quick-service outlets like Thai Express and Tiki-Ming, for example, became staples in shopping mall food courts. Those restaurants belonged to a growing stable owned by Montreal-based MTY Food Group. MTY was a new-on-the-scene consolidator that had been launched in 1979 by a twenty-nine-year-old Hong Kong immigrant named Stanley Ma. His company had gone public in 1995.

Ma wasn't Cara's only aspiring consolidator competitor. In 1980, "after years of working for other people, opening and running restaurants," Sudbury entrepreneur Nick Perpick and two partners launched their own restaurant/bar hybrid called Casey's Roadhouse. Its concept—built around the literary character Casey from the "Casey at the Bat" poem and Casey the train engineer—featured a limited menu with oversized drinks. "It was successful from the start," Perpick recalled years later. "People just recognized it was a new and great experience."

Casey's Sudbury success spawned more Roadhouses and, ultimately, other brands. By the early 2000s, Perpick was the president and CEO of Prime Restaurants, yet another consolidator competitor for Cara whose popular brands by then included not only Casey's but also Irish-flavoured restaurants like Paddy Flaherty's, D'Arcy McGee's, and Fionn MacCool's, the gastropub chain Bier Markt, and its flagship chain—East Side Mario's—a family-friendly Italian American–themed eatery that claimed to have been inspired by New York's Little Italy.

Even as MTY and Prime nibbled away at Cara's restaurant market share, Starbucks, the Seattle-based coffeehouse chain that had only opened its first five Toronto locations in 1996, began expanding exponentially and expeditiously across Canada. "It became a game changer in the quick service coffee category," remembers Robert Carter, one of Canada's leading food retail consultants, whose NPD Group often provided strategic advice to Cara. Starbucks, he recalls, "put a huge amount of pressure on Second Cup because Starbucks kept stealing its customers."

Suddenly, Cara's Second Cup seemed passé, dissed and dismissed by younger consumers as "your parents'" coffee shop. "The millennial cohort, which was a huge segment of that market, wasn't going into Second Cup," Carter points out. "Starbucks and other specialty coffee places kept popping up, and Second Cup just couldn't keep up with the marketplace changes that were taking place."

To complicate matters, Cara CEO Gabe Tsampalieros, who'd worked closely with Gail for more than a decade through the buyouts of PJ and PD and then the privatization process, left Cara in 2006. Tsampalieros was already suffering from amyloidosis, a rare disorder that would kill him three years later. Though he could no longer cope with the complexities of running a multi-faceted Cara, recalls Gail, "he still loved business and believed he could handle one concept." He purchased Cara's interest in Second Cup and became the chain's owner, chair, and CEO.

Offloading Second Cup to Tsampalieros—and selling off its Air Terminal Restaurants division for $62 million—should have helped Cara refocus its limited resources on growing its restaurant business. But that didn't happen.

Don Robinson, Tsampalieros's successor as Cara's CEO, did not succeed.

In the beginning, Robinson must have seemed like a smart choice to run Cara. He was not only family—a cousin to the Phelan sisters—but he'd also spent over three successful decades in the global consumer packaged goods industry. As CEO and president of Mars Canada, in fact, he had transformed that business from an unprofitable operation losing $20 million annually to one with $25 million in profit on sales of over $500 million.

But the restaurant business turned out to be a very different world than consumer packaged goods.

"Don was a visionary," says Robert Carter. "He had a lot of big ideas and he really wanted to expand and grow the business. He was always moving at a million miles an hour with a thousand things on the go." He pauses. "It was just his execution was ... There were some challenges in him just executing properly."

One problem was that Robinson blithely continued down the growth-without-pause path even as Cara Operations' balance sheet groaned under an ever-increasing debt load, leading some inside the company to question whether it could even survive.

Consider Cara's environmentally friendly, state-of-the-art, $35-million, 100,000-square-foot head office complex, which Robinson had constructed in Vaughan, a city just north of Toronto. Spectacularly expensive and spectacularly overbuilt, it came on stream smack in the middle of the 2008 financial crisis.

"It was massive," Carter recalls, "the largest restaurant head office I'd ever seen. I think it was designed with acquisitions down the road in mind because it had a ton of space that wasn't being utilized."

But those acquisitions failed to materialize. In 2011, for example, Robinson thought he had a deal to buy Nick Perpick's Prime Restaurants. At first, Prime's board of directors "unanimously supported" Cara's $58.9-million offer, but changed their minds after their rival bidder sweetened the purchase price pot to $71 million plus expenses, including the price Prime would have to pay Cara for reneging on the original deal.

The suitor? Fairfax Financial. At first blush, Fairfax seemed a most unlikely rival suitor for Prime.

Fairfax was an investment vehicle for Prem Watsa, an Indian-born immigrant who arrived in Canada in his twenties with $8 in his pocket. He sold air conditioners and furnaces door to door to pay his way through business school. In 1984, he'd refinanced a failing insurance company, renamed it Fairfax Financial Holdings, which stood for "Fair, Friendly and Family," and made his—and Fairfax's—fortune in the insurance and reinsurance business. By 2010, Fairfax, with assets of $31.7 billion and annual revenues of more than $6 billion, was on the prowl to diversify its investments.

What did an insurance company want with restaurants? And why Prime? According to a 2019 story in the *Globe and Mail,* that acquisition had been just the first move in a larger chess match. Watsa's eventual goal was to consolidate as much of the Canadian chain-restaurant business under his control as possible.[79]

Two years after stealing Prime from under Cara's nose, Fairfax approached the company with a different scheme—a merger of their two operations that would combine Cara's restaurant management expertise with Fairfax's deep pockets. Fairfax agreed to sell its stake in Prime to Cara for roughly the price it had paid for it two years earlier, and Prime became a wholly owned subsidiary of Cara. To give the newly merged company fiscal room to operate, Fairfax would invest $100 million in the recapitalized business. And, oh yes, Fairfax wanted to appoint Bill Gregson, a former chief executive at The Brick who had been widely credited with rescuing the furniture chain when it was a Fairfax investment, as the merged company's CEO.

Don Robinson was out; Bill Gregson was in.

Things moved quickly after that. In 2015, Cara not only returned to being a publicly traded company, but also—guided by Gregson and Watsa—went on a buying spree, adding New York Fries, St-Hubert, State & Main, Elephant & Castle, The Pickle Barrel, and The Burger's Priest to its stable.

In 2018, Cara acquired The Keg Restaurants Ltd., a popular steakhouse chain, but no one was fooled about who was behind the purchase or its import.

"The press release says that Cara Operations Ltd. is buying privately held Keg Restaurants for $200 million in cash and stock," reported online investment adviser the Motley Fool, "but it just as easily could say Fairfax Financial Holdings Ltd. CEO Prem Watsa is consolidating his company's restaurant holdings ... With this latest move to increase Fairfax's hold on Cara while Cara consolidates its hold on the industry, shareholders in both companies ought to be happy about the news, because from where I sit, the acquisition's a winner."

As part of that acquisition, Cara also rebranded itself Recipe Unlimited Corporation and boasted it had become Canada's largest operator of full-service restaurants. It now owns control of two dozen fast-casual and fast-food chains boasting more than 1,200 outlets.

When the COVID-19 pandemic slowed its expansion, forcing Recipe to shut down in-restaurant dining at many of its full-service restaurants and even close some outlets permanently in 2020–2022, Fairfax plucked a page from Cara's playbook. It announced plans to take the company private again. The difference was that Fairfax had the resources to do it successfully.

The fact that Recipe offered shareholders a significant premium to sell their shares, says Robert Gill, a senior vice-president and portfolio manager with Toronto-based Goodreid Investment Counsel, "indicates that Fairfax is confident that the asset is priced well below fair value, and that they see plenty of upside for the portfolio of brands. With the economy reopening, the Fairfax team clearly sees a bright future for casual dining."[80]

The Fairfax team ... Cara Operations was dead. Long live Cara Holdings.

On May 20, 2021, Paul David Phelan "passed peacefully in the early morning surrounded by his children in the family home of over 30 years, just a few blocks from where his parents, Paul J. Phelan and Helen Gardiner Phelan, raised him." PD was seventy years old. The ultimate cause was liver disease, an all-too-familiar Phelan family curse.

It had been seventeen years since his final, failed attempt to take his place in the family business and more than twelve years since he gave up the fight to buy the house where his parents had "raised him." Over that time, Paul had sought other ways to connect and pay homage to the complicated, larger-than-life father who'd loved his son as a prince and desperately claimed to want him to lead the family into its next generation but never trusted him enough to give him the keys to the castle.

According to Paul David's only son—another Paul, known as PW—his father had donated "a lot of money" to Upper Canada College during his lifetime, including for the school's new arena. "My father joked that his father didn't always come to watch his games," PW told the *Globe and Mail*'s Fred Langan, "but now he can watch them for eternity."[81] It was, seemingly, a throwaway line, but one that also seemed freighted with meaning. Perhaps now, father and son could finally watch together.

PJ's and PD's most visceral father-son connection, of course, had always been their shared love for sailing. From a young age, PJ had imbued in his son that love. In the *Globe and Mail*, when Langan catalogued Paul David's many accomplishments as "a businessman, sailor, athlete, early personal computer user, devoted family man and bon vivant," he was quick to add that the list was "not necessarily in that order, as his huge successes in business were certainly matched by his passions for sailing, other sports and family."[82]

Like father, like son.

Following his father's death, in fact, Paul David took the tiller at the P.J. Phelan Sailing Foundation. The foundation provided money, equipment, coaching, and mentoring for Canada's up-and-coming as well as Olympic sailors. Paul David himself became the "inspiration" for the establishment of Wind Athletes Canada, an organization set up to further support Canadian sailing athletes, teams, and programs.

He also sponsored the construction of *O Canada*, a purpose-built Open 60(-foot) sailboat. The vessel was designed to be sailed by one person in a non-stop around-the-world race, the Vendée Globe, that was considered so difficult "more people have been to space than have successfully completed the race." Paul David had created a "unique platform ... to demonstrate that Canadian sailors can hold their own in the international offshore arena." He then helped finance high-performance-sailing documentaries to document the race, showcase the skills of the country's best, and further promote the sport in Canada.[83]

In 2011, the Canadian Yachting Association awarded Paul David Sail Canada's Rolex Sailor of the Year award, Canadian sailing's most prestigious award, "in recognition of his vital contribution, unique achievements and unforgettable presence around the docks and slips in marinas across the country."

Unforgettable presence...

Alan Lombard, president of the Canadian Yachting Association, praised Paul David's "stewardship of his father's legacy" and described his commitment to serve Canada's sailors as "exemplary."

John Curtis, president of Wind Athletes Canada, called him "an unconventional thinker and visionary." Later, he would tell the *Globe and Mail*, "Paul was a bit of a Zen master. He was not a perfect person, but he could teach people things. He did not look at things with a dollar figure. You could say that was because he was rich, but it was more than that. He wanted to think things through before someone could say you can't do that."

Not a perfect person...

He wasn't. He was complicated.

In the right circumstances—mostly outside his family circle—Paul David could show himself to be smart, personable, funny, charming, and engaging, the kind of leader he would eventually become in the sailing world. Early friends—people like his former brother-in-law Michael Robbins, and one-time fellow windsurfer Stephen Christie—could still conjure memories of that happy-go-lucky, larger-than-life personality. But as his life-of-the-party drug dabbling in the 1970s descended deeper into addiction and paranoia during the 1980s and '90s, fewer and fewer of those traces remained.

There was always that other Paul David lurking at the edges, the one who could, even in the best of times, turn on a dime. He was the "spoiled rich kid" who grew up privileged with parents who offered him unfettered freedom and indulged his sense of entitlement while failing to provide him with the parental love and limits he needed.

"I think Paul got bent over the years," suggests Michael Robbins, "because he thought he was going to inherit this family business and be the PJ of the next generation. But it didn't happen. PJ liked to play with people. I think he played with Paul, teasing him. That had consequences."

Paul David sank into self-pity. He blamed his sisters and his mother—the "feminazis," as he sometimes called them—for plotting against him, denying him his birthright.

At some point, probably during the 1990s fights over the farm, those grievances passed the point of no return. There would never be a reconciliation between brother and sisters, son and mother.

In his obituary and beyond, Paul David's children unsurprisingly focused on personal aspects of the man they called their father, a "truly original character, colorful storyteller, loving father, fireworks enthusiast, devoted sailor, and perennial life of the party."

They told stories. One of his daughters, Hayley, told the *Globe and Mail* about her father's "playful side. On Canada Day he liked to strap dozens of fireworks to a chair, douse it with gasoline, then stand back and toss a Roman candle at it and watch the show ... 'It was known in the family as the burning chair. I don't know what our neighbours thought.'"

In his later years, Paul David worked on a book he titled "The Water's Edge," whose thesis was that mankind migrated around the world by sailing rather than trekking overland. "This is my way of giving back to the sea, which had given so much to me," he wrote, crediting his father for introducing him at an early age to the sport that he would remain passionate about for the rest of his life. The book was never published.

In the book, he described a time when he had lived alone on a sailboat. Paul David claimed it had more computing power on board than the Apollo 11 mission to the moon. But "on some evenings," he wrote, "the darkness of the water merged with the darkness of space, providing me with a spiritual experience that is still hard to describe."

Added his children: "We know he's out there now, sailing through that inky expanse, finally at peace."

At 10 a.m. on the morning of May 12, 2022, the members of the board of directors of Cara Holdings Ltd. gathered for their biannual meeting. The meeting took place not in the elegant living room of the long-ago-bulldozed Phelan family mansion at 8 Old Forest Hill Road but around the dining room table in Rose Phelan's comfortable but not ostentatious Rosedale home. Rose herself served refreshments.

It was, befitting a family business, a family affair. Holdings president Sean Regan presented his report to the board, which now consisted of Sean's mother Gail, the company treasurer, as well as his aunt Rose and his cousin Holly, both vice-presidents. "Also present at the invitation of the board" were Gail's daughter and Sean's sister, Honor Ireland, whose husband Sam was Recipe's director of vendor management and design, and Rose's daughter, Raewyn Robbins. Stephen Christie, still a friend to all, served as board chair and secretary.

Cara Holdings board meetings were no longer contentious affairs, in part, of course, because Paul David was no longer at the table. But the stakes were different too. Cara Holdings no longer controlled Cara Operations Limited. In fact, Operations itself no longer existed as a distinct entity, having been subsumed into Recipe Unlimited in 2018.

The decades of what Rose remembers as "frustration, family estrangement, anger, tears, and heartbreak" were now themselves nearly two decades in the rear-view mirror.

The time in between offered everyone the chance to finally put all that corporate and family history into perspective. What had been gained? What had been lost? And what was the financial—and human—cost of it all?

Those calculations are complicated.

Start with the sisters' pivotal decision back in 2003 to take Cara private. While many analysts agreed the decision was the right one at the time, the price they ultimately agreed to pay added substantially to Cara's debt. That limited not only the company's ability to, in Gail's words, "do something stupid," but also its opportunities to continue to grow by acquisition at a time when the rest of the big restaurant players were consolidating the industry in fewer and fewer hands.

There wasn't anything the sisters could have done to duck the global recession, of course, but even they acknowledge that their decision to hire their cousin Don Robinson to replace Gabe Tsampalieros was an expensive mistake. As was their subsequent failure to curb his expansionist ambitions, which further eroded Cara's financial position. The situation got so dire by

2012 that some inside the executive suite wondered if the company could continue to pay its bills.

All of which, of course, made Cara ripe for the plucking when Prem Watsa's Fairfax came calling in 2013. By 2018, its absorption into newly christened Recipe Unlimited was not only complete but also seemed somehow inevitable.

Such an ignominious ending, of course, could certainly be considered a failure. Cara Operations, the venerable family business their great-grandfather created with his own sweat back in 1883 and that their father had transformed into a food industry giant in the 1960s and '70s, had disappeared.

But it could also be seen as a success—from the family finance perspective. Cara Holdings Ltd., their investment company, remained a significant minority owner of Recipe, an almost billion-dollar enterprise nestled inside a $24.4-billion Fairfax behemoth. Holdings may now own less than 20 per cent of the shares of Recipe, but that is no trifling matter; its stake in Recipe is worth more than $200 million. More importantly, Fairfax has the wherewithal Cara didn't to keep growing their shared business.

In the end, whatever decisions the Phelan sisters made or didn't make, Rose believes Cara would have eventually had to become part of a larger, deeper-pocketed entity anyway. "We live in times of consolidation, and Cara was just too small a fish to compete with the big boys. So, it was inevitable."

But what about the "family" in the family business?

Gail and Rose had rescued Cara from the clutches of their father, who had seemed hell-bent for so long on following Leon Danco's "corpor-euthanasia" dictum and taking his family's business "right into the grave with him." They had saved Cara Operations, its executives, managers, and employees from the increasingly erratic behaviour of their brother, Paul David. Rose is still convinced Paul David would have run the business into the ground if left to his own devices.

That must be considered a win, a vindication of the choice Rose and Gail made back in the late 1980s to challenge their father's will and all the choices that inevitably flowed from that. Rose herself doesn't think of the "choices" she and her sister made as choices at all. "We had no choice," she says. "We were forced into positions, and we reacted."

Sean Regan, for one, is thankful. "I'm so grateful to the women for actually getting control of the business," he says today. He remembers well when that future was in its most significant jeopardy. While he was still a young man, he says, his mother would trot him out at family meetings—like that one at Old Forest Hill Road in the spring of 1988—"to plead the case that my grandfather's 1,000 preferred shares should not be given to PD. This became a regular occurrence, a Sunday dinner act by my grandfather, with him announcing what he was going to do with his preferred shares and my mother trying to convince him not to...

"When I think about our history, that was the single greatest thing that ever happened, when the women pulled themselves together and they said, 'No.' And eventually they got control of it. Which was also amazing for me too. Because I fell in love with this business, and I've been here twenty-five years."

With no encouragement from his own family, Sean Regan navigated his way into the operating company and scaled his way to its top rungs before helping negotiate the deal that made Fairfax its controlling chairholder and finally assuming his place as head of the family's holding company.

When you ask him what he fell in love with about Cara, he tells a story from his boyhood. He and his brother were often chauffeured in their grandparents' Cadillac to visit their father at Cara's Toronto flight kitchen. At the time, Tim Regan was a Cara personnel manager working out of the kitchen. "My brother and I would see Dad and run around, and the chefs would serve us these great steaks...

"I don't remember whether it was my grandfather or my father, but I remember one of them talking to us about the impact Cara had on all these first-generation Canadians who worked for the company, and what these jobs really meant for stability for their families. It became really, really powerful to me. We were having this huge impact on families and on the Canadian economy by bringing stability. So, when people ask me today—like my children ask me—about Cara, I always say, 'Start counting to sixty thousand ... one, two, three, four ... Because that's how many paycheques go out every two weeks. That is our job."

He stops, laughs. "That's why I love the business."

It's a voice that echoes back through the Phelan generations.

Sean, of course, now seems fated to have been the last blood member of the Phelan family to play a role in running the family business empire his great-great-grandfather created 140 years ago.

You might think that Gail and Rose would consider that a loss on the family heritage balance sheet. They don't. In part, that is because they understand better than most the price family members so often pay in family businesses. Although the sisters never fully reconciled with their brother by the time of his death, their children—and now their children's children—have been able to establish their own independent relationships with one another. Rose and Rundi have rekindled their friendship too.

All of that, says Rose, is more important than continuing the Phelan business line.

They also insist they did not set out to save the business for their children to run; they set out to preserve the family's wealth and its possibilities so that the next generation—and the generation after that and, hopefully, the one after that—will be able to make their own business, financial, and personal choices.

Choices ... Those, in fact, were on the agenda of this morning's meeting of Cara Holdings Ltd.'s board. In his report, Sean provided the directors with "a general overview of Recipe's plans for expansion and growth," including privatization, but he also noted family members' "reliance on the corporation's investment in Recipe for income." He "encouraged the directors and their families to consider diversification of their indirect investment in Recipe if the opportunity arises...

"There being no further business, on motion made by Gail Regan, seconded by Holiday R. Phelan-Johnson, and unanimously carried, the meeting terminated."

The business—and the family—continues.

Endnotes

1. Much of the information in this section comes from Pyfrom's "Notes Re: Cara Holdings & Phelan Family Meeting," May 12, 1988.
2. To avoid confusion, the family-owned holding company is referred to as Cara Holdings, Cara Holdings Ltd., or simply Holdings, while the publicly traded company is identified as Cara, Cara Operations, or Cara Operations Ltd.
3. "Cara Expected to Serve Up Appetizing Earnings," *Financial Post*, May 19, 1988.
4. Correspondence, Gail Regan to PJ Phelan, April 10, 1988.
5. "Family Firms Perish When Big Daddy Dies," *Deseret News*, September 25, 1988, www.deseret.com/1988/9/25/18779274/family-firms-perish-when-big-daddy-dies-br-most-founders-fail-to-leave-a-viable-organization-with-cl.
6. Lloyd Steier, "Family Advantage: Why All the Doom and Gloom," *FFI Practitioner*, February 26, 2014, https://ffipractitioner.org/family-advantage-why-all-the-doom-and-gloom/.

7. Most, but not all. Hoshi Ryokan, a family-owned Japanese hotel, has been owned and operated by members of the same family since AD 718.
8. Gordon Pitts, "Eaton's Path to Family Business Infamy," *Globe and Mail*, August 24, 1999.
9. Leah McLaren, "The $500-Million Family Feud," *Toronto Life,* June 2019, https://torontolife.com/city/inside-500-million-family-feud/.
10. "The Rogers Family Feud: From a Butt-Dial to a B.C. Supreme Court Case," *Globe and Mail*, November 5, 2021, www.theglobeandmail.com/business/article-the-rogers-family-drama-from-a-butt-dial-to-a-bc-supreme-court-case/.
11. Amanda Coletta, "Canada Riveted to a Real-Life 'Succession': A Family Empire's Internal War with Billions at Stake," *Washington Post*, November 5, 2021.
12. Much of the material for this chapter is taken from H. Kenneth Edwards, *Cara: 100 Years* (Toronto: Key Porter Books, 1983).
13. In addition to Frederick, two of TP's other brothers, Eugene and Charles, would later become directors of CRNCo. Charles also served as its vice-president.
14. Two of his great-granddaughters, Rosemary and Sharon, would inherit TP's love for horses.
15. Sandy Naiman, "Feminist Realities," *Sunday Sun* (Toronto), May 9, 1993.
16. Green College Staff posting, "Behind Graham House," University of British Columbia, accessed February 4, 2024, https://greencollege.ubc.ca/blog/gc-building-history-part-4-behind-graham-house.
17. In 1957, Percy, by then the sole owner of Canada's Bowles Lunches, renamed the eateries Scott's Restaurants. Three years after that, he bought the rights to sell Kentucky Fried Chicken in Canada. Scott's would become not only a key source of the Gardiner family's wealth but also a competitive flashpoint with PJ's own fast-food ambitions.

18. Ian Brown, "The Great Canadian Chicken Wars," *Quest*, October 1984.

19. Wallace Immen, "Touring in Style: Hiding Out's Easy at 'Snobbo' Windermere," *Globe and Mail*, February 21, 1987.

20. "They," as we will see later in the narrative, is more complicated and helped trigger yet another dispute among family members.

21. In that history, PJ is referred to only as an "aspiring hotelier." There is no reference at all to his role at Cara. "Hotel Victoria History: The Phelan Era and Beyond, 1971–2019"—Hotel Victoria Toronto." www.hotel-victoria-toronto.com/2019/10/hotel-victoria-history-the-phelan-era-and-beyond-1971-2019/.

22. Peter C. Newman, "Rallying Around Canada," *Maclean's*, October 3, 1983.

23. Doug Hunter, "The Hand on *Canada II's* Helm," *Financial Post*, November 24, 1986.

24. Hal Quinn, "The Race for the America's Cup Begins," *Maclean's*, June 27, 1983.

25. Tom Maloney, "Sail Past," *Financial Post Moneywise Magazine*, July 1986.

26. PJ was not the first in the family to be named to the Order of Canada. In 1982, Helen was named to the Order for what was described as a "lifetime of voluntary service" to the arts, health, and education.

27. "Three Hot Stocks," *The Albertan*, October 29, 1978.

28. "Food Giant Has Growth on the Menu," *Windsor Star*, August 22, 1981.

29. Ian Brown, "The Great Canadian Chicken Wars," *Quest*, October 1984.

30. Scott's ultimately sold to Laidlaw in 1996 for C$836 million. Laidlaw, in turn, made a deal to sell Scott's Hospitality's four hundred Kentucky Fried Chicken restaurants and more than fifty highway rest-stop franchises to A&W Food Services of Canada.

31. The story of Paul and Liz's relationship is told in Elizabeth Smythe Brinton's unpublished 2019 memoir, "Four Stanley Cups and a Funeral." In the memoir, Smythe Brinton disguised the Phelans as the Baileys, but she says the story is true.

32. Ballard was ultimately convicted of tax evasion and sentenced to nine years in prison, but he served only a little more than a year.

33. Years later, Sean Regan recalls seeing father and son come to blows at the family farm in Collingwood. "It was on the stairs leading to the basement," he remembers. "I don't know what it was about, but they got into fisticuffs for sure."

34. Phelan's *Mia VI* was defeated in the preliminary races by Don Green's *Evergreen*, which went on to win the 1978 Cup.

35. Seven months later, in March 1984, Paul David finally got his wish. He was permitted to "butterfly" his funds out of their Langar cocoon. David Bork reported to Helen and PJ in a March 5, 1984, letter that their son "seemed very pleased with the autonomy it gives him. The issue of when adult children take full control of their holdings," Bork wrote, "is complex. I have dealt with cases where young people have responsibly managed their financial affairs early on as well as the other extreme where individuals are irresponsible and may never be ready. I believe," he added hopefully, "Paul David is fully responsible and am pleased for him that this next step has been taken."

36. Helen would later become part of the succession discussions with Bork.

37. Correspondence, Paul David Phelan letter to David Bork, July 5, 1983.

38. Correspondence, PD Phelan letter to PJ Phelan and Gail Regan, March 28, 1984.

39. Collingwood would turn out to be a much more successful venture.

40. Correspondence, David Bork memo to Phelan family members and Cara executives, September 6, 1983.

41. Correspondence, Paul J. Phelan to Paul D. Phelan, November 18, 1986.

42. Correspondence, Coopers & Lybrand to Paul J. Phelan, October 17, 1986.

43. Correspondence, Lawrence Hynes to Paul James Phelan, October 21, 1986.

44. In October 1941, Weir, a fighter pilot, was shot down over Normandy and captured by the Germans, and spent four years as a prisoner of war. Imprisoned at Stalag Luft III, 150 kilometres from Berlin, he helped engineer and dig the tunnel used in "the Great Escape" and later became a survivor of a forced march across Germany in the dying days of the war.

45. The idea that Weir would help facilitate succession within the Phelan family seems ironic. His own father had co-founded another financial services firm, McLeod Young Weir, in 1921. One of its founding principles was that "no father and son alliances were permitted." After Weir returned from the Second World War, he was forced to seek employment at Wood Gundy because he wasn't welcomed at the firm that carried his father's name.

46. Correspondence, PJ Phelan to Gail Regan, Sharon Phelan, Paul David Phelan, and Rosemary Robbins, May 30, 1988.

47. Anthony Reinhart, "The Little Eatery That Cooked Up an Empire," *Globe and Mail*, September 9, 2006.

48. The condominium development, known as One Bedford Place, incorporated the original façade of Cara's behind-the-restaurant head office in its design.

49. Correspondence, Paul David Phelan to PJ Phelan, November 21, 1994.

50. Correspondence, Gail Regan to Paul David Phelan, February 22, 1994.

51. Correspondence, Brian Levett to Peter Gaunt, vice-president, Cara Holdings, June 8, 1994.

52. Correspondence, John Evans to Brian Levett, September 27, 1994.

53. "Canadian Tire Gets an Offer," *New York Times*, December 9, 1986.

54. Jennifer Hunter, "Curious George," *Report on Business Magazine*, September 15, 1989.

55. Ron Joyce, with Robert Thompson, *Always Fresh: The Untold Story of Tim Hortons by the Man Who Created a Canadian Empire* (Toronto: HarperCollins, 2006).

56. Minutes, Cara Holdings board, September 19, 1995.

57. Barbara Schecter, "Desperately Seeking Sizzle," *National Post*, October 26, 1996.

58. James Chen, "What Is a Shareholders' Agreement? Included Sections and Example," Investopedia, updated March 23, 2022, www.investopedia.com/terms/s/shareholdersagreement.asp.

59. Correspondence, Christina Medland to Lindsay Histrop (Paul David Phelan's lawyer), April 16, 1996.

60. Correspondence, Lindsay Histrop to Christina Medland, April 4, 1996.

61. Correspondence, Christina Medland to Paul David Phelan, November 25, 1996.

62. Correspondence, Christina Medland to Paul D. Phelan, June 19, 1997.

63. "Phelan Son to Sell Indirect Stake in Cara Operations," *Globe and Mail*, September 12, 1998.

64. "A Woman of Many Causes," *The Globe and Mail*, July 1, 1999.

65. J. Paul Mills affidavit, June 28, 2006.

66. Correspondence, Peter Lockie (lawyer for Paul David) to Bernadette Dietrich (lawyer for Rosemary), February 10, 2005.

67. Nola M. Ries, "Chapter 3: The 2003 SARS Outbreak in Canada: Legal and Ethical Lessons about the Use of Quarantine," in *Ethics and Epidemics*, ed. J. Balint, S. Philpott, R. Baker, and M. Strosberg,

vol. 9, Advances in Bioethics (Leeds: Emerald Group Publishing, 2006), 43–67, https://doi.org/10.1016S1479-3709(06)09003-0.

68. Marcus Richard Keogh-Brown and Richard David Smith, "The Economic Impact of SARS: How Does the Reality Match the Predictions?," *Health Policy* 88, no. 1 (October 2008): 110–20, https://doi.org/10.1016/j.healthpol.2008.03.003.

69. "Sidelined on the Floor," *Financial Post Magazine*, May 24, 1997.

70. Mark Brown, "Inside the Phelan Family's Restaurant Empire," *Canadian Business*, June 24, 2004.

71. Sean Silcoff, "Long-Term Rise in Cara No Mistake, Unlike Latest Spike," *National Post*, May 11, 2001.

72. Paul Vieira, "Phelan Family Takes Run at Privatizing Cara," *Financial Post*, August 30, 2003.

73. "Paul Phelan Sits on Fence over Cara Privatization Plan," Dow Jones, September 8, 2003.

74. Mark Brown, "Inside the Phelan Family's Restaurant Empire," *Canadian Business*, June 24, 2004.

75. Gordon Pitts, "The Fight for Cara's Soul," *Globe and Mail*, October 11, 2003.

76. Cara Operations Ltd.'s board had not approved the deal at this point.

77. Paul David didn't walk away empty-handed, of course. Gail estimates he made about $80 million as a result of the privatization.

78. Paul David helped his nephew get his helicopter pilot's licence.

79. "Prem Watsa Hoped to Revive a Restaurant Giant. But Recipe Unlimited's Turnaround Has Hit a Wall," *Globe and Mail*, December 22, 2019.

80. "Fairfax Proposes Taking Swiss Chalet Owner Recipe Unlimited Private in $1.2-Billion Deal," *Globe and Mail*, August 9, 2022.

81. Fred Langan, "Cara Food Empire Heir Paul David Phelan Was an Astute Investor and Avid Sportsman," *Globe and Mail*, June 7, 2021.

82. Paul David did continue to be active in business in his later years too, not only as a Harvey's franchisee and stock market investor but also as the founder of Chartright, which owned and managed private planes and became the second-largest private jet business in Canada.

83. "Paul D. Phelan Has Passed Away," Sail Canada statement, May 25, 2021, www.sailing.ca/paul-d-phelan-has-passed-away/.

Index